www.wadsworth.com

wadsworth.com is the World Wide Web site for Wadsworth and is your direct source to dozens of online resources.

At *wadsworth.com* you can find out about supplements, demonstration software, and student resources. You can also send email to many of our authors and preview new publications and exciting new technologies.

wadsworth.com
Changing the way the world learns®

From the Bush

The Front Line of Health Care in a Caribbean Village

Marsha B. Quinlan
Ball State University

 Case Studies in Cultural Anthropology: George Spindler, Series Editor

THOMSON

WADSWORTH

Australia • Canada • Mexico • Singapore • Spain
United Kingdom • United States

Anthropology Editor: *Lin Marshall*
Assistant Editor: *Analie Barnett*
Editorial Assistant: *Amanda Santana*
Marketing Manager: *Diane Wenckebach*
Project Manager, Editorial Production:
  Catherine Morris
Print/Media Buyer: *Rebecca Cross*
Permissions Editor: *Kiely Sexton*

Production Service: *Mary E. Deeg,*
  Buuji, Inc.
Copy Editor: *Alan DeNiro, Buuji, Inc.*
Cover Designer: *Rob Hugel*
Cover Image: *Marsha B. Quinlan*
Text and Cover Printer: *Webcom*
Compositor: *Buuji, Inc.*

The logo for the Cultural Anthropology series is based on an ancient symbol representing the family: man, woman, and children.

For more information about our products,
contact us at:
Thomson Learning Academic Resource Center
1-800-423-0563

For permission to use material from this text,
contact us by:
Phone: 1-800-730-2214 **Fax:** 1-800-730-2215
Web: http://www.thomsonrights.com

Library of Congress Control Number: 2002113893

ISBN 0-15-508567-0

Wadsworth/Thomson Learning
10 Davis Drive
Belmont, CA 94002-3098
USA

Asia
Thomson Learning
5 Shenton Way #01-01
UIC Building
Singapore 068808

Australia/New Zealand
Thomson Learning
102 Dodds Street
Southbank, Victoria 3006
Australia

Canada
Nelson
1120 Birchmount Road
Toronto, Ontario M1K 5G4
Canada

Europe/Middle East/Africa
Thomson Learning
High Holborn House
50/51 Bedford Row
London WC1R 4LR
United Kingdom

Latin America
Thomson Learning
Seneca, 53
Colonia Polanco
11560 Mexico D.F.
Mexico

Spain/Portugal
Paraninfo
Calle/Magallanes, 25
28015 Madrid, Spain

For Rob and Maggie

Contents

List of Figures and Tables   ix

Foreword   xi

Preface   xiv

Chapter 1   The Importance of Home Remedies   1
Ethnomedicine   2
Why Use Ethnomedicine to Study Ethnobotany?   4
From the Bush   5

Chapter 2   Dominica and Dominicans   8
The Island   8
The Physical Environment   9
Ethnohistory of Dominican People   13
Language in Dominica: Commingling Creoles   16
Island Socioeconomics   19
Conclusion   20

Chapter 3   Bwa Mawego   21
The Village Site   22
Population   24
Residences   26
Physical Appearance of Bwa Mawegans   28
Earning a Living in Bwa Mawego   29
Village Family Life   31
An Abbreviated Daily Round   31

Chapter 4   Methods   36
Rapport: The First Concern   37
Membership in a Research Team   37
Stage I Research: Fundamental Exploration   40
Stage II Research: Systematic Exploration   46
Freelist of Remedies   49

Chapter 5   Disease and Illness in Bwa Mawego   51
The Disease–Illness Dichotomy   51
Diseases in Bwa Mawego   52
Illnesses in Bwa Mawego   54

Chapter 6   Bwa Mawego's Sectors of Health Care   62

Bwa Mawego's Popular Sector: Bush Medicine   63
The Professional Sector: Biomedicine   64
The Folk Sector   67
Path of Treatment Seeking   69
Popular Treatment and Acculturation   69

Chapter 7   Body Image in Bwa Mawego   71

Hot and Cold   71
Rural Dominican Humoral System   72
The Body's Basic Requirements   75
Rural Dominican Ethnophysiology   78
Summary   86

Chapter 8   Bush Medicine in Bwa Mawego:
Illnesses and Their Treatments   87

The Illnesses   88
Illness Domains   89
Cold Illnesses and Their Treatments   92
Hot Illnesses and Their Treatments   103
Buttons and Prickle Heat   109
External Conditions and Their Treatments   112
Stomach Conditions and Their Treatments   113

Chapter 9   Applications and Conclusions   121

Professional Biomedical Care   122
Folk Healing   123
Bush Medicine   124

Appendix A   131

Appendix B   134

Appendix C   136

Glossary   137

Bibliography   140

Index   149

Figures and Tables

FIGURES

1.1   A man examines his buckets of medicinal and food seedlings   3
1.2   A woman shaves cinnamon bark to make a diarrhea treatment   6
2.1   Map of the Caribbean and Dominica   9
2.2   Diagram of Dominica's wind, rain, and vegetal patterning   11
2.3   Cultivated land   12
3.1   Population pyramid for Bwa Mawego, 1997   25
3.2   Traditional wood plank house   27
3.3   A woman rests against the rail of her modern cinderblock house   27
3.4   House extremes in Bwa Mawego   28
3.5   A family compound   28
3.6   A man heads for his garden in the bush   32
3.7   Girls carry water from the spring to their homes   32
3.8   Bathing and doing laundry   34
6.1   Young woman cuts some *pwev jine*   65
6.2   Bwa Mawego–St. Pierre Health Center   65
6.3   The path of healthcare seeking in Bwa Mawego   70
8.1   Crushing *glorisida* (*Papilion glirisida*) to treat "prickle heat"   88
8.2   Grinding *set vil* (*Ambrosia hispida*) to treat a sprained ankle   88
8.3   Illness domains in Bwa Mawego   91
8.4   *Pachurí*   95
8.5   A bottle of bay oil held in front of a bay leaf tree   101
8.6   *Kojourouk*   103
8.7   *Malestomak*   111
8.8   *Malvina*, or *san dwagó*   114
8.9   *Sime kontwá*   116
8.10   *Goiyav* or guava   118
8.11   *Twef*   120

TABLES

5.1   Disease conditions present in Bwa Mawego   53
5.2   Common Caribbean diseases of crowding and still water   54
5.3   Herbs used in infusions to ward off witches   59
7.1   Humoral quality of common illnesses   76
8.1   Freelisted illnesses treatable with bush medicine (n = 30)   90
8.2   Principal prescriptions for common illnesses   93

Appendix A   Plants mentioned in freelists   131
Appendix B   Nonherbal bush medicine treatments and ingredients for common
                illnesses in Bwa Mawego   134
Appendix C   Principal plant species used to treat common illnesses   136

Foreword

ABOUT THE SERIES

These case studies in cultural anthropology are designed for students in beginning and intermediate courses in the social sciences, to bring them insights into the richness and complexity of human life as it is lived in different ways in different places. The authors are men and women who have lived in the societies that they write about and who are professionally trained as observers and interpreters of human behavior. Also, the authors are teachers; in their writing, the needs of the student reader remain foremost. It is our belief that when one gains an understanding of ways of life very different from one's own, abstractions and generalizations about the human condition become meaningful.

The scope and character of the series has changed constantly since we published the first case studies in 1960, in keeping with our intention to represent anthropology as it is. We are concerned with the ways in which human groups and communities are coping with the massive changes wrought in their physical and sociopolitical environments in recent decades. We are also concerned with the ways in which established cultures have solved life's problems. And we want to include representation of the various modes of communication and emphasis that are being formed and reformed as anthropology itself changes.

We think of this series as an instructional series, intended for use in the classroom. We, the editors, have always used case studies in our teaching, whether for beginning students or advanced graduate students. We start with case studies, whether from our own series or from elsewhere, make our way into theory, and then turn again to cases. For us, they are the grounding of our discipline.

ABOUT THE AUTHOR

Marsha Bogar Quinlan was born Marsha Louise Bogar in 1964. She grew up in the Northeastern United States near extended family. She attended private lower school outside Philadelphia and public secondary school across the Delaware River in New Jersey. She was an exchange student to Venezuela in 1982 and graduated from high school in 1983. She majored in International Studies and Spanish Studies at American University and spent her junior year at the University of Valencia, Spain before graduating from American University in 1987.

After working a few years in the financial industry, she enrolled at Memphis State University to study anthropology. There, she met and married fellow student Robert Quinlan. She received an M.A. in Applied Medical Anthropology from the University of Memphis in 1994, and a Ph.D. in Anthropology from the University of Missouri–Columbia in 2000. She has conducted anthropological field work in the United States, Dominica, and Venezuela. Quinlan enjoys gardening, music, and the outdoors with her daughter Maggie, her husband Rob, and her Labrador retriever, Mary. She teaches anthropology at Ball State University in Muncie, Indiana.

ABOUT THE CASE STUDY

This case study by Marsha Quinlan describes a cultural pattern that is universal in some form, not only in Third- or Fourth-World cultures, but also in thoroughly advanced and complex cultures. In the United States this pattern is probably less developed—in at least some sectors of our society—than in most of the world's cultures, but even here there are broad social segments where it is widely practiced. I am referring to folk medicine, home remedies used by people to cure cuts and bruises, colds and headaches, assorted pains, malaise, and more.

In some societies folk medicine is all that is available, but even in countries where modern medicine is available, folk medicine may continue to flourish. Such is the case in Germany. The data for what I am about to say were collected in the seventies, so we may assume that changes have occurred since then and that folk medicine has lost ground to scientifically rationalized medical practice. But we may be equally sure that folk medicine is still practiced in Germany, less so in the thoroughly urban parts of the country, but still practiced. As the author of one of the *Volksheilkunde* books wrote, "He who trusts nature has not built on sand." The nature-is-health movement is very strong in Germany.

The term *volksheiklunde* covers the remedies, infusions, and substances often used by anxious mothers and fathers to treat relatively minor health problems of their children or themselves. *Das Artzliche Hausbuck*, or *Unser Hausfreund*, may be found in the homes of almost every family, including the highly educated.

But one does not need a book to know what to do. For infections and fever, drink plenty of water, or camomile, peppermint, or Lindenbluten teas; for headache, wrap the head with a compress soaked in water, vinegar, and milk, drink various teas, take a cool foot bath; for stomach aches, cramps, and heartburn, drink various cognacs and schnapps, eat zwieback, drink Baldrian and bloodroot teas; and so on and so on.

Gemans are also fond of therapeutic bathing and for that one needs some direction. Germans regard therapeutic bathing as aiding nature in the disposal of body poisons, strengthening nerves, arousing appetite, improving digestion, and enlivening circulation and metabolism. For example, the *Sitzbad* is a simple tub bath that achieves maximum results with the coldest possible water. The mud bath is a tub bath with mud mixed with water. The *Luftlichtsbad* requires sprinkling the body with water and running around naked while breathing deeply. And so on through the *Reibebad*, *Damfbad*, *Bettdampfbad*, and the *Ganzwaschung*. The latter requires a ritualistic procedure that begins with washing the right foot and then the left foot. This continues on up to the hips on the foresides of the legs, followed by the backsides, and finally to the upper body starting with the right arm, followed by the left arm, and so on. Various herbs with therapeutic value may be added to the water used in the various baths. And then there are the *Heilkrauter-tee* (teas made from medicinal herbs). There are at least eighty of them, including anise, fennel, camomile, mint, and sage.

It is difficult to separate out precisely what is "sound" medical treatment and what is ritualized or magical practice in these folk remedies. Regardless of their medical efficacy these remedies will be used without objective evidence of their effectiveness. Most people who get mildly ill or receive cuts or bruises, or simply don't feel good, do get well. If the practice does not kill the patient there is a self-validating sequence to complaint-treatment-result. Meanwhile, the procedures give people something to do that is inexpensive and handy.

I do not mean to imply that in the homes where folk remedies are used professional medical help is not also employed. All German families are covered by medical insurance. Hospitals and clinics are readily available. The conditions treated by folk medicine are mostly minor. When a serious condition develops, professional medical help is always used. To the German user of *Volksheilkunde* there is no necessary contradiction between the use of professional medical help and the use of home remedies of the type described here.

In the same way, fundamentally there is no difference between the uses of folk medicine in Bwa Mawego and in Germany. Parallels can be drawn between both cultures' practices. If we can accept this point of view, then Bwa Mawego practices become much more understandable.

It is remarkable that anthropologists have not paid more attention to folk medicine. Marsha Quinlan has done us all a service of considerable magnitude. This case study places folk medicine in the context of the local culture as well as presents the information about the many herbal cures and other practices that make up folk medicine in the bush in Bwa Mawego, a village in Dominica.

George Spindler
Series Editor

Preface

My first stay in Dominica was the summer of 1993, when I was a graduate student. I did not go to the village of Bwa Mawego with intentions of working on a book or even the doctoral dissertation that I ended up doing there. My husband and colleague (Robert Quinlan) and I went to Dominica to work with Mark Flinn. Dr. Flinn (University of Missouri–Columbia) is the Primary Investigator of the Dominica Child Health Project in Bwa Mawego. He offers his advisees foreign fieldwork and experience as researchers on his project. In addition, he expects his students to propose and work on their own research project while in the field.

My position was somewhat different from other student researchers on the Child Health Project. I was neither a University of Missouri student, nor a Flinn advisee (I was a new advisee's wife). I went to Dominica to help out and to experience fieldwork in a swidden village. I did not go to Dominica looking for a project of my own. In fact, as enthused as I was about this fieldwork opportunity, I felt guilty that while I was in Dominica, the data I collected for my University of Memphis MA practicum (in medical anthropology) was forsaken and unanalyzed in a storage shed. With MA work hanging over my head, other projects seemed distant. Rather than conduct my own formal research, I volunteered to assist the others so I could try out their research techniques. For the majority of that summer, I had the old-fashioned luxury of engaging in plenty of participant-observation.

While spending time with village women, I noticed that a great deal of their conversation dealt with medical topics (who was ill, the "hot" or "cold" event that caused the illness, which "bush" they used as a remedy, the possibility of witchcraft, etc.). These conversations seemed to surround me. As a medical anthropologist, I felt compelled to learn more about and describe this system of curing that Bwa Mawegans call *bush medicine*.

Perhaps this village and I were a good mix, since plants and medicine interested me as well as them. I began gathering my own data almost by accident and it motivated me to study ethnobotany during my doctoral training. Still, to a large degree, I feel that the people of Bwa Mawego chose the topic of "bush medicine" for me, or with me. I hope you find it interesting too.

ACKNOWLEDGMENTS

I am forever grateful to Mark Flinn, who first brought me to Dominica, and who has consistently done all that he could to support my research efforts in Dominica and in anthropology in general. I also appreciate the overwhelmingly friendly and forgiving spirit that people in the village extended towards me. Martina, Onia, Jean, and Amatos Warrington, Edith Coipel, and Juranie, Margillia and Lilia Durand were crucial to this work and I owe them many thanks. Special thanks also goes to MacField Coipel, Avie Constant, Catherine and Sarah Durand, Indira Durand, Jonathan Durand, Wilford Durand, Verona L'Homme, Constance Thomas, and

Beltina Warrington. I thankfully acknowledge Dominica's Ministry of Health for sponsoring this research. Dr. Robert Nasiiro, Dr. Dorian Shillingford, and Nurse Dorothy James were particularly helpful to me during my fieldwork. Work for this book was funded in part by the Earthwatch Center for Field Research[1] and by the National Science Foundation.[2] I am very grateful to George Spindler for supporting and editing *From the Bush*. My doctoral advisor, Deborah Pearsall, and my master's advisor, Ruthbeth Finerman, encouraged me to write this book and offered extensive comments on early versions. Theresa Quinlan reviewed a late version. Judith and Robert Bogar, Robert Domingos, Mark Flinn, Robin Kennedy, Michael Robbins, Gery Ryan, and Ross Sackett also contributed useful suggestions. Justin Nolan introduced me to several analytical techniques. In the field, Kathryn Gentner photographed, conducted interviews, and assisted me with entering and analyzing preliminary data. Robin Kennedy and Baadi Tadych helped curate my plant specimens at the University of Missouri Dunn-Palmer Herbarium. Steven Hill (Center for Biodiversity of the Illinois Natural History Survey) helped me with plant identifications. Work in ethnopharmacology by Nina Etkin and ethnophysiology by Elisa Sobo heavily influenced the very topics and approach of this research. Thank you all.

My deepest gratitude goes to Robert Quinlan for his extraordinary effort and steadfast support for this project. His teamwork at home and in the field and his thoughtful, thorough reviewing made this book a far better product.

[1] 1998 Grant for "Dominica Family Environment and Child Health Project" to M. Flinn, R. Quinlan and M. Quinlan.
[2] Grants BNS 8920569 and SBR 9205373 to M. Flinn.

1/The Importance
of Home Remedies

Think about the last few times that you felt sick or got hurt. If you're a college or university student, you may well have experienced a cold, sore muscles, a headache, or a hangover this past week. You may have even had the flu recently. How did you deal with your condition? Did you call your doctor's office the first time you sneezed or noticed a headache? Probably not. In our culture (Western industrial culture), we have a host of over-the-counter pharmaceuticals available to us at our local drugstore, discount mart, or grocery store. American gas station convenience stores even carry basic pain killers, antacids, first aid products, diarrhea medicine, and cold medications (and, if the gas station is near a highway, it likely stocks caffeine pills). A lot of Western industry and culture focuses on self-medication; for example, think of TV commercials that promote these products. We rarely seek immediate, professional medical care unless we have a cut needing sutures, a broken bone, or an illness with serious symptoms (e.g., acute appendicitis). Instead, we change our behavior. We rest, baby ourselves (or the affected body part), possibly eat special food (e.g., chicken soup), and probably take or apply some nonprescription medicines. Then, if the condition does not improve, we reluctantly visit our doctor.

The same basic pattern exists the world over. People avoid the hassle of going to an expert healer when they can more easily and more efficiently take care of themselves. Self-treatment, or home-based health care, is almost always a person's first line of defense against illness. Perhaps because it is so usual and so common, we give home health care little attention as a topic worthy of serious inquiry.

In Western culture, we don't even think of home treatment as "medical care" (which usually has a sterile, professional, white coat-and-scrubs sort of connotation). Yet the pills we pop at home are real and powerful medications, most of which were only available through prescription originally. Further, our first response to illness can be critical. For example, a baby's fever can become dangerously high very quickly. Administering pain/fever medication in time (at home) can prevent a fever from rising high enough to damage a baby's organs. Yet giving an infant too large a dose of pain/fever medication can also cause organ damage. Part of Western medical culture, therefore, involves looking for and following directions on medicine labels.

Medical anthropologists often seek information from a society's medical specialists (e.g., medicine men—folk healers and **shamans**—and biomedical physicians). It is also important, however, to investigate the medicinal practices of regular community members. After all, people take care of themselves much more often than they rely on a physician's (or other expert's) care. For example, about 70–90% of all medical treatment in the United States and Taiwan occurs at home (Kleinman 1980), and among the Saraguro of Ecuador, mothers treat 86% of family illness complaints (Finerman 1991). Home treatment has the power to improve, mask, or exacerbate a condition—or to create a new problem, as in the infant fever example. Home treatment behavior, and the beliefs and attitudes surrounding self-treatment, deserve the attention of social scientists.

From the Bush is a medical ethnography. It aims to explain the common theories and practice of home-based health care in Bwa Mawego,[1] a rural and remote village in Dominica. The book's main thesis is that cultural notions of the body—its function and malfunction—map onto local botanical treatments. In Dominica, notions of hot, cold, obstruction, and pollution account for most illness. Locals associate medicinal plants with cooling, heating, loosening, and cleansing properties that counteract the perceived causes of illness (see Figure 1.1). Manufactured pharmaceuticals, they assume, work similarly.

Dominicans refer to their rural medical system as *bush medicine*. As with any medical system, practice of bush medicine requires three-fold knowledge. First, one must know the **internal logic** of the local healing system, including concepts of normal body functioning and the body's response to various pathogens. Second, one must know treatments for maladies. In Dominican bush medicine, locals treat the majority of recognized illnesses with medicinal plants, or *bush*. A large part of this study involved collection, identification, and description of Bwa Mawego's medicinal plant species. *From the Bush*, then, is an ethnobotanical study as well as an ethnography. Finally, one must know the limitations of bush medicine, and when to seek help from outside the system of home-based care. For example, when is it appropriate to seek help from a physician rather than treating with "bush"? The internal logic, the local knowledge, and the boundaries of knowledge comprise the elements of an ethnomedical system.

ETHNOMEDICINE

Every society has a body of beliefs about sickness that includes ideas about what we need to do to stay healthy, how we catch certain sicknesses, and what we need to do to get better. These ideas—together with our thinking on who, when, and why we seek medical help—comprise our culture of medicine, or **ethnomedicine**. When I was young, my grandmother would come to our house and scold me for not wearing my slippers. "You'll catch cold running around in your stocking feet," she said. My grandmother's warnings were part of my medical **enculturation**, as was eating the chicken soup she brought over when I did actually "catch cold," and my learning to sit up straight, stick my tongue out, and say "ah" for the doctor.

---

[1]For reasons of confidentiality, the name "Bwa Mawego" (Patwa for the French "Bois Marigot") is a pseudonym for the research site, per anthropological tradition. Individuals' names are also pseudonyms.

Figure 1.1 A man examines his buckets of medicinal and food seedlings for transplant in his bush garden. He grows these plants for himself and his family, and to give to friends.

From the early days of anthropology, ethnomedicine intrigued Western researchers who studied non-Western societies. Non-Western medicine, which may include dancing, hallucinogenic tripping, and shouting, can be much more charismatic than the relatively stoic Western medical tradition. Early ethnomedicine consisted of ethnographic descriptions of exotic medical practices (e.g., Evans-Pritchard 1937), cross-cultural comparison of far-flung ethnomedical features (e.g., Frazer 1911), and generalizing and classifying traits of "primitive medicine" (Rivers 1924, Clements 1932). Later, anthropologists studied ethnomedicine as an important part of whole, interrelated cultural systems. For example, Whiting and Child (1953) found cross-cultural associations between the kinds of anxiety children experience through socialization and a culture's dominant explanations for disease. For example, societies with harsh weaning practices often point to oral disease origins (e.g., bad food or drink, or poison). Some societies have ways of handling aggressive or disobedient impulses that leave individuals with unresolved anxiety. Such cultures tend to have disease explanations that involve disobedience or aggression toward spirits or others (as in witchcraft).

Beyond its ethnographic interest, knowledge of ethnomedicine has become increasingly relevant for public health, particularly as the world system develops and stretches into areas of the globe in which the traditions of Western biomedicine are new, foreign, and in some cases suspect.

WHY USE ETHNOMEDICINE TO STUDY ETHNOBOTANY?

Ethnomedicine and medical ethnobotany are natural compliments. Ethnomedicine examines cultural notions and behavior surrounding illness and medical treatment (Fabrega 1975, Foster and Anderson 1978, Rubel and Hass 1990, Nichter 1992). Medical ethnobotany examines plant remedies used within particular cultures (Lewis and Elvin-Lewis 1977, Etkin 1988, Schultes and Raffauf 1990). And, the vast majority of the world's traditional medicines come from plants (Farnsworth 1988). Basically, ethnomedicine deals with behavior whereas medical ethnobotany, or **ethnopharmacology**, deals with medication. Yet medicine or treatment equally involves behavior and concepts as well as medication. When observing someone making an herbal tea or applying an herbal salve, it is difficult to distinguish behavior from medication. So it makes perfect sense to combine ethnomedicine with ethnobotany. Local concepts of plants and illnesses are related to one another. Thus, ethnobotanists interested in identifying bioactive plants may find it expedient to identify maladies of ethnic importance that are accompanied by well-developed local conceptions of physiologic processes. These are culturally prominent illnesses of a population, which map on to common botanical treatments (Quinlan, et al. 2002). And culturally significant plant species may be more efficacious than species collected by random sampling (Balick and Cox 1996, Khafagi and Dewedar 2000).

Further, ethnomedicine offers an anthropological perspective that allows ethnobotanists to understand cultural rationales for illness behaviors, including remedy administration and preparation. It likewise behooves medical anthropologists to adopt ethnobotany so that they can identify, collect, and research plants that are useful to humans. Further, ethnobotany offers a way of testing the efficacy of the material products (herbal remedies) of the ethnomedical system. Even the existence of medicines without demonstrable pharmaceutical properties raises very interesting questions for cultural anthropologists.

Some leading ethnobotanists recommend taking a biobehavioral approach to ethnobotany. This approach entails interdisciplinary work and broader research designs that incorporate medical studies with behavioral observation and **emic** description (Alcorn 1995, Brown 1987, Etkin 1996, Prance 1995). A popular ethnobotanist, E. Wade Davis (1995), suggests that the future of ethnobotany holds two challenges: (1) documenting plants that are important to a society, and (2) understanding the group's perceptions about the plant or the disease it treats, and how those perceptions influence behavior.

This book takes up these challenges by uniting ethnobotany with ethnomedicine in a study of the Dominican folk medical system. I begin with the premise that ethnographers researching medical treatment should view medicine **holistically** as a system, and should account for the cultural and scientific perspectives on healing. The anthropologists Browner, Ortiz de Montellano and Rubel (1988) propose a way to "combine the emic perspective of ethnomedicine with the **etic** measures of bioscience" (p. 681). Following their methods, the researcher (1) identifies the health problem and how it is conceivably healed according to locals, (2) objectively assesses the remedy's ability to produce the emically desired effect, and (3) identifies the areas of convergence and divergence between the emic and the etic assessments. For example, these authors suggest that Aztecs envisioned some headaches as the result of a build-up of blood in the head. Many Aztec headache medicines produced nasal bleeding, which was presumably thought to release the feeling of pressure allegedly caused by the excess blood in the head. These medicines were effective in Aztec terms because they achieved the desired result (i.e., a bloody nose). From the etic perspective, Aztec medications have chemical properties empirically capable of causing nosebleeds; however, most remain scientifically unproven as headache remedies (Browner, et al. 1988).

The science-minded may ponder the utility of a qualitative study of body image. Investigation and description of exotic medical beliefs may initially appear frivolous, esoteric, or unnecessary. Nevertheless, it is important to consider the context in which treatment takes place. Dismissal of the value of beliefs can lead to errors. When investigators do not first learn their subjects' views and vocabulary surrounding illness and the body, conceptual misinterpretations occur. This is true even in circumstances where both the researcher and the informants speak the same official language.[2] For example, without knowledge of the Dominican concept of "pressure" (worry-driven heating and reduction of blood, discussed in Chapters 7 and 8), researchers might well assume that plants used to treat "pressure" (sometimes called "high pressure" or "blood pressure") alleviate "high blood pressure" (hypertension). In reality, the two constitute different conditions.

In Dominica, there are many opportunities for misunderstandings because many local common names for plants and illnesses sound like, but differ from, Standard English terms (i.e., the words are actually homonyms). For example, when Dominicans talk about planting "fig trees" and eating "figs" (as they often do), they are not referring to the fruit that we Standard English speakers call a "fig," but what we call a "banana." The aforementioned "blood pressure," which is not hypertension for Dominicans, is another example. This misalignment in dialects demonstrates why accurate medical ethnobotanical research requires that researchers consider local vocabulary and meanings of illness. A researcher must tease out the core cultural understandings about the body's form and function and views on illness in order to fully comprehend the local language and logic of illness. One must learn what symptoms members of a culture recognize and what illnesses they link to those symptoms. Only with this requisite information can a scientist hope to recognize the applications and effects of a remedy for a given illness (see Figure 1.2).

Ethnomedicine provided me with a framework to study body and disease concepts and curing roles. **Ethnobotany** provided methods for systematic collection, identification and preservation of plant voucher specimens, and literature on plant usage and chemical properties. My data on remedies include the ailments each plant treats, dosage, emic rationale for the plant's selection, and who is best qualified to use the plant in treatments. This biobehavioral approach combining ethnomedicine and ethnobotany adds a degree of depth to the understanding of human medicinal practice and environmental exploitation.

FROM THE BUSH

This book is about the theories and plants that ordinary Dominican villagers use in home remedies. *From the Bush* thus looks at population-wide data, rather than

---

[2]Such is the case of an American ethnographer working in Dominica; however, the same phenomenon might occur to an ethnographer working with a subculture in one's own country.

Figure 1.2 A woman shaves the outer bark from a cinnamon tree to boil as a "bush tea" treatment for diarrhea.

relying solely on key informants. I collected the data during four field trips (and to a lesser degree by mail and telephone) over a six-year period (1993–1999). The bulk of my description comes from information I gathered during participant-observation and informal discussions with residents of Bwa Mawego. I support these impressions with data that I collected (1) in recall interviews with every village mother, (2) in key informant interviews with village experts on bush medicine, and (3) in freelist interviews with nearly every adult residing in the village from June through October of 1998 (see Chapter 4).

Chapters 2 and 3 of *From the Bush* introduce the research setting. Chapter 2 describes the Commonwealth of Dominica and its inhabitants. It gives an overview of the island's physical and social environments, describes the sociolinguistics of this bilingual society, and offers an ethnohistorical account of the peoples who came to inhabit the area. Chapter 3 concentrates on the village of Bwa Mawego, the study site, including the village's ecology, demography, economy, and general lifeways.

Chapter 4 details the methods used to collect qualitative and quantitative data on Bwa Mawegan bush medicine. It is, to some degree, a narrative of the fieldwork process. Additionally, the chapter evaluates advantageous and disadvantageous aspects of each method and each stage of the fieldwork for this project.

Chapter 5 describes the ailments that afflict residents of Bwa Mawego. It discusses Dominican pathologies from the etic and emic perspectives. The chapter presents the disease risks that occur in Bwa Mawego, and defines and discusses personalistic and naturalistic illnesses as they affect residents there.

Chapter 6 details the healthcare options available to villagers. The chapter discusses the various medical practitioners and how Bwa Mawegans generally perceive the practitioners' utility for managing particular illnesses.

Chapter 7 explains how the people of Bwa Mawego envision human anatomy and physiology. Local body concepts underlie village notions of the **etiologiy** of the illness and appropriate treatment. This chapter describes the local hot–cold **humoral system** of health, and its relation to illnesses and medicinals. The chapter also presents local explanations of the body's requirements and metabolic systems.

Chapter 8 presents the illnesses that Bwa Mawegans commonly treat at home with bush medicine and the plants they use to treat them. It discusses how those illnesses fall into four domains: cold, hot, external, and stomach disorders. Then, domain by domain, the chapter describes each illness with respect to its primary bush treatments.

Finally, Chapter 9 offers an applied synthesis of the practice of bush medicine in Bwa Mawego. It discusses biomedicine, folk medicine, and bush medicine in terms of their accessibility and acceptability to rural Dominicans. It offers some suggestions to make professional biomedicine less intimidating and more intuitive for West Indian patients. It also discusses the unique health benefits Bwa Mawegans receive from using bush medicine.

2/Dominica
and Dominicans

I peered out the window of the small, twin-engine prop plane at my first sight of Dominica. The mountainous island appeared to rise vertically from the deep blue Caribbean. Fissured and steeply graded, the terrain seemed carpeted with lush vegetation right down to the windswept shores. Mist clung among the peaks of the interior rain forest. A pair of swiftly flowing rivers snaked down through the mountains and out onto narrow coastal plains. The "twin otter," our small aircraft, bounced through the turbulent air along the island's coast. The copilot handled the approach clumsily (apparently in training) while the pilot chain-smoked cigarettes, chuckling to himself as he nervously flicked ashes out the small, open window in the cockpit. The twin otter banked hard before leveling off. The sudden turn was so severe it caused my heart to race and my palms to sweat as I gripped my seat. But the unexpected move gave me a spectacular view of the ground below, a verdant mix of forest and gardens in red soil with banana trees and large, heart-shaped taro leaves that I could see from the plane. The landing on the short airstrip was abrupt and violent, much like landing on an aircraft carrier, or so I imagined. I could hardly wait to climb out of the twin otter and set my feet on the red dirt of Dominica.

THE ISLAND

The Commonwealth of Dominica (see Figure 2.1) is the most mountainous, most rural, and least developed country in the Caribbean (Honychurch 1995). About 71,700[1] people live in this independent democracy centered at 15°25' N by 61°20' W between the French islands of Guadeloupe to the north and Martinique to the south. Dominica is one of the Windward Islands[2] and forms the midpoint of the arc of the Lesser Antilles in the southeast Caribbean. Measured at its longest point, the island is 29 miles long with a maximum width of 16 miles. Its area is about 300 square

[1]Projection of the 2001 census figures, available at http://www.delphis.dm/stats.htm#P2001.

[2] As the island in the keystone position of the Lesser Antilles, Dominica has been administered as both the southernmost Leeward island and the northernmost Windward island. Today Dominica is considered a Windward isle, although no longer a colonial holding.

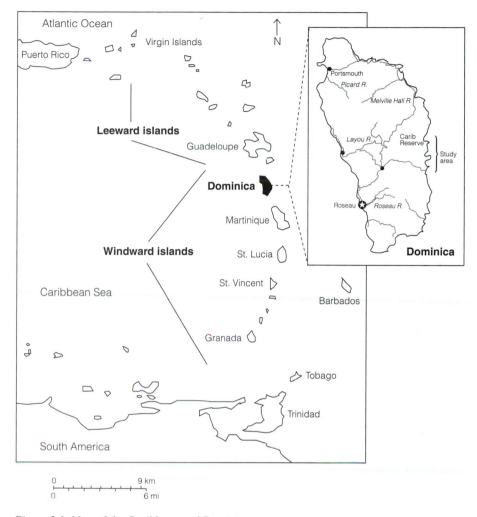

Figure 2.1 Map of the Caribbean and Dominica

miles (Honychurch 1995). Dominican citizens have Native American, African, and European ancestry. The country's official language is English, but a French Patois is the first language of most citizens (Lowenthal 1972). Dominica has one town, Roseau, the capital, and approximately 90 villages scattered throughout its hills and shoreline.

THE PHYSICAL ENVIRONMENT

Dominica is entirely comprised of volcanic mountains that rise directly out of the ocean to an average central-island height of about 3,000 feet. Plains and valleys are rare and relatively narrow. For someone unfamiliar with the appearance of volcanic islands, Christopher Columbus made a remarkably helpful illustration in 1493. To describe Dominica's physical appearance from a distance to King Ferdinand and

Queen Isabella, he simply crumpled a sheet of paper and held it out (Honychurch 1995).

Climate

Dominica is a tropical island. June is the hottest month (average high of 90°F, average low of 74°F) and January (84°F high, 68°F low) is the coolest (Honychurch 1995).

A fairly constant, moist northeast trade wind blows from the Atlantic side of the island. This makes the east coast the island's windward side and the west coast leeward. The east coast's mountains force the moist winds to rise, cool, and precipitate almost immediately upon hitting the island (Hodge 1954). Rain showers thus fall mainly on the windward side of the island (the location of the present study) and over the island's high interior (see Figure 2.2).

Rain is the most outstanding aspect of Dominica's climate. Even when neighboring islands experience drought, Dominica often remains watered. Rainfall ranges between 100 and 152 inches (250 and 380 cm) per annum on the east coast, and reaches over 200 inches (510 cm) in the island's central mountain range. The island's leeward side, in the rain shadow of the central mountains, is noticeably drier (120 and 250 cm per annum) than the windward side and has scrubbier vegetation. Still, Dominica's "dry" coast receives more annual rainfall than the U.S. East Coast, and more than any other leeward coast in the Caribbean (Honychurch 1995). There is a seasonal aspect to the rain pattern with a July to December rainy season, followed by a drier season from January to June. Even during the dry season there is no noticeable lack of water (Hodge 1954).

Vegetation

Dominica has a rich **neotropical** flora that is probably closer to its original state than any other Caribbean island (Adjanohoun, et al. 1985, Hodge 1954). Botanists generally accept that most of the island's plant life came from seeds that floated up from South America on the "south equatorial current" that flows into the Caribbean (Honychurch 1995).

The island has seven vegetative communities, which correspond with the island's altitude and rainfall zones (see Figure 2.2). The study site, Bwa Mawego, lies within *bel mawché* (a nice day-hike) to five out of seven of these zones (littoral forest, cultivated land, montane rainforest, rainforest proper, and secondary forest).[3] The characteristic plants of the zones are discussed below.

Most of the soil on the island is the color of red bricks. The "red earth" (a technical soil type) is almost pure clay; it has poor drainage and is acidic. Crops do not grow well in red earth, but it supports a "lower montane" rain forest that covers most of the island (Beard 1949). In places, red clay gives way to browner, copper-colored

---

[3]The two zones not readily accessible to Bwa Mawegans are (1) the Elfin Forest (the "cloud forest"—a low, thick forest in which the trees are covered with many mosses, ferns, orchids, bromeliads—which occurs on summits and slopes of the highest mountains), and (2) the Dry Scrub/Deciduous Woodland (low trees and many grasses, which occurs in the leeward rain shadow areas). Though rare, Bwa Mawegans have access to plants from the Elfin and Dry Scrub zones through long hikes, family, and trade.

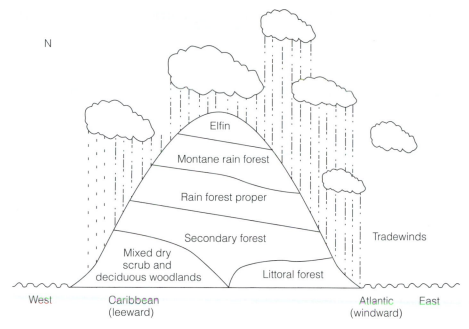

N

Elfin

Montane rain forest

Rain forest proper

Secondary forest

Mixed dry
scrub and
deciduous woodlands

Littoral forest

Tradewinds

West   Caribbean   Atlantic   East
              (leeward)   (windward)

Figure 2.2 Diagram of Dominica's wind, rain, and vegetal patterning

earth, and yellower earth (about the color of pumpkin pie). The brown and yellow
soils are free-draining and highly fertile, so crops are frequently planted there.

Like most windward coast villages, the village of Bwa Mawego is carved out of
littoral forest. This zone is a narrow band of woodlands along the Atlantic coast.
Under the trees, the littoral forest is similar to a typical shrubby neotropical mountain forest. There are various hardwood trees (up to about 50 feet tall), vines, small
wildflowers, many grasses and, in shady spots, ferns and begonias. From a distance,
when one looks down the coast, the effect of the constant westward winds becomes
apparent. The whole forest appears gnarled and serrated, and forced in a downward
lean against the bluffs.

Walking through the village of Bwa Mawego, the most common vegetative zone
is *cultivated land*. People plant flower, herb and vegetable (carrots, onions, and cab-
bage) gardens near their houses. Though most people have large subsistence gardens
(one or more acres) burned out of the bush surrounding the village, there are numerous subsistence gardens inside the village too (usually plots between 1/4 and 1/2 acre
of mostly taro, plantain, and yams). In rocky and very steep village areas, there are
orchards. This cultivated zone is altered by slash-and-burn gardening (see Figure
2.3). Human gardening activities like burning and weeding change the environment,
making the secondary or weedy plant communities different from communities in
primary, undisturbed areas with otherwise similar growing conditions.

Walking the slippery trails, climbing inland, out of the village and into the bush,
one enters the *montane rain forest*. This evergreen or semi-evergreen zone (i.e., there
is no seasonal leaf loss) begins above elevations of about 700 feet, and occurs in wet,

Figure 2.3 Cultivated land; a subsistence garden with visible, burned tree stumps and newly planted dasheen (taro)

windy areas near exposed mountain ridges and summits of smaller peaks. Montane rain forests are dense. They have 40- to 80-foot trees, many climbing plants or vines, a thick shrub layer, and epiphytes or "air plants," such as orchids and bromeliads, throughout.

Climbing further inland to around 1,000 feet above sea level, one comes to the zone of the *rain forest proper*. This is the most extensive and luxuriant of all Dominican forests. Rain in this zone averages between 175 and 300 inches. The heavy red soil covers a hard clay subsoil and is constantly moist. There are several layers of trees. For the most part, different species comprise each layer. The canopy has trees around 100 feet tall with 5- to 10-foot diameters at breast height. Beneath these there are medium-sized trees of 40–80 feet, followed by a layer of short, 15- to 35-foot trees. It is very shady and there are few plants on the forest floor because little sunlight permeates the layers of trees. Ferns are the most common plants that do live on the forest floor.

On a long hike, climbing through wide stretches of montane rain forest and rain forest proper, one happens on numerous subsistence "bush gardens." One also notices forested zones where the soil is browner (less red) and where the trees are further apart. These "interzones" are called *secondary forests* where rain forest areas have been cultivated and later abandoned. Trees in secondary forests are similar to those in the rain forest and lower montane rain forest; however, they are more spread out. There is also more shrubby ground cover in secondary forests than in the rain forests (Beard 1949).

ETHNOHISTORY OF DOMINICAN PEOPLE

Amerindians

Before Europeans and Africans came to Dominica, the island was settled by at least two migrations of South American natives. Local legend stereotypes these groups as the "peaceful Arawaks" and the "cannibal Caribs." Actually, both groups were from the Arawak language and culture group of lowland South America, and the so-called Caribs were probably not cannibals (Allaire 1985).

The earliest settlers known on Dominica were from a migration of Arawaks who slowly colonized their way up the West Indian island chain from Venezuela's Orinoco Delta and settled in Dominica around A.D. 400 (Haviser 1997). Like Arawakan speakers in South America, these people were fishing and hunting horti-culturalists that relied heavily on processed **manioc** (also called cassava). They also grew maize, beans, sweet potatoes, peppers, pineapple, papaya, custard apple, and soursop. They cultivated calabash gourds for containers, cotton to weave, and annatto for body paint. Their technology included ceramics, hammock and basket weaving, and construction of wooden huts with thatched roofs. The most important aspect of their technology was canoe building. They built various types and sizes of dugouts, which may have carried up to forty people. Canoes were necessary for trade, fishing and coastal hunting, inter-island visits, and migration. These first settlers lived in small, presumably egalitarian communities, each with one headman (Honychurch 1995).

Dominica's second migration of Native Americans took place around A.D. 1000 when, like their predecessors, another group left South America from the Orinoco Delta and began to proceed north up the Lesser Antilles island chain (Beckles 1990). Anthropologists generally refer to people from this migration as Island-Caribs. The Island-Caribs were an Arawakan tribe who, in South America, had been conquered by a Carib language/culture group so that their language contained many Carib elements (Taylor 1977). Historical reports of these so-called Island-Caribs begin with accounts from Columbus' expeditions and are undoubtedly tainted by fears, biases, and language confusion of those first European explorers. A large group of Indians in the Greater Antilles told Columbus that among the smaller islands to the South were islands called "Caniba," "Cariba," "Caribi," or "Caribe" (there is some name discrepancy among the Columbian texts). The Northern islanders allegedly told Columbus that these Southern islanders stole people from other islands and ate them (Honychurch 1995). Whether this was truth, myth, hyperbole, or a language mis-understanding by the Europeans is undocumented. However, in November of 1493, the day after Columbus first sighted Dominica, he landed on Guadeloupe where he saw his first Island-Caribs. Columbus' men reported finding great quantities of human bones hanging in the houses, with skulls used as vessels to hold things. The men assumed they had found "Caniba" (the place with man-eaters), or as others called it, "Caribe." In the case of the first pronunciation, our legacy is the word *cannibal* as the Spanish *canibal* refers to a native of Caniba. The pronunciation "Caribe" stuck as place names for the Caribbean Sea and islands and the name "Carib" to refer to the tribe of people there (Honychurch 1995). The skeletal material in Island-Carib houses may have been evidence not of cannibalism but of mourning rituals involving dead family members' bones. Later accounts revealed that other Caribbean tribes also kept ancestral bones in their houses (Myers 1984).

From Columbus' accounts and other early accounts we can deduce that the Island-Caribs were a mobile, seafaring, canoe-building, chiefdom-level society with a tradition of bride capturing. Males lived in large, central huts while wives and children lived in surrounding smaller huts. Columbus' surgeon noted that the Caribs seemed "more civilized than those elsewhere. All have straw houses, but these people build them much better, and have larger stocks of provisions, and show more signs of industry practiced by both men and women" (Honychurch 1995).

After Columbus, the Spanish began to enslave Indians to the north in the Greater Antilles. Aggression and disease killed most natives there. Some allegedly escaped to the Lesser Antilles where they warned inhabitants about the Spanish. At this point, remnant Indians from the Greater Antilles and descendants of the first Arawak settlers joined the Island-Caribs in Dominica to amass a defense against the Spanish (Honychurch 1995). The Spanish never bothered to colonize Dominica. Neither the terrain nor the inhabitants of the island were hospitable.

About 200 years after the first European contact, some French people began to settle on the island. The Island-Caribs withdrew to Dominica's rugged East Coast, where escaped European indentured servants and African slaves sometimes joined them. The Island-Caribs, locally referred to as "Caribs," remain on the island's East Coast to this day. In 1903 the government granted them 3,700 acres of land (Honychurch 1995). This territory, the Carib Reserve, is just north of Bwa Mawego, the study site.

Maroons[4]

People of African descent settled on the island before Europeans did. Most were escaped slaves from other islands. Some formed their own communities on Dominica while others joined Island-Carib communities. The Island-Caribs captured still more Africans and re-enslaved them on Dominica.

More Africans came to the island as slaves when the French started the first coffee plantations in the middle of the eighteenth century. When Dominica became British in 1763, Roseau and Portsmouth (both on the West Coast) became free ports where foreign merchants could make tax-free purchases of slaves and other British commodities. During this time, many more slaves escaped and settled in the island's rugged interior and East Coast. Also during this period, English colonists established the island's first sugar growing and manufacturing estates. One can assume that a trickle of slaves escaped from both the French coffee and the English sugar operations.

In the Caribbean, French colonialists used the term *marron* for a fugitive slave. The borrowed English term became "Maroon." By 1785, the Maroons had expanded into 13 chief-led camps in the mountainous center and toward the eastern part of Dominica. Colonial slaveholders attempted to destroy these camps and recapture slaves. Maroons plundered and set fire to colonial estates in rebellion. As a result, the British increased their arms and the frequency and severity of raids on Maroon camps. Maroons retreated into the hills.

[4]Discussion from Honychurch 1995.

Slave escapes and planter raids increased during the early nineteenth century. In 1812, 75 slaves escaped from the Castle Bruce estate, not far from Bwa Mawego, the present study site. Around this same time, Maroons began raiding and looting larger estates. In response to this rebellion, the Governor ordered extermination of the Maroon forces. Five hundred seventy-seven Maroons were either beaten and returned to estates, jailed, or killed. The heads of eleven Maroons were displayed on poles at various strategic island spots. Any remaining Maroons went back into hiding until 1838, which marked the emancipation of the island's approximately 14,000 slaves.

Colonial Europeans[5]

European colonization of Dominica began in 1627 when England and France simultaneously claimed Dominica. These opposing claims caused no real conflict as the steep, forested island offered little promise for cash-crop profits to either nation. Ships from both empires used Dominica as a place to resupply food and water. The French established trade relations with the Island-Caribs on the island's eastern coast while the English established trade with Island-Caribs on the western coast. On both sides of the island, trade primarily consisted of cutlasses (machetes), nails, and beads in exchange for produce—especially cassava [manioc] cakes, plantains and bananas, potatoes, pineapples and papayas—and barrels of water that the Indians would carry in exchange for goods. Often there was no need for the Europeans to set foot on the island as the Island-Caribs rowed their canoes out to meet the European ships.

Around 1700, French lumbermen (some with families) were the first Europeans to stay on the island. They encroached on the Caribs peacefully by buying their land with rum and trade goods. They built plank houses on the leeward coast by the present site of Roseau (the capital) and cleared provision gardens and small cotton and tobacco gardens.

These French settlements paved the way for other imperialist pursuits. By 1725 French coffee growers and their African slaves moved to Dominica (coffee trees were one of the few cash-crop plants that took hold on the steep mountainsides). In 1763, France ceded the island to Britain as partial settlement over war in Canada. The English introduced sugar estates[6] in the broader coastal river valleys during this period.

Dominican sugar "estates" were different from sugar "plantations" on other islands. They came relatively late and were small. More importantly, Dominican sugar estate owners were absent—they lived in England or on more developed islands and hired local managers to run their estates. As a result, the typical Caribbean legacy of white aristocracy remains reduced on Dominica compared to other islands (Lowenthal 1972).

France recaptured Dominica in 1778 while England was preoccupied fighting the American Revolution. Six years later, England regained the island. Dominica remained a British colony until it achieved independent Commonwealth status in 1978.

Dominica shares so many social traditions with French Caribbean islands that it seems unbelievable that French rule ended over two hundred years ago. Dominica has a long history of English rule, yet the island lies within eyesight of two French

[5]Except where otherwise noted, discussion is from Honychurch 1995.
[6]The study village is located in the hills between two former sugar estates.

départements (Guadeloupe and Martinique) and most citizens claim at least partial French ancestry. Relations between Dominica and its French neighbors continue through trade, kinship, and migration. In terms of language and culture, Dominica is as similar to French Caribbean islands as it is to English Caribbean ones.

LANGUAGE IN DOMINICA: COMMINGLING CREOLES

Some language discussion is important to this book—not only because of its inherent ethnographic value—but because the languages have implications for health care. Most Dominicans are bilingual in a West Indian English **Creole** and Patwa,[7] a French Creole. In rural villages, Patwa tends to be the language of bush medicine, while English tends to be reserved for biomedicine.

Almost all rural Dominicans are bilingual in two Creole languages. Creoles have vocabularies based on a colonial or trade language. A Creole **dialect** may not be mutually intelligible with the standard dialect because some of the vocabulary and all of the grammar is unique to the Creole form. Such is the case with both the English and French Creoles of Dominica (Taylor 1977). In a simple example, Patwa and Creole English share grammar in which the verb "to be" is absent before an adjective (and, technically, the adjective functions as both a verb and predicate). This linguistic phenomenon (called *predicative adjective use*) is a universal indicator of Creole languages (Taylor 1977). Some Dominican examples are:

> English: "Di boy stupid." (The boy's stupid.)
> "Di cat not fat." (The cat's not fat.)
> Patwa: "Ou sou." (You're drunk. *ou* = you and *sou* = drunk)
> "Manje yo fwet." (Their food is cold. *manje* = food, *yo* = their,
> fwet = "cold")

Various dialects of English coexist in Dominica. The English form that most Dominicans speak is called Dominican English Creole (Christie 1990, Roberts 1988, Taylor 1977). All English-speaking residents of the study community speak Dominican English Creole. This form of English shares features (e.g., word order) with Patwa that are foreign to Standard English and other Caribbean dialects. English varieties in Dominica range from Dominican English Creole, spoken by the general public, to West Indian English (Standard English with West Indian accent), spoken by the most elite and educated (Roberts 1988).

While English is Dominica's official language, most Dominicans speak Patwa as a first language (Christie 1990). English is the more formal language—the language of government, commerce, and school. Patwa is the language of the populace—an informal, conversational (mostly unwritten) language—and the only language necessary if one has no direct contact with schools, government, or commerce.

Dominican French Patwa (a.k.a. Patois, or Kwéyòl) is a holdover from the days of the French plantations. It was the language of Dominican slaves and the slaves who escaped to Dominica from the French islands (Taylor 1977). The language is a

---

[7]There is some debate about the official name of this language. Following linguist Stephanie Stuart (1993) I use the term Patwa. This is the name that Dominicans use for their own language spelled in the most standardized way to write the language to date (Fontaine 1992).

Creole based on French **lexicon** (vocabulary) with **syntax** (grammar) showing similarities to several West African languages (Fontaine 1992).

Before going to Dominica, I had taken three years of French. After one summer, I could comprehend some Patwa and use a few key expressions. Now, I can comprehend more Patwa; I have a moderate vocabulary of everyday words, and a specialized vocabulary of medical words. But I am not close to fluent in Patwa.

There are some obvious differences between Standard French and Patwa. For example, the French *r* is a *w* in Patwa so that the French word *aprés* (after) is *apwe* in Patwa. Swallowed or unemphasized sounds in French words are completely absent in Patwa. Thus, the French word *quatre* (four) is *kat*, and the French word *petite* (small) reduces to *ti* in Patwa. Finally, French nouns that would normally occur with their definite articles *le*, *la*, or *les* (the) retain the French article as part of the Patwa noun. Thus the French word *pluie* (rain) is *lapli* in Patwa.

Dominican Patwa is mutually intelligible with the French Creoles of Guadeloupe, Martinique, St. Lucia, Grenada, Trinidad, and to a lesser degree with the better-known Haitian French Creole. It is not identical to any of the other Creoles although it remains structurally closest to the dialects spoken in Guadeloupe and Martinique (Taylor 1977).

For many years, the Dominican government thought Patwa was a deterrent to education and development, and discouraged its use. Teachers used to beat children for speaking Patwa. During the 1980s, Dominican government policy began to embrace Patwa as part of local cultural identity. The new policy and national attitudes resulted in a fragmented language system. Now, Dominica has elderly people, especially in the remote areas, who only speak Patwa. In rural areas, young and middle-aged people are fluent in Patwa but often view their fluency as a hindrance. These rural young and middle-agers speak English more than their parents, but have restricted English vocabularies (Stuart 1993). Meanwhile, in Roseau, the only "town" and capital, people speak little Patwa, although they comprehend it and value the language.

Patwa is Dominica's folk language. It is the language of folk traditions, including the better part of folk medicine. It is the language of the folk songs, proverbs, and the *kont* (folktales) that people recite at village feasts and wakes (Christie 1990). Village Dominicans prefer to speak Patwa when telling jokes, gossiping, and cursing at each other.

To a degree, Dominicans associate Patwa with nationalism. For instance, most place names in the country are in Patwa or French. The national motto, *Apwé Bondié Se La Ter* ("After God, It Is the Land") is in Patwa, as are the slogans of many products made in Dominica and marketed to Dominicans. Older and rural Dominicans regard speaking English informally (e.g., in passing or while drinking alcohol) as pretentious. At the same time, Dominicans view those who regularly use Patwa, through lack of English proficiency, as uneducated or countrified.

Often Dominicans switch languages in the same breath. A Dominican might repeat a statement in Patwa and English Creole for emphasis, such as: "Mwen pa ka ve'y! I not seeing it!" ("I don't see it! I don't see it!"). Or, they might switch from one language to the other, as in: "What happen you? Ou malad?" ("What's happened to you [What's wrong]? Are you ill?") (Christie 1990).

In the study site, both the English and Patwa language situations appear to be changing. Patwa use appears to be on the increase. Young adults speak Patwa much more often, or more publicly, than they did when I first went to Dominica. This is partly due to Patwa's acceptance in schools. Seeing Patwa in print also undoubtedly increases the language's status.

Meanwhile, village acculturation is leading to more contact with Standard English. In the six years that I traveled to and from the village, two additional mini-buses began daily, or nearly daily, trips to town. Further, electronic media increased dramatically. In 1993 almost all villagers had some kind of radio (typically a transistor), a few villagers had stereo jamboxes, and two (maybe three) families had stereos. Now, *most* villagers have jamboxes, several have stereos, and several (maybe 10 families) have televisions with VCRs.[8]

During my second summer in the village, our landlords had a working television (a gift from U.S. cousins). They rigged up a giant TV antenna so they could get reception.[9] People gathered from all over the village to watch the television. One show that came in clearly was *World News Tonight* with Peter Jennings. The villagers could not understand Peter Jennings's Standard American English and often asked us anthropologists to translate (no doubt difficulty stemmed from unfamiliarity with U.S. and world geography, technology, etc., but the primary problem was language). Even the few high school graduates present were unable to follow the broadcast entirely. They said they understood "almost" everything, but they still could not understand some of the language. During the summer of 1998, I gathered that comprehension of Standard English was increasing from the way villagers acted while watching videos and while speaking with American and British Earthwatch volunteers.

Few villagers speak an English form close to West Indian (Standard) English. Those who speak West Indian English have lived in town or on another island for an extended period. They are often high school graduates, and two of them attended the two-year teachers' college. Typically, these people speak Standard English with the members of our anthropological team. All but the members of one family (locally reckoned as snobs) shift to a more creolized English when their neighbors are around.

It took about three weeks of village living for me to understand almost all Dominican English Creole speech (and make myself understood by those with little experience with American English).

Dominican English Creole and Standard English have different syntax. For example, Dominicans use the "-ing" gerund verb form (without the helping verb "to be") to show habitual present tense, as in, "They calling that bush *sime kontwa*." Also, prepositions in Dominican English Creole are often absent and generally different than Standard English ones:

"My moda afraid snakes." (My mother's afraid of snakes.)
"I going at home." (I'm going home.)

---

[8] There is no TV reception in the village without a tall antenna. People who have televisions use them to watch videos, generally sent from relatives in the United States, Canada, England, or other islands (as were the televisions).

[9] The antenna was subsequently destroyed in a tropical storm. No villager has attempted the antenna since.

"Trow di soap behind me." (Throw me the soap.)
"I hiding my broda." (I'm hiding from my brother.)

Dominican English Creole shares many grammar and syntax traits with Patwa. Some examples are (1) the Dominican use of "it have" (*there is* in Standard English, *i ni* in Patwa), as in "It have a man in town who wearing dresses"; and (2) the use of "it making" (*it is* in Standard English, *i fe* in Patwa), as in, "It making sun today" (It is sunny today); and (3) generally French-like word choice and order, as in "How many years you have?" (How old are you?).

Phoneme (sound) shifts from Standard English to Dominican English Creole follow certain rules (Roberts 1988). The accents are generally different because of shifts in vowel sounds and shifts in some consonants. There are three obvious phonetic differences between Creole and American Standard English. First, Dominicans do not pronounce *r* after vowel sounds made in the middle or back of the mouth (not even as a voiceless semi-vowel, as in some British or New England accents). Thus, "hard" is pronounced *had*, "chord" is pronounced *cod*, "bigger" is *biga*, "pepper" is *pepa*, and so forth. Second, Standard English *th* is pronounced either as *t* or *d* (before a vowel) or *f* or *v* (after a vowel). "Thief" is thus pronounced *teef*, and "them" is *dem*; "arthritis" is *afraitis*, and "bathe" is *beiv*. The third obvious difference between Standard and Dominican Creole dialects is that final consonant sounds are often swallowed. When a consonant blend occurs after a vowel, the second consonant generally disappears. "Last" is thus pronounced as *las*, and "find" is *fain*.

As an American English speaker, I had the most trouble with the Dominican accent when a couple of phoneme differences occurred in the same sentence, or in the same word. During my first summer in Dominica, our landlord's 12-year-old son, Henry, came to the door and said to me, "*Mahsha* (my name there), my *moda* (mother) ask if you have *fren*." Confused, I said, "Well, do you mean like Mark is my friend?" I said, swinging my thumb toward Flinn. "What?!" the boy said, knitting his brow and looking at me as if discerning whether I was crazy, stupid, or joking. "I'm sorry, Henry, I guess I don't understand. What's *fren*?" I said. Then, looking at me with the realization that I was just stupid, he looked right in my eyes and slowly said what sounded to me like "*Fren. Fren to so cloves.*" "What?" I still didn't get it. I was embarrassed. "Fren. FREN to put in a needle to sew *cloves*!" "Oh, thread to sew clothes! Yes, I have thread. Sorry, Henry," I laughed. The boy waited for the thread, never unknitting his eyebrows, and left shaking his head. Henry thought I was amazingly dumb then. We became pals later.

ISLAND SOCIOECONOMICS

Most West Indian islands have class hierarchies that correspond to skin color gradations with white as the highest class, blacks at the lowest, and the various brown to red shades in the middle (Lowenthal 1972). Dominica is one of four islands (along with Grenada, St. Lucia, and Haiti) where racial relations are distinct from the rest of the Caribbean because resident upper-class whites are nearly, if not completely, absent.

There are a few Dominican white families who have disproportionate wealth and power. These make up .5% of the total population yet make up 14% of the "influential" people (Lowenthal 1972). Still, this means that non-whites, mostly mulattos, comprise the vast majority (86%) of the elite. These people are racially similar to people of the poorest peasantry, which is also a mix of European and African descent (and Amerindian in parts).

In most of the Caribbean, the light-colored elite socializes and marries amongst itself; the darker poor do likewise. Dominicans also tend to socialize within their class. However, at least among the agricultural class, complexion is a secondary concern. Poor Dominicans recognize color difference and consider "fair" or "clear" (paler) complexions attractive and a blessing. However, color appears to affect mate and friendship choice little in comparison with other attributes such as wealth, family status, dependability, and personality.

The hierarchical social class situation that exists on the island is not racially fueled. Dominicans distinguish between the commercial (high and middle) classes, and the agricultural (low) class. This is essentially a rural-urban[10] dichotomy. In Dominica, language ability, not color, indicates one's class. The bilingual language split corresponds to the historical social strata and parallels the separation of the agricultural class from the town class (Stuart 1993). People of the upper classes speak West Indian English, not Dominican English Creole, and speak no or little Patwa. Middle class people tend to speak some Patwa (primarily as a trade language), and can code shift (switch dialects) easily between West Indian English and English Creole. Poor, agricultural people speak only the two Creole languages. Those few who speak only Patwa are of Dominica's most rural, isolated class. These people live in villages like the study site, Bwa Mawego.

CONCLUSION

Dominica is a small, Caribbean country with rugged volcanic mountain terrain that limits agriculture and development. It is a warm and rainy island, which is almost entirely covered with either cultivated land or some kind of tropical forest.

The island was first settled by Arawakan Indians around 1,600 years ago. French and English and their African slaves settled on the island (in small numbers) during the eighteenth century. At this point, the Native Americans withdrew to the mountainous windward side. Because the island's terrain was so rugged, Dominica became a haven for many escaped African slaves and European indentured servants. The population of Dominica became a racially mixed (mulatto) one in which most people speak two Creole languages—Dominican English Creole, and French Patwa. The culture of Dominica shares traits with societies in the English-speaking and French-speaking Caribbean. Dominican culture also includes Island-Carib traits, especially on the island's East Coast in and around the Carib Reserve.

During the chapters to come, we see that Dominica's ethnic integration reveals itself in the medical beliefs and practices of the island. Rural Dominicans live in fear of illnesses sent by **syncretic** Native American and Africanized versions of the witches and werewolves that alarmed colonial Europeans. They seek healing and protection from Catholic priests. And they make "bush medicines" (herbal remedies) from some European herbs (e.g., rosemary), plants found throughout the tropics (e.g., coconuts), and many plants of the American tropics that may have been used by Island-Caribs for a thousand years.

---

[10]I hesitate to employ the word "urban" to Roseau, with its municipal population totaling only 15,853 (Maxwell 1997). It is, however, the island's governmental and commercial center.

3/Bwa Mawego

We rented an old Subaru station wagon in Roseau, and after winding through lush and beautiful Dominican tropical mountain forests, we arrived in Bwa Mawego on an early Saturday evening. By the time we unloaded our things and quickly surveyed our lodgings, the sun had set. Then our team leader, Mark Flinn, took us through some of Bwa Mawego to meet some people. Walking around on steep trails with flashlights in the dark was disorienting and fantastic. Dim light from a bare, hanging light bulb or a homemade oil lantern occasionally spilled out of shacks along the paths. We walked by an open-air shop where men bellowed out rapid-fire Patwa at the top of their lungs as they slammed dominoes down hard on a homemade table. As we stopped to meet people, it seemed to me that every man in Bwa Mawego was drunk, overly friendly, and fuming with the sweet, stale stench of rum-infused sweat. The women were coolly reserved. I could only understand about one in four words of the local English Creole. I felt quite out of place.

The first days I spent in the village were a difficult time of adjustment. My feelings early on were a mix of excitement and dread. The trails around the village are steep and slippery, so even walking from one hamlet (neighborhood) of Bwa Mawego to another was tough. I had to really concentrate to understand the English Creole. Sometimes I had to ask people to repeat themselves multiple times, which sometimes miffed them and always made me uncomfortable. The food was very different. The vegetables were mostly new to me and the meat seemed more suitable for pet food. One of our first days there, our village host asked if "all you eating pork?" After hesitating a moment I said, "Yes, I like pork, I think we all do." Later that evening my spirits sank—how was I supposed to eat a boiled pig snout with grace and tact?

Our bathing spot was a beautiful little waterfall about a half-mile from our accommodations, down in the bottom of a steep-sided gorge. During the rainy season, the seemingly ice-cold water slammed down from above. We were supposed to bathe under the waterfall while standing on a slanted rock covered with slick, slimy algae. My first "shower" in Bwa Mawego ended when I slipped, fell hard, and lost my eyeglasses in the stream. As I crawled to the side of the stream, I got a sharp, long intestinal cramp (I thought I was diseased. Actually, it was just dish soap in my gut.

A housemate ran out of water before rinsing our plates and we all got diarrhea). I am ashamed to admit that I wept like a child as Rob Quinlan, my coworker and husband, dutifully searched the stream for my glasses. He found them. After the steep hike out of the ravine, I was sweaty again and half covered with mud. But when we arrived at the crest of that ravine, the view of the blue Atlantic and the scattered village homes and garden plots was spectacular, and there was a lovely, revitalizing breeze. Clearly, life in Bwa Mawego was going to take some adjustment, but finally I was doing fieldwork in a horticultural village.

On my third day in Dominica, we set out for Roseau to return the rental car, pick up provisions in town, and return to the village on the afternoon "transport" (Toyota van). On our way out of the village, one of the women I had met on that first night came running to our car to flag us down. She asked Mark Flinn if he could drop her daughter, Aileen, off at the "health center" in a larger village 45 minutes away. The mother said that Aileen was having "terrible belly pains." Aileen, a tall 19-year-old in baggy clothes, weakly walked toward the Subaru, crying, and twice doubling over to scream, "Why! Why! Why!" I sprang out of the front left passenger seat (Dominicans drive British-style), helped Aileen into that seat, then climbed into the back of the wagon. As Flinn started to pull away, Aileen turned to him and said, "The water bag broke about half an hour ago. We were waiting for the ambulance when you came past." As wide-eyed as I have ever seen a person, Flinn negotiated the winding, bumpy, treacherous road deftly and quickly, with the girl next to him panting and screaming "Why! Why! Why!"[1] every two minutes. My husband, sitting behind Flinn, was extending a hand for the girl to squeeze and looking desperately at David Tedeschi, another graduate student in the back seat, who pointed to his watch and returned the desperate look. About halfway to the health center, Aileen began to take off her panties and shouted "Stop the car! I making the baby now!" Flinn stopped the car and we all jumped out, except for Rob—Aileen was squeezing his hand. David Tedeschi, who had been sitting behind Aileen, rounded her car door to find the baby's head all the way out. He shouted, "Mark! The head's out! What do I do?!" "Is the chord around the neck?", Flinn asked as he rounded the front of the car. "No!" Tedeschi shouted. "Then help pull it out!" Flinn said. And that was it. Aileen pushed, David pulled, and we all saw a perfect baby girl born on the side of that dirt road. My job was the less prestigious one of catching the afterbirth in a bowl that someone brought from the road. But I was thrilled, all the same. We joyfully continued to the health center. I suppose an ethnographer has never had a sweeter, more exciting welcome to a community than that.

THE VILLAGE SITE

The village of Bwa Mawego is on the East Coast, tucked between 1,400 foot mountain ridges that slope steeply to the sea (Beard 1949:108). It is primarily a subsistence horticultural village with a resident population of about 500 people.[2] To Dominicans, Bwa Mawego's most remarkable feature is its geographic situation. It is remote—a village in the bush—even by rural Dominican standards. For a for-

---

[1]At the time I thought that "Why! Why! Why!" was a desperate, imploring statement. I later found out that it is the standard pain exclamation, similar to "Ow!" or "Ay! Ay! Ay!"

[2]Though 200 additional individuals call Bwa Mawego home (discussed later in the chapter).

eigner, Bwa Mawego's most noteworthy feature might be its geological situation. It is steep, slippery, and lush.

Ecology

Bwa Mawego is community nestled in a veritable tropic garden. Essentially all land in the village is cultivated and covered with greenery. The village's soil is fairly fertile[3] and usually moist because Dominica's Atlantic coast gets between 100 and 150 inches of rain per year[4]. The primary crops are two kinds of taro—"dasheen" (*Colocasia esculenta* (L.) Schott)[5] and "tannia" (*Xanthosoma* ssp.), which are both boiled and eaten like potatoes. Other crops include banana and plantain (*Musa* ssp.), manioc (*Manihot*) and yams (*Dioscorea*). Cultivated trees, including coconut palm, mango, breadfruit, soursop, avocado, coffee and cocoa, are common. Various types of bay (or bay leaf) trees (*Pimenta racemosa* (Mill) J. W. Moore) grow in otherwise fallow garden plots and in areas that are too steep and rocky for other plantings. Bay leaf trees are grown to extract and sell the fragrant oil in their leaves, a perfume ingredient. The margins of the village are mostly Littoral Forest (Littoral Woodland) with pockets of permanently cultivated land and Lower Montane Rain Forest (Beard 1949:109–122). I described these zones in Chapter 2.

History

According to village oral history, the Fabb family from Canada founded Bwa Mawego on the Atlantic coast in the hills between two large sugar estates. The village was settled sometime after 1787[6] and before about 1840.[7] It is likely that the village was founded (or grew larger) shortly after Emancipation (1838), when many new Dominican villages were formed (Honychurch 1995).

Situation

By land, Bwa Mawego lies at the dead end of a mostly unpaved (formerly paved, now washed out) lane, about a 45 minute drive from one of the island's main roads. Bwa Mawegans call this lane the "big road" and it winds more or less through the middle of the village. Otherwise, there is no grid or formal layout pattern to the village. Terrain determines feasible house sites. Footpaths wind off the big road and pass by all of the village's houses, bathing and water fetching spots, and the "factories."[8]

---

[3]Most of the village's soil appears to be the brown earth type (stony clay), although yellow earth and red earth also occur.

[4]Compare to annual rainfalls of 60" in Miami, 48.6" in Memphis, 47.3" in New York, 37.4" in Chicago, 37.2" in Seattle, 22" in Honolulu, 12.4" in Los Angeles, and 29.7" in London, England (from http://www.weather.com).

[5]Latin species names, in their full form, are followed by an **authority**. Authorities are the botanists who named the plants. The authority's name is usually abbreviated (e.g., Linnaeus is "L."). Sometimes a new botanist renames a plant because, say, he or she finds that the species should be included in a different genus than its original name indicated. Then, the original authority remains in parentheses, followed by the new authority, as in *Hyptis pectinata* (L.) Poiteau.

[6]A 1786 map documenting a nearby Maroon revolt (Honychurch 1995:95) shows the two sugar estates and two neighboring villages, but not Bwa Mawego.

[7]Robert Quinlan's genealogical oral history (2000) goes back to a Fabb descendant born around 1845. This woman is not the village's first generation, but either a daughter or granddaughter of the founders.

[8]"Factories" are pavilions built over bay oil stills and a manioc grinding/roasting area.

Once I was tip-toeing and occasionally sliding down a footpath that leads to the "big road" from a cluster of houses atop a village crest. On my way down, I met Alfea,[9] one of the women in this study. She was climbing up the path to visit her own mother. Alfea and I were both sweating, she from the exertion of the steep climb up, and I from fear of the steep fall down. In passing, Alfea told me, "They say that here in Bwa Mawego, if you're not walking up, then you *must* be walking down." The saying is not profound, but so plainly true that I associate it with the core of life in Bwa Mawego, where the only apparent level spots are manmade. "If you're not walking up, then you *must* be walking down" ran through my head at least a hundred times while I climbed, scrambled, crawled, trotted and slid along Bwa Mawego's steep clay trails.

The residential part of Bwa Mawego is about 1 by 1½ miles as the crow flies. The time it takes to walk around the village varies greatly depending on whether the trip is predominantly up or downhill, and the age, sex, and load of the walker. Children and young men typically run down the slippery slopes. The elderly walk very slowly using long staffs for balance. Women and middle-aged men walk at a moderate speed taking deliberately placed steps, and running only to avoid a fall after skidding. Walking from residences at opposite extremes of the village might take a Bwa Mawegan anywhere from 15 minutes to an hour.

Bwa Mawegans refer to their village's wider footpaths (3–8 ft.) as "roads" and smaller paths (6 in.–2½ ft.) as "tracks." The "roads" and "tracks" have a friendly air to them as it is polite for passersby to greet each other, and preferably disclose destinations. It is it is also customary to yell out a greeting when passing a house or a yard. One who is seen by another's house without announcing his presence may be suspect of being a *mako* (homosexual spy), or a witch.

Most village households (85%) have electricity. One-third of the households own a stereo or a boom box. As one walks through the village any time before 9 PM, one hears music[10] emanating from open windows of at least every fourth house. At about the same frequency, one hears laughter from a group of playing children or a woman screaming at someone.

POPULATION

Because of a lack of financial opportunities in the village, Bwa Mawego's population is in constant flux as work becomes available elsewhere. A community census that we (Dominica Child Health Project, M. Flinn, Primary Investigator) compiled during 1997 showed a total population of almost 700. As one can see in Figure 3.1, the population is a young one, fairly typical of Third World communities. Eighteen percent of the village population is under ten years of age; almost half (46%) is under twenty years of age. I believe that the rapid population growth potential of this community declined in recent years because of (1) migration of whole families to other

---

[9] First and last names of all individuals mentioned in this text are pseudonyms.

[10] Types of music heard include: reggae (in English, rapidly gaining popularity), zouk (in French—like soukous of Central Africa), soka (usually French, sometimes English lyrics to a driving, Latin-Caribbean, salsa-like beat), calypso (in English—most popular around Carnival time), classic U.S. country and western from 1950–1960 (with emphasis on Charley Pride), and occasional American/English Top 40 hits.

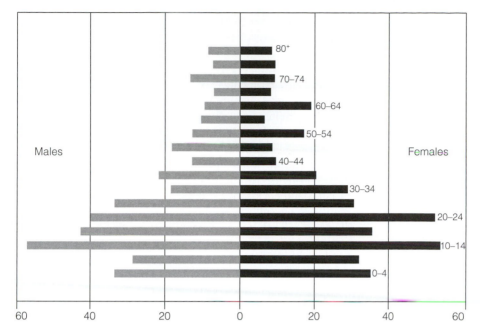

Figure 3.1 Population pyramid for Bwa Mawego, 1997

countries, and (2) recent introduction of accessible and acceptable birth control (Norplant contraceptive implants) at the village clinic.[11]

The census counts all individuals who villagers consider Bwa Mawegans. Some individuals recorded are not full-time village residents. At the time of the census, and every trip that I have taken to Bwa Mawego, the total population in residence was between 500 and 600. Of this group, approximately 490 individuals (about 70%) were in the village every time and during the entire length of each of my four stays. These are, for the most part, the village's permanent residents. An additional 75 or so people resided in the village at least part-time during each of my stays.[12]

The range of part-time living in Bwa Mawego might be illustrated by the example of the Duncan family. Abraham Duncan works 40 hours a week for a Roseau construction company. He works ten-hour days, so he only works Monday through Thursday. His schedule lets him stay in the village with his wife and children Thursday through Sunday nights. Abraham's cousin, Paul Duncan, leaves Bwa Mawego for three and four months at a time for construction jobs in the Virgin Islands. When Paul returns to his five children and Sarah Sebastien, his common-law wife of eighteen years, Paul has enough money to keep his two eldest daughters in

[11] While other forms of birth control come from a pharmacy two hours away, the village nurse administers Norplant. Unlike the pill, which village women feared as medicine that was "too strong," Norplant is acceptable to women. Norplant does not change the male sexual experience, unlike condoms, and thus is acceptable to most village men.

[12] This group of about 75 people consisted of different individuals in each trip. Thus, I have at least met (though I do not necessarily know) nearly every individual in the census.

high school[13] for another semester, and to buy some materials for the cinderblock house he has been building for years (each trip abroad buys him another wall or so). Paul only lives in Bwa Mawego for about half of the year, but the village is his home. Another of Abraham and Paul's cousins, Lily Duncan, lives in Roseau where she works in an office and rents an apartment. Lily's three-year-old daughter, Olivia JnoFin, lives in Bwa Mawego with Lily's mother and father. Lily returns to Bwa Mawego for one weekend every month or so. When Lily comes to Bwa Mawego, she brings money for her parents' household (including her daughter and her younger brother and sisters). Lily considers herself a Bwa Mawegan, as do other villagers.

As in the Duncan family, part-time residents leave the village for jobs in town (i.e., Roseau) or in other villages (primarily as construction and domestic workers). Some people work on other islands and occasionally in the United States, Canada, or the United Kingdom (primarily as agricultural hands, laborers, and domestic workers). The most educated villagers (high school graduates) rarely reside in the village full time. They tend to get jobs (primarily as clerks) in town where they rent a room from family or a family friend. Many of these people consider themselves commuting Bwa Mawegans. At Christmas, Carnival, and funeral days, when many people come home at the same time, there may be as many as 650 villagers in Bwa Mawego at once.

RESIDENCES

Houses in the village have one to three rooms and may be solitary or in a family compound. Most houses are built out of hand-cut wood planks which are usually brightly painted or covered with shingles (see Figure 3.2). Newer, more expensive houses are cinderblock (see Figures 3.3 and 3.4). All roofs are corrugated tin or galvanized steel. In addition to the house, most families have two outbuildings—a kitchen and a latrine. The kitchen is a shed with a food-chopping table, one or two stools or a wooden bench, and either a hearth for cooking with wood, a propane stove, or both. The latrines are deep with a stool over the hole. Poorer families have no outhouse around the latrine. Instead, they conceal this area within available topography and plantings.

Every house has a cleared yard where most of the family activity takes place. Families frequently edge their yards with colorful ti plant (*Cordyline*) or croton hedges. Most yards contain herb and flower gardens (though the majority of gardening takes place in larger subsistence gardens in the bush surrounding the village).

People frequently build their houses in family compounds (see Figure 3.5). These compounds vary in their construction and composition. A typical configuration might have a grandparents' house with three surrounding households containing the grandparents' children (usually daughters) and grandchildren. Shared resources within these compounds vary. Some houses share a latrine or a kitchen with another house in the compound. Some houses share yards. Generally, however, each house in a compound has its own yard, latrine, and kitchen.[14]

An ordinary household contains a mother and her children, sometimes with the mother's spouse. People often live in households with some twist on the traditional

---

[13] While middle school is free and within walking distance, secondary school requires tuition and daily transport to (or boarding in) Roseau.

[14] For the purpose of my study, I employ the traditional definition of a household as having its own hearth. If a pair of houses shares a kitchen, I count that as one household.

Figure 3.2 Traditional wood plank house

Figure 3.3 After a day of laundering at the river, a woman rests against the rail of her modern cinderblock house.

nuclear unit, including extended family such as: a pair of grandparents and a grandchild; a woman, her child, and two of her sister's children; or a woman, her husband, their child, and the woman's brother. Sometimes single men (of any age), and elderly widows live in a house of their own (though usually still within the family compound). Everyone else shares a household with family or a spouse. Couples do not live together until their first child is born. No friends live as housemates.

Figure 3.4 House extremes in Bwa Mawego. The block house on the right is the most valuable house in the village. The builder said he "worked like a donkey" in England for years then returned to Dominica with a large retirement nest egg. He died at age 70, leaving this year-old house to his family. The traditional plank house on the left, one of the village's least valuable, belonged to the oldest man in the village, who recently died at age 96.

*Figure 3.5 A family compound surrounded by a grove of bay leaf (*Pimenta racemosa*) trees*

PHYSICAL APPEARANCE OF BWA MAWEGANS

Nearly everyone born in Dominica is racially mixed. Bwa Mawegans refer to straight hair (even my own thin, blond hair) as Carib hair. Carib hair is relatively rare. In fact, to a visitor from the United States, Bwa Mawegans would at first appear to be of mostly African ancestry due to predominance of very curly, "Afro" hair. However, at second glance, people look more Native American. Amerindian skin tone, cheek shape, and eyelids abound.[15] The village is only about five miles south of the Carib

---

[15] Bwa Mawegans appear physically similar to the Black Caribs, or Garífuna, in Central America (see Gonzalez 1969 and Kerns 1997).

Reserve, the only Native American reservation in the Caribbean. Island history suggests that Bwa Mawegans (and most East Coast villagers) are ancestors of the Maroons and Caribs who hid from European colonialists on the island's rugged eastern seaboard. There is also obvious European admixture in this population, evidenced by several villagers with sun-bleached blond hair and green or blue eyes.

EARNING A LIVING IN BWA MAWEGO

The majority of Bwa Mawego's inhabitants are subsistence gardeners. Gardens in Bwa Mawego are the slash-and-burn type. Matches, cutlasses (machetes), and digging sticks are the standard gardening tools. Some villagers have shovels or gardening forks. A few own handheld sprayers, which they use to spray gramazone (an herbicide). Many villagers own "fowls" (chickens) that are kept more for eggs than for meat. Almost half of the households own one or more goats, and 15% of households have at least one cow or pig. The large animals are for eventual meat sale or consumption, not for milk. Occasionally, Bwa Mawegans hunt in the bush for agouti, *manikou* (opossum), small birds, land crabs and *kwapó* (giant frogs). Individuals also collect shellfish and fish the village reefs with hooks and lines and spear guns. Still, villagers buy the majority of their meat (primarily frozen turkey legs, chicken wings, and pig snouts) from village rum shops.

Even though many villagers of Bwa Mawego are nearly self-sufficient, everyone requires some spending money for buying meat, cloth or clothing, and school and gardening supplies. Families in Bwa Mawego supplement their subsistence with cash they earn from several "penny capitalist" enterprises such as selling fruits and vegetables to fellow villagers, selling baked goods, doing other people's laundry, building furniture, sewing clothes, weaving baskets, and working in other people's gardens. Villagers also produce bay oil, which they sell to a cooperative. They harvest and dry cinnamon bark, nutmeg, and cocoa on a small scale (from one or two trees), which they generally have to go to town to sell.

Bwa Mawego is a fishing village to some extent. Fishing is a male occupation. For the most part, Bwa Mawego fishermen build large, Carib-style, ocean-faring dugouts (18–25 ft.) with raised plank sides. They power these boats by oars and sails though most fishermen have outboard motors too (which they use sparingly due to high petrol prices). As of 1998, two villagers had fiberglass boats with outboard motors. Fishermen use casting nets that they weave from nylon thread. Bwa Mawegan fishermen are relatively well-off, despite selling fish for at least $1 EC less per pound than any other village in the country (an Eastern Caribbean dollar is about .70 of a U.S. dollar). I know of no fishermen who have quit fishing to pursue other forms of income. Yet young men are no longer becoming fishermen. Fishing is variable in productivity and dangerous (two fishermen died at sea between 1993–1998). Further, fishermen can often afford to send their sons to secondary school, thereby opening work alternatives for them other than fishing.[16]

---

[16] One might suspect that the shift away from fishing would result in a less educated future village population because fishermen can afford to educate their children. This is not the case because fishermen's children (like most people) who go to high school typically leave the village anyway. The shift away from fishing reflects a general trend of people abandoning Bwa Mawego for locales where earning a living is more lucrative and involves less risk or labor.

The village has eight "factories"—five are bay oil stills and three are for processing bitter manioc into flour. Manioc (*Manihot esculenta* Crantz), a staple root crop in the American tropics, comes in two basic types: "bitter manioc" and "sweet manioc," which are not really bitter and sweet, but toxic and nontoxic. Whereas sweet manioc can be eaten whole like a potato, bitter manioc must be grated, washed, and squeezed to leach out cyanide poison in the tuber. Though bitter manioc requires processing once it is out of the garden, the roots are so hardy and easy to grow that people tolerate some extra work at the end. Bwa Mawegans process manioc in sheds they call "*farín* factories." *Farín* (manioc flour) factories are 15- by 20-foot tin-roofed pavilions covering three workstations. The first station is a foot-spun manioc grinder made from a piece of nail-pierced tin wrapped around a log on an axle. The second station is a screen press that leaches water and juices out of the manioc pulp. The third station is a flour toaster made from a 5-foot diameter iron pan (the bottom third of a large mooring buoy) on masonry supports.

The other five village "factories," the bay oil stills, produce bay oil, a fragrance sold for use in colognes, soaps, and so forth. Like *farín* factories, all "bay factories" are near streams, as water is required to boil the bay leaves. "Bay factories" are also beneath tin-roofed pavilions that are about twice as long as the *farín* factories. Most of the space is used to keep rain off the firewood that fuels the still. Villagers make the still kettles out of steel drums (pounded and riveted together). The hearths are masonry, and the collection kettle is another large buoy pan, like the toasting pan at the *farín* factory. Factory owners who process their own crop of manioc or bay get to keep all of the profits of their yield. Villagers who do not own a factory of their own pay the factory owner with a portion of their yield.

Nearly 10% of Bwa Mawegan adults are part-time, small-scale merchants. The village has ten shops. These are one-room structures, either part of the owner's home, or a nearby out-building. Shop merchandise ranges from little more than cask rum to varied (but scant amounts of) supplies including canned meats, bouillon, hard biscuits, hard candy, sugar, flour, salt, lye soap, bleach, and matches. Some shopkeepers sell eggs, onions, garlic, and baguettes of bread when they can buy them from other villagers. At least half of the shops have a refrigerator or freezer. These shops sell frozen meats and cold sodas, malts, and beer. Shop owners have higher socioeconomic status than the rest of the village. They are simultaneously village leaders and targets of suspicion and jealousy. They are frequently fingered as witches and accused of "wickedness."

The richest, highest status men in the village are transport drivers. There are five in the village—four with minibuses and one with a pick-up truck.[17] Transport drivers own (or have a loan against) their vehicles, which are quite expensive in Dominica. They leave for Roseau every morning at about 5:30 and arrive in town around 7:30. Round-trip fare to town costs a villager EC$18.00, about one day's earnings as a laborer. Town trips are necessary to buy supplies like tools, cooking equipment, provisions, school supplies, and pharmaceuticals.

---

[17] Besides these five men, there are three other villagers who know how to drive—one who drives a dump truck for a company in town; one elderly retired truck driver, and one ruined alcoholic who used to drive a transport.

VILLAGE FAMILY LIFE

Almost everyone in the village is related to everyone else (Quinlan 2000). Kinship forms the basis of most reciprocal exchange and inheritance (mostly of land, along patrilineal lines). The amount and kind of kin cooperation depends largely on house location and a household's family structure. When adult sisters live and raise their children together in one household, they regularly cooperate with chores and child-care. In contrast, when a woman moves into her husband's extended family compound, she can expect little direct assistance from her affines. Yet, the woman's children receive significant care and support from their relatives in the compound.

There is little stigma in Bwa Mawego associated with having children out of wedlock. A man legitimizes his children by simply claiming paternity and giving the children his "surname." Formal marriage is an institution of the past in Bwa Mawego. In the six years I worked there, the only wedding was a second marriage of two elderly villagers. Villagers cannot recall the last young Bwa Mawegan couple who married (it was about twenty years ago). Residents nevertheless form durable conjugal unions in which the woman sometimes refers to the man as her "husband" (though it is rare for a man to call the woman his "wife"). Currently, approximately 40% of households in Bwa Mawego are male-headed (or coheaded), and around 30% of reproductive-aged women are in long-term unions (Quinlan 2000).

One can find a full spectrum of father involvement in the village. Differences in father-presence occur partly because temporary migration makes male residence variable. Many village fathers earn their livings right in Bwa Mawego as subsistence gardeners, perhaps supplemented with village bay leaf distilling or gardening jobs. These fathers can, if they want to take their children along to the garden, spend nearly constant time with their children. Some fathers work in villages that are more prosperous or on wealthier islands and return to their families at regular intervals. There are fathers who work abroad, send money to their family in Bwa Mawego, and intend to either return to the village with savings or send for their families when they can afford to do so. Some fathers work abroad, send money for their children, and have no plans of further involvement. Other fathers' involvement with their children ends entirely when the man leaves the village. At any given time, more than half of village females are raising children without a father present (Quinlan 2000).

AN ABBREVIATED DAILY ROUND[18]

Bwa Mawegans rise between 5:00 AM and 6:00 AM, although this varies from house-hold to household—some rise earlier and a few sleep till after 7:00 AM. The first act of the day is to go outside to the kitchen and light the stove to boil water (half of the households cook on propane stoves, half on wood fires) for "tea" (usually coffee, "bush tea," or cocoa). People who have breakfast eat *farín* (manioc flour) mixed with water or milk, leftover dasheen (taro) and gravy, or bread they bought from the village baker the night before.

---

[18] For a more detailed breakdown of individuals' activity budgets, see Quinlan 1995.

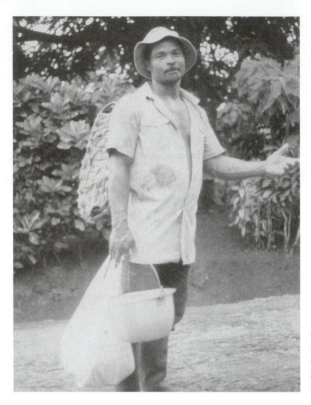

Figure 3.6 A man heads for his garden in the bush with a cooking pot to make his lunch and a Carib-style pack for carrying food home.

Figure 3.7 Girls carry water from the spring to their homes

Frequently, before dressing, people wash their faces or their bodies, if need be, in the yard. This is usually done with water that collects in a barrel under the house roof.[19]

After tea and dressing, children go to school. From October through June, children between the ages of four and fourteen are supposed to attend school. However, attendance is weakly enforced. The government school is in Saint Pierre, the neighboring village. Going to school is a fifteen-minute to over an hour-long walk, depending on the child's age and house location.

Once the older children have gone to school, a mother begins her daily chores. The extent of her chores varies according to whether she has a baby or not, or a female relative in the compound to share in childcare activities. Chores include: fetching drinking and cooking water from the closest spring or standpipe, washing plates, hand-washing clothes, sweeping the house and the cleared clay yard, scrubbing the house floors, feeding chickens, chopping wood, preparing food, and gardening, primarily around the home. By 10:30 AM, nearly all village women are working on some aspect of lunch preparation.

People eat lunch around noon. If a man has a lot of garden work to do, and his garden is a long hike from his home, he will cook his own lunch in the bush (see Figure 3.6). In other cases, the man will come home for lunch, as will all of the children.

Lunch is always a boiled meal—usually in two pots. One pot contains what villagers call "food." Food includes dasheen and tannia (kinds of taro), yams, breadfruit, and plantains. Women boil these foods together in any combination in one large pot. The second pot contains gravy (usually bouillon-based broth with onion, garlic, and peppers—thickened with arrowroot or wheat flour) and meat, if the family can afford meat that day. Meat is one of the following: goat (on special occasions); turkey and chicken legs or wings; pig face or feet; fresh, dried, or salted fish; or canned Vienna sausages, mackerel, or corned beef. The village's stricter Rastafarians eat only fish for meat.

After lunch, people often rest in the shade on a bench or in a fishing net strung hammock-style in a shade tree. They play with babies, talk about their mornings, and often sit silently in the breeze.

Around the village, children under ten spend most of their time either playing or resting. However, at about age four they begin to help their mothers with scaled-down household chores. For example, children under ten generally carry water in gallon-sized jerry cans, whereas adults carry five-gallon plastic buckets (see Figure 3.7). Children also wash their own food plates, wash their own underwear, and help in the garden.

Adult men also do household chores, especially home and out-building maintenance and wood chopping. However, men spend a lot of time working away from home. Primarily this involves gardening. Men work in their own subsistence garden about twice a week. However, men also work in other people's gardens. Men tend to help their cousins and friends out on a reciprocal basis. Men also work for sisters or elderly parents out of duty and in exchange for a cut of the garden's yield. Men without close friends or family to help them on a reciprocal basis must either have very small gardens or pay helpers. Thus, men occasionally do garden work as a cash-paying job.

---

[19] This standing water poses a risk for mosquito-borne diseases, though the water is rarely still because it is used copiously for cleaning, and because it rains so often.

Figure 3.8 Women and children bathing and doing laundry

When older children are not in school, they spend more time playing or resting than adults do. Parents expect all children to help with household chores, however. When chores are finished, older girls assume much of the care for their younger siblings. Older boys spend more time away from the house where their activities include playing cricket or soccer, swimming and spearfishing in the sea, foraging for fruit and killing bird snacks with slingshots.

During the school year, children head back to school after lunch and women and men (if they are home) continue with their chores. Women need to go to "the river" (one of the village streams) to wash clothes about three times a week. Many women do this on hot afternoons so they can enjoy the cool water and shaded stream as they work (see Figure 3.8). People usually go to the river to bathe in the afternoon for the same reason.

In the late afternoon, between 4 and 5 PM, most people end their chores and have a cup of coffee. Later, they might eat. There is no set dinner, but people generally eat something (some bread or leftovers) anywhere from 5 to 9 o'clock in the evening. A lot of people use the evening for relaxing with their families and visiting friends and neighbors. People go to local shops and socialize. They talk, buy each other "shoots" (shots) of rum and play dominoes. More men than women hang out at the shops, but women and children do socialize at the shops as well. People at the shops tend to segregate by age and sex.

As in all tropical locales, darkness comes at nearly the same time all year long. It is fully dark by 7:00 PM every night. The majority of villagers stop socializing by then so they can avoid walking home in the dark. Some people, especially hard core drinkers and single men, stay at the shops later, where they either play instruments and sing or listen to jambox music, play games (usually dominoes), and *lime*.[20] Most people are in their houses with the shutters closed (so that insects and witches cannot come in) by nightfall.

Between 7:00 and 9:00 PM people sit in their houses—most by electric light, some by candlelight, and some in the dark. During this time one can hear families telling stories and jokes and singing songs (especially lullabies to babies) until they go to sleep. Almost everyone goes to bed between 8:00 and 10:00 PM.

---

[20] To "lime" is a Caribbean term meaning to relax while engaging in creative conversation and repartee.

4/Methods

In the early days of ethnographic fieldwork, a lone anthropologist would set out with a notebook (and maybe a camera) to live among the natives. Researchers had the vaguest research questions in mind—"how does the so-and-so group live?" There was little attention given to research methods. Ethnographers simply observed whatever they could and hoped to ask the right questions of the right people. Sometimes "fieldworkers" did not even stay in the communities they studied. As the twentieth century wore on, some experienced ethnographers lamented their lack of training in the early days of their fieldwork. And students were eager to set off for their own field sites with some research tools in hand. A movement began to teach research methods as a part of anthropological training. By the 1970s there were several texts devoted to ethnographic methods (such as Chagnon 1974, Naroll and Cohen 1970, Pelto 1970). Today, even the smallest anthropology programs offer courses in ethnographic methods. In fact, at the beginning of the twenty-first century, "methodology" is a specialty for many anthropologists. So, in contemporary anthropology, no ethnography is complete without a detailed discussion of its methods.

This chapter tells the story of my fieldwork in Bwa Mawego and details the techniques I used to collect and analyze data. In addition to reporting on research findings, scientists present their research design or **methodology**. Disclosure of each method used lets a reader evaluate the research. It allows future investigators to improve on the techniques or use the same methods to replicate the research (either to check for accuracy or—often in anthropology—to look for similar or contrasting phenomena in different conditions or societies). The methods that I used allowed me to (1) identify the illnesses that occur in Bwa Mawego, (2) record their (usually herbal) remedies, and (3) document their perceived **etiologies** (causes). The book results from the research process I describe in this chapter.

The fieldwork for this book spans a five-year period. I worked in Dominica during the months of June–August of 1993, May–August of 1994, December of 1997, and June–August of 1998. I was in the village of Bwa Mawego during 11 separate months, with my total time in the village adding up to almost 9 months. I maintained contact with certain villagers between visits. From September 1998 through

September of 1999, I augmented data that local research assistants and I collected in the field with data that I gathered through mail and telephone correspondence with Bwa Mawegan research assistants and key informants.

RAPPORT: THE FIRST CONCERN

Most ethnographic data comes from one of two sources: direct observation and informant statements. As in psychology and other social sciences, the quality and quantity of observational and reported data depend on relationships between individual human personalities. A social scientist need not be close friends with every research subject, but he does need to be trustworthy. Few other scientists live, work, and interact with their subjects continually the way that anthropologists do. An ethnographer always has to bear his or her reputation in mind—not so much his reputation as a good researcher, but his reputation as a good person.

For a cultural anthropologist in the field, **rapport** (harmonious understanding and trust) with people in the study site must be a constant, primary concern. An ethnographer with bad rapport in a community gets shut out. No one wants to talk to him or her, and this person might be asked to leave the group. Good rapport allows people in the study population to feel comfortable with a researcher, to trust him or her with information about their family life, their economic situation, their fears, and so forth. It also makes the fieldwork experience fun and rewarding. For me, maintaining rapport meant finding a balance between kindness (I was sympathetic and would help out when I could) and professionalism (I was there to do a job, pay research participants for helping me, and remain neutral in some social issues). Fieldwork can be emotionally taxing for anthropologists because they are always at work to some degree. I was always listening and observing and I was constantly being evaluated also. I knew that a disagreeable opinion made its way through village gossip channels in short order. Yet a quiet person who does not offer opinions is reckoned sneaky, untrustworthy, and perhaps a witch. Thus, I offered considered (hopefully considerate) opinions with rapport ever in mind, just as I tried to do *everything* with rapport in mind. Publicly, anthropologists are probably finer people in the field than when they are home because rapport issues require them to be.

MEMBERSHIP IN A RESEARCH TEAM

I consider this research my own. I conceived of the project, conducted most of the research, and oversaw all other data collection. However, I was never on my own in Dominica in that I never lived in Bwa Mawego alone, without other anthropologists. I conducted all of the present research while living and working as part of a research team. For thirteen weeks, the team was minimal, consisting only of myself and my husband, Robert Quinlan. During a two-week Earthwatch project, the research team topped out at five Bwa Mawegan research assistants and 18 foreign researchers.[1] For the majority of my time in Bwa Mawego, I was part of a research quartet led by Mark

---

[1]Other than observations I made myself during this period, no data for the book was collected during the Earthwatch project.

Flinn, who studies the stress, family relationships, and health of Bwa Mawegan children (see Flinn 1999; Flinn and England 1995, 1997; and Flinn et al. 1996, 1999).

Mark Flinn began ongoing research in Bwa Mawego in 1987, six years before I went to Dominica. My husband and colleague, Robert (Rob) Quinlan and I were the fifth and sixth graduate students that Flinn brought to the village. By the time Rob and I got there, Bwa Mawegans had developed a long-lasting rapport with Flinn, and were accustomed to meeting and dealing with Flinn's students. Ordinarily, work in a subsistence gardening Caribbean village like Bwa Mawego requires an initial period of very basic rapport building. These villages are rife with suspicion about neighbors and strangers alike. A researcher must show that he or she respects the local people and holds no malice for them, and must also convince villagers that he or she has no intentions to steal their land, or dominate or bewitch them. Time is the best proof of trustworthiness. The longer a researcher associates with a community, causes no harm, and continues to return, the more residents trust him. By the time I came to Bwa Mawego, the vast majority of residents already trusted Flinn and were comfortable having anthropologists in their midst. Because of the friend-of-a-friend principle, villagers offered me at least superficial acceptance almost immediately. I was able to conduct **participant-observation** and informal interviews, take photographs and take notes as soon as I got a handle on Dominican English Creole.

Coming to work on an established team project was generally advantageous to rapport-building. However, team research also carries rapport risks. First, a group coming to the village is more disrupting than an individual or two would be. Rather than going about their business, villagers flock to see the anthropologists—visit the old ones, meet the new ones, and check out everything that everybody brought into the village (computers, books, shoes, pen knives—all foreign field gear is interesting). Further, an anthropologist who works as part of a team gains collective acceptance as "one of them" rather than in his or her own right. Initially, this is an asset. Yet bridging cultural gaps to connect with people from another society is a special challenge of cultural anthropology. It is an aspect of fieldwork that I find particularly fulfilling. There is some advantage to autonomy, and some risk in membership.

Dominicans naturally generalized about the members of our team. Just as team members gained acceptance by association, we also lost approval because of colleague's gaffs. For example, one anthropologist stated (without explanation) that he was not a Christian. This led one Bwa Mawegan to undertake a campaign against us. "All them white people with Satan," he shouted to fellow villagers. The anthropologist had not realized that in rural Dominica, one is either "with Jesus" or "with Satan." I thus learned that working in a team compromises control over one's own rapport with the community. I paid for others' mistakes and they paid for mine.

I expected some villagers to be distant (indeed, those who were aloof at first often became the best informants later). Some villagers, however, went beyond acting distant to acting outright antagonistic, such as the man in the previous paragraph's example. Every time I ran across such an individual, I could not help but wonder if one of my colleagues or predecessors had offended that villager. Without team members to scapegoat, I might have either put due blame on myself, or accepted a villager's intolerance as an unpleasant aspect of that individual's personality. After all, I expected suspicions. Our team was an oddity in the village. Like many anthropologists, we were occasionally accused of practicing evil magic with our data or colluding with the CIA. Were these accusations spurred by something a colleague said? Probably not, but as one member of a group, I sometimes wondered.

For each of our stays in Bwa Mawego, my husband and I lived in the home of Amicus and Justina Welton. We benefited from these accommodations because (1) the house is centrally located in the village, and (2) the Welton family is fairly neutral in terms of village factions, helpful, witty, and generally pleasant to rent from and live with. Flinn has been renting space from the Weltons since 1987. The Weltons are a relatively wealthy Bwa Mawegan family (Amicus is a part-time carpenter and Justina, in addition to gardening, runs a small but popular rum-and-snack shop). Their house is one of the largest in the village and one of the few houses with two floors. Flinn traditionally rents the Welton's second story for his research team. In December of 1997, my husband and I stayed in one of the Weltons' downstairs bedrooms. Otherwise, we lived in the Weltons' upstairs space whether we were in the village alone, or with other anthropologists.

The Weltons' second floor has its own entrance located under a narrow porch that runs across the front of the house. Like locals, we use the porch to hang out and to exchange hellos with villagers as they pass. We also hang our laundry under the roof there. The inside space upstairs is approximately 450 square feet (18' × 25') divided into five rooms (a central hall and four side rooms). The turquoise-painted walls are wooden planks that Amicus cut himself. We use the 9- by 18-foot central hallway as general living and working space. For the most part, we eat and talk in four chairs in the front half of the hall, and we work at a table and chairs in the back half of the hallway. There are two rooms along each side of the hall. Three of these rooms—the bedrooms—each contain a queen or full sized foam mattress bed, a shelf, and strings across the wall where one can drape clothes. The other room is a makeshift kitchen. In it there is a small electric refrigerator and a counter (a linoleum-covered shelf) supporting a dish rack and a two-burner propane stove (we wash dishes outside by the cistern).

Most Bwa Mawegans would find this space adequate for a family of six or more. Bwa Mawegans do not work in their houses however. They do not have computers, notebooks, racks of test tubes, and plant presses cluttering their homes. Moreover, they do not attract a constant stream of visitors, first-aid seekers, and onlookers like anthropologists do (especially for the first couple of weeks of each visit). In my experience, the space in Weltons' upstairs has been roomy for two, decent for three, and stressful for four or more anthropologists.

For me, living with other anthropologists provided some advantages and some disadvantages. There were certainly logistic and schedule advantages to living together when we were also attempting to work together. It was also beneficial to have other anthropologists around to share our experiences and ideas. Indeed, when there was a comfortable mesh of personalities together in the field, it was tempting to spend time with people with whom I had a lot in common, rather than interview, or even do participant-observation with Dominicans. I occasionally wasted field time at home with my husband and anthropologist friends when I could have been out collecting some kind of data. I wanted to minimize this behavior because I feared that spending time with colleagues instead of continually circulating with villagers might make me (or us) appear snobbish. At the same time, it is difficult to live in close quarters with nonrelatives, even during optimal convergences of personalities.

Sometimes greed for data kept all of us from keeping up with household duties, such as carrying water and washing dishes. Moreover, we all had different tolerances and requirements in terms of sociability, culture shock, and cleanliness. Consequently, I may have gone out and collected the most data during times when I was most frustrated with my housing circumstances.

STAGE I RESEARCH: FUNDAMENTAL EXPLORATION

To a certain degree, the research format I followed was traditional, as it took the form that Agar calls the ethnographic cone (1980). Here, one's research starts with making the most basic observations while developing rapport in the study community. Then, with rapport still very much in mind, one conducts participant-observation (joining activities and recording information; see Bernard 1995), coupled with informal interviewing (i.e., directed conversations). The anthropologist thus begins to understand general workings of the community. Next, one focuses on his topic, moving from the general to the specific. This involves conducting interviews in stages of increasing structure and formality. Each stage contains more informants than the stage before.

Participant-Observation

My first participant-observation (P-O) in the village was to join Justina Welton, our landlady, and her two teenage daughters as they peeled coffee beans on their front stoop. I was nervous and felt awkward when I asked if I could help them. They laughed at me for volunteering to do something so boring, but welcomed me to sit down. The neighbor woman from across the road came over to help. We all sat, talked, and peeled for a couple of hours that morning. Around five o'clock that afternoon, Justina called me over to join her daughters, the neighbor and her for a cup of coffee—the first of many afternoon coffees we would drink together.

After that, I began going to hang out with (and help, when possible) the Welton women—both during the day in their kitchen, and in the evening when they were liming, sitting on their front stoop or on benches along the "big road."

I had been in the village about ten days when, as part of Flinn's Child Health Project, our team began collecting saliva samples from village children twice daily. I became familiar with the village trails and met many women while collecting saliva. After a few days collecting their children's' saliva, I felt comfortable enough with some of the women to visit them later or ask if I could tag along with them (to do P-O). The more people I met, and the more I got used to doing P-O, the easier it became to do informal interviewing in the context of P-O.

I started talking to people about general life in the village. Then, as I learned more about local medicine through general discussions, I began to focus my informal questions on health-related issues. I started to direct conversations so that people could recount their own health experiences and elaborate in detail on the circumstances surrounding illness events in their family's and friends' life histories.

I began looking at gardens informally. I started asking about peoples' house gardens while visiting with them. I asked about planting procedures and names and uses of certain plants. Later, I began going with people to their bush gardens, both for tours and to help.

The bush is not only a place to make gardens, but a place for sex. It is neither safe nor proper for a woman to go into the bush alone, or with a nonrelated man. Unless I was working specifically with a woman, trips in the bush were a joint venture between my husband and me. We worked as co-interviewers as we did our P-O. We both enjoyed this format and seemed to get a lot of information out of these days. For one thing, we helped one another to direct conversations and explored each other's areas of interest (his was families, e.g., Quinlan 2001). Also, with two people asking questions, the tone of the excursion was informal and conversational. One person paused while the other asked a question. One of us might inquire on an aspect of something that the other missed. At the end of the day, we debriefed together. This added to our understanding and memory of the day.

My longest stay in Bwa Mawego was my second trip to the village. This trip lasted almost four months, from the beginning of May through the end of August 1994. This time, my husband and I showed up in the village alone, without Flinn. We wanted to start our stay by taking a few weeks to establish our own rapport in the village. During this time we decided to try to do what villagers do, rather than conduct formal research.

I was twenty-nine years old that summer. A Bwa Mawegan woman of that age generally has about three children and spends much of her day doing childcare and related household activities. I spent some time with women and their children. I also spent time pursuing the activities more common among teenage and menopausal women. For example, I went to work with people in their gardens. I did not clear any new swidden gardens (which was men's work). However, I did some second-stage fire clearing,[2] planting, and weeding. My husband bought a spearfishing gun in Roseau. We went spearfishing a few times a week. This is a fairly typical young male activity. When women go along, they generally carry the bag of dead fish. If there were Bwa Mawegans watching, this was my role too. We gave our quarry away, mostly to old or sick people. On days when we gardened, we lent our snorkeling equipment to village teenagers. They then brought fish home to their own families, and generally brought us some seafood (often lobster) in exchange for the use of the equipment. As that summer progressed, we each developed increasingly formal research methods and spent less time doing fishing P-O. That meant we lent our equipment out more often. We consequently ate increasing amounts of fresh seafood as our quantitative data mounted. By August, we laughed about actually being sick of lobster.

Instantaneous Behavioral Scans

Participant-observation is the foundation of ethnographic fieldwork; however, observing *without* participating gives a researcher another vantage point to learn about a society and its goings-on. Instantaneous behavioral scans are a formal method for collecting quantitative data on people's behavior and time allocation (i.e., the percentages of time people spend engaged in particular activities; see Gross

---

[2]During the first clearing stage, men cut trees and start fires across a swath of land. Because much of the vegetation is green, many plants wilt and die but do not burn. During the second stage, men and women return to the garden (several weeks later) and burn the remaining, now dead trees and ground cover.

1985, Hames 1991, Johnson and Sackett 1998). The method provides a researcher with a large body of observations of everyday activities and interactions. One way to collect scan data is for a researcher to establish a set route for observation, then walk the route daily, beginning at randomized times and route locations. Every time the researcher encounters a person, she records the time and the individual's name, location, and observable activity. The behaviors are later coded for data management and analysis. Collecting enough observations of enough people for statistical analysis is a big job requiring thousands of observations. Hence, instantaneous behavioral scans are not a typical ethnographic method, but are reserved for research in which peoples' time allocation is the *specific* topic of the study. I began conducting scans to help my husband gather thesis data, which turned out to be an unexpected boon for my own work.

Behavioral scanning did three things for me. First, by doing scans at various times of the day, I quickly developed a good understanding of village activities. This includes the following: who does what kind of activity; when and how often they do it; and the nature and amount of work, relaxation, and recreation people in the village take part in. Second, I observed many personal interactions that I would not have seen had I been doing P-O with just one or a few people. Scans gave me the opportunity to catch candid snapshots of behavior and relationships. I began to grasp Bwa Mawegan styles of parenting, spousal and sibling relationships, and friendships through these opportunistic observations of interactions. Finally, doing scans made me more familiar to people in the hamlet we scanned, increasing my rapport with them.

The first time we did a scan, Rob wanted me to come with him, to possibly soften his presence. His thesis focused on the hamlet of Mt. Zion, which is approximately one-fifth of the village. We stopped at each house in the hamlet and explained this scan project and the kinds of things we would write down. If people seemed suspicious, we showed our notebook to a family member. No one objected. We did subsequent scans alone. At first, scanning was slightly uncomfortable, as we would sometimes catch people fighting or doing some other private or deviant thing (such as finding a woman smoking a cigarette). However, after a week or two when we obviously had neither spread gossip nor changed our demeanor towards anyone, people began to trust us.

I must caution readers that formal behavioral scanning is an extremely time- and energy-intensive, often tedious field method that should be reserved for specific research questions. However, one can achieve the informal benefits of scan sampling (such as those I just mentioned) in the first ten or fifteen hours of observations. Given my experience, I think that a modified, informal scanning procedure conducted for several weeks should be an excellent tool for general ethnography in environments where the method is feasible.

Family Health Surveys

The first formal method of my study involved asking a series of structured questions of every village mother regarding the health of her family members. Before meeting with the women, I went over my questions with a key informant to make sure they were worded clearly for speakers of the local English dialect. I also took a well-liked Standard English–speaking high school student with me as a guide, to help me with people's names, and to translate. I asked women about the general health history and condition of all members of her household. Then I asked them to recall any illnesses or injuries their family members had suffered in the past week, month, or year. This gave me a great deal of insight into common illnesses among villagers.

Each time a mother mentioned an illness event, I first asked her how the person got the illness and probed to find the mother's perceived cause of the illness. Next, I asked what, if anything, anyone did to treat the sick person. In this manner, I began to uncover patterns in who treated what kinds of illnesses. If someone at home treated the sick person (which was usually the case), I inquired as to the treatment. The treatment was usually some kind of bush tea. I asked what kind of herb the tea contained, and where the person obtained the herb. Often, the mother showed me the herb right away, as the plant was growing in her house garden. During this early stage, I did not want to deplete anyone's house garden. However, I did tag and take home several small clippings from the herbs mothers showed me; not to use as voucher specimens, but simply to familiarize myself and memorize the appearance, names, and uses of the most popular cures. I also asked mothers to list the village's bush doctors, or people who know "plenty bush."

As this was my first village-wide formal interview, and as villagers tend to shy away from clinical and bureaucratic types, I felt uncomfortable conducting the interview with a clipboard and photocopied interview instruments. Instead, I wrote my questions on a cheat-sheet and used a small stenographer-type notebook to take notes. Villagers received me well. However, in retrospect, I do not know if a Bwa Mawegan would really recognize any formality difference between a notebook and a clipboard. Perhaps the real issue was that I felt less formal, and therefore more comfortable with the small notebook. Unfortunately, I forgot to look at my cheat-sheet for each question. The informality of my instrument resulted in me doing several interviews where I did not ask every mother every question.

Health Record Collection

At the same time that I conducted the above interviews, I asked each mother/caretaker if I could borrow her children's health records for our research team to look at. Families keep children's health records in their homes. Each record contains information on the child's growth, inoculations, and presenting complaints and diagnoses from clinic visits. Though it would be interesting to see the records that the clinic keeps, as these would contain adult health histories and potentially be more detailed, this would be problematic for privacy reasons. Collecting health records from caretakers eliminated this concern since every caretaker had the option not to loan me her child's health record. Back at the house, we anthropologists took turns recording each record on videotape. The contents were later entered into a database that we have all used for various questions. For this project, my knowledge from the health records gave me an accurate idea of the kinds of problems for which villagers seek biomedical care, and the diseases that occur (at least among children) in Bwa Mawego.

Key Informant Interviews on Bush Medicine

Earlier, in my health surveys with mothers, I had identified people that other villagers sought out for bush-medical advice. Seven villagers stood out as village experts. One of the experts was hospitalized in Guadeloupe for what later turned out to be a terminal disease. I could not interview him. Another expert suffered from some mental irregularities and was going through an especially incoherent few months. I did not interview him during that trip. The remaining five experts became my key informants. These experts were both men and women of various ages and from different parts of the village. I knew them all already and, luckily, rapport was not a problem.

Indeed, one expert was my 39-year-old friend and landlady, Justina. Another was a friendly woman in her sixties who I already knew well. She had worked with Flinn for years and she and I had worked together as partners collecting children's saliva samples for Flinn's Child Health Project. The remaining female expert was a 55-year-old mother and grandmother who lived in one of the family compounds on our instantaneous behavioral scan route. She and both of her daughters were always exceptionally friendly with my husband and me. We had an affable, joking relationship before the interviews. My younger male informant was already a good friend of my husband and mine. He was an intelligent 25-year-old who, though he was not a full-fledged Rastafarian, appreciated the Rasta back-to-nature ideal. He decided to become a "bush doctor" of sorts, out of interests in self-reliance and historic preservation. He started learning as many cures as he could—first from his parents, then from his grandparents, then from his friends' parents and grandparents. Many of the young parents and single young men in the village, especially the Rastafarians and Seventh Day Adventists, sought his advice for remedies. The elder of my male expert key informants was a 49-year-old father and grandfather. He was one of the best educated and most respected men in the village. This man pursued medicine as a hobby. In addition to learning medicine from other villagers, he owned and consulted two paperback books on herbal medicine (these were Kloss 1972 and Lust 1974). I did not know this man as well as my other key informants. However, he was cordial and easy to work with.

I paid all of my key informants the same pay as a laborer receives for a day's work. I arrived at this amount because, theoretically, the informant might have missed a whole day of work to do the interview (although no one actually did miss work to interview with me). All of these key informants appeared to enjoy their role in this project. They were glad for the extra cash, and seemed proud to share their expertise.

I spent three days interviewing each key informant. On the first day, I did a long, descriptive interview on the medical system. I asked general questions that stemmed from the Caribbean **ethnology** of medicine (especially Laguerre 1987) and from my own knowledge of village medicine (from informal interviews). Each initial long interview took up most of one morning. I took notes on informants' responses and tape-recorded the interviews. I arranged the questions according to types of treatment—clinic, folk healer, and self-treatment (the "sectors of health care"; see Chapter 6). The questions address the sectors from the most to least formal in terms of practitioner training. Thus, as the informant got used to being interviewed (the tape-recorder, etc.), they could address areas of their increasing expertise as bush practitioners. The questions I asked were as follows:

1. What kinds of sickness do people here need to go to a doctor or nurse for?
2. What kinds of sickness do people here need to go to a Pastor or Priest for?

3. People tell me there is no obeahman[3] in the village.
    Is there obeah going on in the village?
    Where is an obeahman that people here can use?
    What kind of sickness do people here go to an obeahman for?
4. Explain the importance of keeping clean.
5. How do people get dirty blood?
    What happens to people with dirty blood?
6. What other kinds of things do people here have with their blood?

    Pressure
    Color
    Temperature
    Other

    How do these occur? How do you cure them?

7. What are the sicknesses that you or a bush doctor can treat with bush remedies?

On the afternoon of the first interview, I reviewed the notes and tape of the interview. From these, I compiled a list of each illness the expert said he or she treated with bush medicine. I also made another list of all medicinals the key informant mentioned during the interview. These individualized lists formed the basis of my second interview with each informant.

On day two, I asked the experts to tell me the bush remedies they used for each sickness they listed the day before. I added these bush medicines to my compiled list from the first day's interview. Next, I asked them to tell me the use(s) of medicinals they listed the day before, and any additional uses for the plants they listed earlier in the interview. Likewise, with any new plant they mentioned, I inquired for all additional uses of that plant. These interviews took 1.5–3 hours. After the interview, I made a new, clean list of all the plants the informant had mentioned.

Plant Collection

I spent the third day with each informant collecting plants. Together we collected at least one **voucher specimen** (plant sample to preserve and deposit in a public herbarium), of each plant the key informant mentioned during the previous two interviews (see Appendix A for a plant list). For each voucher specimen, I followed the key informant to the place where the plant grew. There, I collected the specimen and requisite information about the plant and its growing conditions (see Martin 1995:28–36). I accumulated these samples in a backpack throughout the day. When I returned to the house, I placed each specimen in a plant press to dry (Pearsall 2000:119–133).

Preserving plants by pressing them dry proved difficult in Dominica. In conditions with normal humidity levels, plants in a press dry within a few days to a week, depending on their thickness. One simply has to keep replacing the damp blotters in

---

[3] *Obeah* is a Caribbean variety of capitalistic sorcery. Practitioners are *obeahmen*. I discuss obeah in detail in Chapter 5 and obeahmen in Chapter 6.

the press with dry ones. Most of my plant collection period was constantly humid, with rain several times a day. The blotters around my pressing plants did not wick well. Even my "fresh" blotters were moist from the air. My press got full but my plants were not drying. During hot, sunny periods I sundried both the blotters and the newspaper-wrapped plants on hot cement areas and on the corrugated metal roof above our cistern. I used this method because locals dry cinnamon and coffee beans similarly. I placed rocks on the papers so that the samples would not blow away. I dropped one specimen in the cistern and a few got rained on, as I could not get everything collected quickly enough when a cloud rolled in. I also overcooked a few samples on the roof. On subsequent trips, I used alcohol preservation to avoid such mishaps. Unfortunately, I was unfamiliar with that method during this second field trip (my first plant-collecting trip) to Dominica.

By the time I went plant-collecting with my fourth and fifth key informants, I had already collected the common remedies with my first three informants. Though I packed what seemed a plethora of corrugates and blotters for my plant press, I was running short because the humidity was slowing the drying rate. Thus, to conserve space in my plant press, I did not collect sets of duplicate species. I did ask the key informant to show me those plants. Seeing an example confirmed that this key informant used the same common name as my previous informants for the same species or variety of plant. On two or three occasions, the plants the later experts showed me were indeed different species from my previous samples, though they had the same common name. For instance, the Patwa common name *malestomak* is used for two plants that both have large, deeply veined leaves. Otherwise, the two plants look dissimilar and are not only different species, but from two separate taxonomic families. If, when conducting the later collections, I was not certain that I had already collected several vouchers of that same species, I collected the plant. Otherwise, I let the plant grow where it was.

As my research continued, I learned about more medicinal plants (through free-listing methods described next) that had not come up in my original long interviews with my key informants. Each time I had accumulated a list of twenty or so new plants, I repeated the previously noted collection procedure with one of my key informants. I repeated the collection with another key informant in case the first informant was not familiar with one of the plant names, and to cross-check. Sometimes, rather that going out on a second trip to cross-check, I asked the second key informant to identify the plants in my plant press that I had collected with a previous key informant.

STAGE II RESEARCH: SYSTEMATIC EXPLORATION

During my first two trips, I concentrated on gathering a general understanding of bush medicine in Bwa Mawego. My methods for this were mostly qualitative and involved key informants. The next stage of my research was to test the generalizability of the data I had already gathered. For this stage, my methods and data became quantitative.

Illness Freelist

My ultimate goal was to compare individuals' knowledge of bush remedies for specific illnesses. My first step in this process was to identify illnesses that Bwa Mawegans tend to treat with bush medicine. I conducted freelist interviews to identify those illnesses. The freelist is an expeditious ethnographic tool that elicits, or prompts responses about, the members of a mental category (called a *semantic domain*; see Bernard 1994, Weller and Romney 1988). A freelist interview simply entails asking a person to list as many members of a domain (e.g., farm animals, stressful driving situations, recreational drugs, etc.) as he or she can think of. There are three assumptions to the freelist method. The first is that individuals tend to list terms within a domain in order of primacy of familiarity (e.g., when listing kinship terms, individuals will tend to list "mother" before "aunt," and "aunt" before "great-aunt"). The second assumption is that individuals who know a lot about a subject will freelist more terms than people who know less (Fleisher and Harrington 1997). Thirdly, terms that many individuals in a community mention refer to prevalent entities in that community.

There is messiness inherent in any attempt to measure people's thoughts. To get the most comparable freelist data, I needed each informant to respond to the same prompt question. For reasons of rapport and understandability, I wanted to ask the question in a way that was friendly and acceptable, as opposed to hauty, governmental, or even biomedical (qualities that can repel Bwa Mawegans). I thought that the easiest way to accomplish this would be to word my question in the local dialect. I asked a few key informants who spoke Standard Caribbean English to help me word my question.

I wanted an easily intuitable stimulus that would elicit a list of conditions that Bwa Mawegans treat with bush medicine. Originally, I wanted to ask, "What kinds of conditions do people in Bwa Mawego treat with bush medicine?" My key informants agreed that a more acceptable phrasing should be: "Here in Bwa Mawego, what things they curing with bush medicine?" This phrasing provided me with a tradeoff. I avoided some informant alienation by using the verb *to cure* rather than the verb *to treat* (my key informants advised that *to treat* was too nurse-like). Otherwise, I would have preferred using the more general verb *to treat*, because *to cure* implies existing ill health. In reality, Bwa Mawegans use bush medicine for more than "sicknesses." My earlier, less structured interviews revealed that people use bush medicines as preventatives, or for conditions that they would not consider illnesses. For example, I know that Bwa Mawegans employ herbs to improve mental acuity, to ensure luck or blessing, for healthy pregnancies, to terminate pregnancies, and to ease hangovers or menstrual discomfort (not really "sicknesses").

References to nonillnesses were uncommon (or nonexistent) responses in the freelist interview. In fact, after hearing my question, most informants began their freelist response with a statement like, "Well, we using bush to cure all them *sickness* like: worms, colds, inflammation . . ." (The emphasis is mine.) My wording therefore influenced my results by prompting people to freelist "sicknesses," or conditions that require "cures."

My impression is that Bwa Mawegans actually do use bush medicine more often for "sickness" than for nonsickness, but my instrument cannot measure whether, or to what degree sickness cures are more salient within the community.

I carried the illness freelist out with a quota sample of 30 adult villagers. This was approximately one-quarter of all adult villagers. For my sample, I interviewed five women from each of the three major village hamlets. In each hamlet I made sure that one woman was in her twenties, one in her thirties, one in her forties, one in her fifties, and one in her sixties or seventies. I did the same with the men. I thus strati-fied the quota equally regarding age, sex, and village location, in case these factors skewed the use of bush medicine.

These freelists were oral. I wrote informant's responses as they listed the ill-nesses. Each freelist took between two and ten minutes. In exchange for their help, I paid informants with their choice of $1EC or one "shoot" of rum.

I used a spreadsheet program to compile this data and ascertain which were the most salient treatable illnesses. This involved ranking, summing, and dividing responses (see Robbins and Nolan 1997) to get a Composite Salience Value score for each illness. The higher this score is, the more salient the illness. This method is use-ful because, in theory, it shows a relative estimation of each illness people treated with bush remedies, accounting for both the number of people who mentioned the illness, and the order of their responses.

Illness Pile Sorts

Analysis of the freelists of illnesses Bwa Mawegans treat with bush medicine showed twenty-one illnesses that were particularly dominant (see results in Chapter 8). These were illnesses that at least 30% of my sample listed in their freelists.[4] The frequently listed illnesses became the focus of my subsequent research.

To get some accurate idea of local typology of these illnesses, I used a variation of the pile sort method (for more on pile sorting, see Bernard 1994). I printed the name of each of the twenty-one illnesses in large, bold letters on index cards. I took the pile of illness terms, a notebook, and a tape recorder to a popular village rum shop. I asked people at the shop to help me in exchange for an EC dollar or a "shoot" of rum apiece (which costs $1EC). They all volunteered.

I went to the domino table and, for the benefit of those who did not read or those with bad vision, I read each illness term aloud as I laid its card on the table. I turned on the tape recorder and asked informants to tell me which of these illnesses go together. As they told me what went together, I sorted the cards into piles, always reading the contents of the piles out loud. I kept asking them to join the piles (some of the piles contained only one term at first) until I had only four piles.

I repeated this same process at another village rum shop. Then, to get input from more sober informants and more females, I went to a ridge where there was excep-tional camaraderie among the households. I went during the afternoon at a time when I knew (from doing scans) that the adults who live there tended to congregate and chat. I did the same sorting procedure with this group, except that I placed the terms

---

[4] Nine informants mentioned these illnesses (composite salience value = .09). The next highest ranked illness was mentioned by only 3 informants (10%), composite salience value = .03.

on a bench rather than a domino table, and I paid each informant $1EC. All of these informants at first attempted to refuse my dollar. However, they accepted it when I explained that it was only fair. All of the previous people at the rum shops wanted their "shoots."

My total informants for this project equaled 24, broken into groups of nine, seven, and eight. Group interviews afforded me two advantages. First, I knew that the results were valid for Bwa Mawegans because villagers came to a consensus on their own. Second, group interviews allow a researcher to hear subjects argue their opinions and rationales for responding the way they did (see Agar 1973). This offers ethnographic depth.

Though most of these informants were inebriated to some degree, I do not believe that my results were qualitatively affected. For one thing, the sober group agreed with the groups from the rum shops. Further, the intoxicated groups were more animated and more vocal about the reasons for their decisions. This worked to my advantage.

FREELIST OF REMEDIES

During the pile sorts, I learned that people were adamant that my original list of most salient illnesses contained three pairs of illnesses that were effectively the same. These pairs contained (1) "prickle heat" and "buttons" (pimples or any pustules), (2) "loose bowel" and diarrhea, and (3) upset stomach and vomiting. Locals said that these illnesses differ in degree, not in kind; and they share the same cures. I thus collapsed those six terms into three categories. Consequently, my final list had 18 illnesses.

Next, my goal was to find the plants that Bwa Mawegans knew about to treat each illness. Again, I chose to use the freelisting method because it is a good way to find out about the plants that people really use. Informants list illness/cure terms from their own active vocabulary, which (unlike being able to recognize a plant or its name) is a strong predictor of familiarity with a subject (Gatewood 1984). Also, as Handwerker and Borgatti (1998:549) argue, "even simple forms of numerical reasoning add important components to ethnographic research." They add that "reasoning with numbers reveals things you'd otherwise miss." Obtaining quantifiable data on the plant knowledge allowed me to find areas of consensus or high modality within the community (Boster 1987, D'Andrade 1987, Weller 1987). Quantitative freelist data provided for a more accurate description of medicine within the community of Bwa Mawego. Freelists have been used successfully in other ethnomedical studies (Crandon-Malamud 1991, Hatfield 1994, Nolan 2002, Nolan and Robbins 1999, Quinlan, Quinlan, and Nolan 2002, Ryan, Nolan, and Yoder 2000).

With this in mind, two local research assistants, another American researcher (Kathryn Gentner), and I set out to ask every adult in the village to give a freelist of bush remedies for each of the 18 illnesses. Together, we obtained 1,826 freelist interviews from 126 adults, yielding 7,235 total responses. For most people, each freelist took less than one minute. Thus, my research assistants and I attempted to do all 18 freelists in one sitting with each villager.

Because Bwa Mawego is a community with varying degrees of literacy, we conducted the freelists orally (rather than asking informants to write their lists). This approach complicated the freelist procedure as subjects solicited help from nearby friends or family who (trying to help) called out various remedies. Sometimes people saw me interviewing another villager, approached out of curiosity, and offered suggestions. These occasions were most frustrating because the whole point of freelisting is to get the items that one individual knows in the order that they come to mind for that individual. I dealt with shared-answer events in several ways, depending on the situation. For example, when I was interviewing Daphne Douglas, she had listed two cures for the common cold when the name of a third slipped her mind. Her aunt was about thirty feet away. Daphne called out, "Auntie! What that bush we using for the cold, na?" "*Timayok!*" the aunt screamed back. Daphne had already listed *timayok*. "No, the other one!" The aunt yelled, "Hibiscus flower." "Yes, but there's another one again," Daphne said to the aunt. Then she turned to me and said, "Hibiscus flower is good too, you know. We using that plenty for colds." "*Pachurí?*" the aunt asked. "THAT is it! *Pachurí*," Daphne said. In this case, I continued with Daphne's freelist, leaving a blank space in the third position. I wrote "hibiscus" in the fourth position. Then, I filled "*pachurí*" in the third position, since that was the one Daphne was thinking of when she involved the aunt. In other cases, I had to abandon the freelist for a later time, as it was less than clear in what order the interviewee would have thought of the herb, had he or she not been prompted. Leaving an interview because of compromised data was discouraging. I knew that the villager might well be irritated, when I returned to do the same interview again, such as the man who said, "I already told you all them bush plants with Baptiste. I telling you things an then you losing the notes, mon. Why should I tell you again, na?" Most of the time, I was able to avoid compromised freelist situations by explaining the project to all the nearby adults, and isolating the interviewee somewhat by stepping around a corner.

In many cases freelist interviews were interrupted. My assistants and I tried to go back to people whose interviews were interrupted to finish the freelists. However, we did not get to obtain every freelist from every individual. Consequently, I have several freelists for every adult in the village from July 15 to October 15, 1998; however, I have some gaps in the data for some individuals.

I used freelist data to determine the most salient and frequently mentioned bush remedies for each of the 18 most commonly treated illnesses. For this, I used ANTHROPAC (Smith 1993) to tabulate for each illness the salience of cures used in the community. The more salient a treatment is, the more consensus there is about that treatment within the community. Consensus regarding a remedy likely occurs when that remedy is efficacious (Trotter and Logan 1986). I detail the salient illnesses and each of their salient treatments in Chapter 8 of this book.

5/Disease and Illness
in Bwa Mawego

Medical anthropology provides a framework for understanding cross-cultural variation in health and illness. Often, medical concepts are so intertwined with other cultural beliefs that disentangling them is a great challenge. This chapter explores the most basic distinctions that anthropologists use as tools for understanding cultural concepts of health and illness. **Pathology** (the departure from a healthy, normal body function) is examined from emic and etic perspectives. **Disease** is distinguished from **illness**. The chapter also examines basic cultural concepts about the causes of illness by distinguishing **personalistic** from **naturalistic** illnesses. These distinctions help anthropologists understand the kinds of health issues that occur in a population and how locals view those problems. These basic concepts of illness are broadly applicable among small-scale societies. Later chapters deal explicitly with the notions associated with ill health in Bwa Mawego, and with specific illnesses there.

THE DISEASE–ILLNESS DICHOTOMY

The distinction between "disease" and "illness" is a key concept in medical anthropology (Eisenberg 1977). Although there is some overlap between disease and illness, "diseases" are in the realm of Western, scientific biomedicine, whereas "illnesses" are in the realm of a local culture. In a sense, disease is the etic perspective of pathology, and illness is the emic perspective of pathology. "Disease" refers to a physiological abnormality that a professional can observe and measure objectively.[1] Biomedical research establishes measurable normal ranges for body parts and functions, such as body temperature, blood pressure, cholesterol level, or gland size. When a patient's condition falls within the normal range, a doctor or nurse can declare the patient "normal," or "healthy." If the clinician observes a condition outside the accepted range, the patient has a "disease" symptom. When symptoms fit into a particular recognized pattern, physicians diagnose a "disease." Because

---

[1]Traditionally, physical abnormalities have been more accessible to objective measurement than mental abnormalities, which are more difficult to define. Thus, in the Western clinical tradition we have "physical diseases" and "mental illnesses."

diseases have recognizable and measurable symptom patterns, they are universal. Any disease (e.g., measles) will be recognized by more or less the same symptoms and will have similar explanations of the disease's cause and process regardless of the society in which it appears (Fabrega and Silver 1973).

In contrast to "disease," culture strongly influences "illness" concepts (Helman 1994). "Illness" is a broader term than "disease" that considers both measurable *and* vague symptoms. "Illness" includes the individual, family, and community perceptions. "Illness" also includes reaction to the ailment in both the physical and social sense (e.g., in terms of what the patient did to "deserve" the illness). Culture shapes the way one recognizes and treats an illness.

Though "disease" and "illness" overlap in Dominica (as elsewhere), a person can experience one without the other. Let's say a Dominican went to a physician for a routine exam (this could occur for a job or a passport application). The doctor detected weight loss despite the patient's increased appetite, took a blood glucose test, and diagnosed the patient with diabetes. This patient, who never felt "sick" and whose previous physical or social life was unaffected by her diabetes, has had a disease with no illness. Another villager might experience the illness "fright" which has no exact biomedical match,[2] and might be immeasurable in biomedical terms. This person experiences illness without disease.

Because this is a book about ethnomedicine, not biomedicine, and the focus here is on home treatment, most of the book deals with illness, as opposed to disease. I conducted the present research not with medical doctors, but with regular village people who, for the most part, self-diagnosed and self-treated their ailments at home. Conditions that have not been evaluated by a doctor or nurse are not termed diseases, but illnesses. Nevertheless, I present Bwa Mawego's disease risks in order to offer an etic glimpse of the village's medical setting.

DISEASES IN BWA MAWEGO

For a Third World village, Bwa Mawego seems exceptionally healthy. In fact, Dominica in general has a relatively healthy population. **Epidemiologists** often use life expectancy and infant mortality rates as basic measures for the health of populations. Life expectancy for Dominicans is 74 years compared to 66 for the Caribbean in general and 77 for the United States. The infant mortality rate is 17 infant deaths per 1,000 live births compared with 46 per 1,000 in the rest of the Caribbean and 7 per 1,000 in the US.[3] The relatively few disease conditions (other than injuries) that villagers reported or that I read about in village health records are presented in Table 5.1.

Though Dominica is one of the poorest Caribbean countries, it is one of the healthiest (see CDC 1998). Caribbean islands typically have high **incidence** rates of diseases associated with crowding and still or slow-moving water. These diseases are listed in Table 5.2. Dominica is rural, not crowded, and only a few water- and mosquito-borne diseases occur (dengue and typhoid fevers, hepatitis, and bacillary and amoebic dysentaries). These are serious, but have a very low incidence in

---

[2] Fright has similar causes and symptoms to what Western practitioners term "post traumatic stress syndrome" (American Psychiatric Association 1994), but this too is a mental illness, not a disease.

[3] These figures are from the U.S. Census Bureau International Database available at http://www.census.gov/ipc/www/idbnew.html.

TABLE 5.1   DISEASE CONDITIONS PRESENT IN BWA MAWEGO

Disease	Description
Asthma	Chronic condition causing breathing difficulties
Cerebral palsy	Disability resulting from brain damage before, during, or shortly after birth—discernible by muscular incoordination and speech disturbances
Chicken pox	Contagious disease caused by a herpesvirus, marked by low-grade fever and blistering red spots
Common influenza	Flu—viral disease characterized by sudden onset, fever, exhaustion, body aches, respiratory congestion
Diabetes	Sugar and starch are not properly absorbed into the body
Elephantiasis	Enormous enlargement of a limb or the scrotum caused by lymph vessel obstruction by filarial worms
Epilepsy	Disorders with disturbed electrical rhythms in the central nervous system and marked by convulsive attacks
Hypertension	Abnormally high arterial blood pressure
Measles	Contagious viral disease producing small red spots across the body
Shingles	Inflammation of the spinal and cranial nerve tissue, with blister eruptions and nerve pain—caused by reactivation of the herpesvirus causing chicken pox
Sinusitis	Inflammation of a sinus of the skull
Tinea, various types	Fungal skin infections such as "athlete's foot" and "jungle rot"
Tuberculosis	Infectious wasting disease affecting various body parts, especially the lungs

Dominica. Influenza is the most common infectious disease risk in Dominica. Other infectious diseases (hepatitis B, tuberculosis, leprosy, and AIDS) occur, but are rare (WHO 1999). Low population density, the local practice of digging deep latrines, and Dominica's steepness (i.e., little standing water) decreases the potential for common Caribbean diseases.

Though it prevents some disease, Dominica's slope presents some danger. Locals of Bwa Mawego face the perpetual risk of falling down steep, often wet and slippery clay paths. Though some individuals are more slip-prone than others, everyone falls from time to time.

In Bwa Mawego, falls tend to provide humor more often than threat. Villagers show their clay-covered pants to friends and neighbors and tell the story of their mishap—often beginning with something like, "Mon, I tell you, I had one good fall today, mon." Another favorite story is that of the extra-long slide with a narrowly evaded fall. When one Bwa Mawegan sees that another has a muddy rump or knees, the routine joke is for the clean villager to ask the dirty one if he succeeded in catching the *kwapo* or "mountain chicken" (a species of giant frog) for his dinner. Despite the abounding jokes, some falls lead to serious injuries like broken bones (especially for the elderly) and serious cuts (by colliding with razor grass or one's own cutlass). Perhaps the most severe fall risk is that of pregnancy miscarriage after a fall. I do not know exactly how common this occurrence is. However, the subject came up on one

TABLE 5.2   COMMON CARIBBEAN DISEASES OF CROWDING AND STILL WATER

Disease	Description
Amoebic dysentery	Amoeba-caused severe diarrhea with passage of mucus and blood
Bacillary dysentery	Bacteria-caused severe diarrhea with passage of mucus and blood
Cholera	Tropical disease carried through contaminated water and causing profuse diarrhea and dehydration
Dengue fever	Acute, mosquito-carried disease with high fevers
Hepatitis A	Acute disease of liver inflammation transmitted mostly in food and water contaminated with infected fecal matter
Malaria	Mosquito-transmitted disease causing fevers that occur at intervals
Schistosomiasis	A tropical parasitic disease caused by parasites that multiply in snails and are released into bathing/drinking/farming water, then bore into human bodies in contact with infested water. The parasites damage human tissues.
Typhoid fever	Infectious disease carried through water or milk and resulting in a high fever, headache, abdominal pain and swelling, and pink patches on the skin

occasion when I was at a river bathing and laundering spot with five neighbor women. Each of them had suffered at least one post-fall miscarriage.

ILLNESSES IN BWA MAWEGO

Ethnomedical anthropologists divide non–Western theories of disease into two categories: *personalistic* and *naturalistic* illnesses (Foster 1976). Both illness forms exist in Bwa Mawego.

Naturalistic illnesses result from exposure to naturally occurring risks in one's environment. Bwa Mawegans have some understanding of contagious diseases, which they call "running sicknesses." Villagers view exposure to a sick person as a natural hazard. Other causes of naturalistic illnesses in Bwa Mawego (and elsewhere) include insults from exposure to hot or cold temperatures, dirt, or blows to the body (see also Helman 1994). These are the majority of illnesses in Bwa Mawego.

Personalistic illnesses are those that are blamed on the supernatural intervention of another—be that a human (i.e., witch or sorcerer) or nonhuman (i.e., a god, ghost, evil spirit, etc.). The sick person with a personalistic illness is not the victim of chance, fate, or the random act of an evildoer. Rather, some existing personal conflict between the perpetrator and his/her victim motivates the evildoer to inflict sickness on an enemy.

There is some variation in the supposed degree of intent of those who cause personalistic illnesses. For example, Navajo people sometimes feared that they were guilty of unconscious witchcraft if they had entertained "bad thoughts" about someone who subsequently died or became ill (White 1928). Similarly, in notions of the "evil eye" (found in Europe, the Middle East, North Africa, and Latin America), a person who possesses the "evil eye" is usually unaware of his supernatural powers to curse or inflict sickness on people whom he envies or admires (Helman 1994). In these cases the curse may be unintentional, but the conflict between individuals still motivates the perpetrator. Victims of personalistic illness can also vary. For example, a perpetrator might cast an illness not on his enemy, but on one of the enemy's closest loved ones. Anthropologists categorize all sicknesses that locals attribute to conflict-driven supernatural intervention as personalistic illnesses (Foster and Anderson 1978).

Personalistic Illness in Bwa Mawego

Sorcery is the vehicle for all personalistic illnesses in Bwa Mawego. Locals identify the sorcerers as either "**obeahmen**" or "witches." In 1937, E. E. Evans-Pritchard drew a distinction between **witchcraft** and **sorcery**. This classification has become an accepted convention in cultural anthropology. In Evans-Pritchard's view, *witches* are practitioners with accepted intrinsic, *inborn* abilities to inflict harm or manipulate reality to one's advantage. *Sorcerers* are reckoned to achieve their status via *learned* rituals and knowledge (Evans-Pritchard 1937). Bwa Mawegans claim that "witches" in their village *learn* how to change their form and do evil. Though accused "witches" tend to run in families, villagers assert that powers of wickedness are not "in the blood"; rather, members of certain families supposedly teach each other the "wicked" techniques. This may seem contradictory to anthropologists who define "witch" differently than Bwa Mawegans. Indeed, to a Bwa Mawegan, *anyone* has the potential to be a witch, and everyone is somewhat suspect. Throughout this book, I employ the local terms "witches" and "obeahmen" to refer to local sorcerers, the only agents of personalistic illnesses in Bwa Mawego.[4]

Bwa Mawegans refer to most personalistic illnesses as "when someone do you something" [i.e., someone does something to you], or "when someone put something on you."[5] They say that someone can "do you something" with either "wickedness" (the work of witches), or with "evil" (**obeah**). Both of these practices invoke the power of Satan, at least in part. Some personalistic illness is said to come as punishment from "The Almighty Father" who is reckoned loving yet strict (much like Dominican parents).

Witchcraft and Personalistic Illness

Bwa Mawegans recognize four kinds of witches. Two kinds of witches, *soukwayans* and *lougawous*, suck blood and can cause "fright," a local **culture-bound syndrome**. The other two types of witches, *djombis* and *diabléses*, only cause "fright."

Before introduction to Bwa Mawegan witch typology, I must introduce fright— a potential consequence of all village witchcraft. I discuss this syndrome further in Chapters 7 and 8. For now, the reader should know that fright is one of the few Bwa Mawegan illnesses that villagers attribute to both personalistic and naturalistic causes. According to local **ethnophysiology**, fright results from a shock so extreme

---

[4] Likewise, the words "witchcraft" and "obeah" here refer to sorcery.
[5] Because of the volatile nature of sorcery, Bwa Mawegans intentionally use unspecific language such as "something" for a "hex" and "someone" rather than "a witch." In general, most discussion of witchcraft is done in hints rather than statements.

it chills one's blood, thus restricting circulation and proper nerve function. Bwa Mawegans attribute some strokes and heart attacks to fright. In most cases, fright does not lead to sudden death. Rather, the victim begins to suffer from long-term anxiety. Both the initial cause of fright (a traumatic event), and its outward symptoms (persistent anxiety and arousal, hypersensitivity, event flashbacks, etc.) are similar to what Western psychology refers to as post traumatic stress syndrome (American Psychiatric Association 1994). In Bwa Mawego, one can contract "fright" naturalistically through any naturally occurring frightening or shocking situation. Alternatively, one can contract "fright" personalistically from an experience involving a witch. A villager could consider a witch encounter a near-death experience as well as a brush with one of Satan's minions.

Bwa Mawegans explain that all witches start their evil in the privacy of the bush, usually at night. There, under cover, the witches do some kind of magic that changes their appearance—usually to look like an animal. A witch's disguise prevents fellow villagers from recognizing him or her. The altered form also gives the witch access to more places because he or she acquires the abilities of the new form (e.g., birds can fly, ants can fit through small cracks, dogs can track people, etc.). Again, one might become frightened by any of the four witch varieties (*djombis, diabléses, soukwayans or lougawous*); however, *djombi* and the *diablés* exist solely to give people fright.

The *djombi* is the least malevolent form of witch. One informant explained that:

> *Djombis* is peoples turning into animals and letting you see them. But they really don't do anything bad. But they can give you fright . . . Maybe they startle you—like a shock. Or, maybe you think you're seeing one of them bad, bad witches. They have no right to frighten you.

If an individual animal with whom a villager is not well-acquainted[6] displays odd behavior, such as approaching unusually near or staring at the villager, the villager suspects that the animal could be a *djombi*. Villagers also suspect snakes near their homes and rats in their homes of being *djombis*. After all, *djombis* like to startle people; and rats and snakes are particularly good startlers. One villager told me that she knew her household rat must be a visiting *djombi* because it knew not to eat the poisoned bread she put out for it.

Another type of fright-giving witch, the *diablés*, never actually enters the village proper. After its transformation (usually into an unrecognizable person), a *diablés* stays in the bush where it hides in the shadows and spies on people. This is a most unacceptable behavior in a village with pervasive peasant paranoia. Spying itself leads to no illness. Danger to one's health comes when the *diablés*' victim begins to sense that he or she is being watched. Here, the victim's creepy sensation can overcome his or her body, especially after looking around and seeing—or thinking to see—the witch duck into a shadow or behind a tree. At this confirmation, a victim could go into all-out fright. The heart might pound; he or she may even suffer a stroke or heart attack. More commonly, he or she starts running away from the witch. The *diablés* tries to chase the victim into a dangerous area—a slippery trail or near a precipice that the victim might fall off.

Bwa Mawegans cite the *soukwayan* and the *lougawou* as the "most dangerous," "most deceitful," and "wickedest" witches. A *soukwayan* is female and a *lougawou*

---

[6] In other words, the villager, or someone close to the villager, does not own the animal.

is male. Otherwise, a *soukwayan* and a *lougawou* are the same kind of witch. When speaking both Patwa and English, villagers use the female term *soukwayan* as the generic term for a blood-sucking witch, as these female witches are allegedly more prevalent than male *lougawous*. A *lougawou*, however, possesses the ability to become a "stronger" and "bigger witch" than his *soukwayan* counterpart, should he choose. In general, *soukwayans* and *lougawous* execute comparable wicked deeds, and the magic both of them use for their metamorphosis is similar. Thus, opposite-sexed witches can learn from each other. A father *lougawou* can teach his daughter to be a *soukwayan*, for example.

Anthropologists have found that in some populations, witches are identifiable. They are often particularly "ugly," deformed, or otherwise outcast (Helman 1994). A Guatemalan Quiché *win* (a witch who transforms into an animal, similar to a Dominican *soukwayan*) is recognized in his human form by having large, protruding canine teeth, bloodshot eyes, and lines forming "letters that no one can read" on his upper torso (Saler 1967:80). In Bwa Mawego, witches bear no distinguishing mark and display no signs of their wicked abilities. Villagers claim that witches keep their identities secret because anyone who discovers evidence that a fellow Bwa Mawegan is a *soukwayan* or *lougawou* must kill the witch to end the witch's satanic ways. Obviously, witches do not want to be killed, so they must be especially deceitful. Particularly friendly people are thus suspects for covering up their witch status. As one Bwa Mawegan stated, "Sometimes them people that does be so nice to your face is the *same ones* who sucking your child's blood at night." Everyone in Bwa Mawego is a potential *soukwayan*. As one woman put it, "Even your own mother or husband might be a witch an' you not suspecting a thing. They not leaving you no clues, now."

According to Bwa Mawegans, *soukwayans* go into the bush at night and seek out a private place, far from the paths. There, they shed their own skins to take on the forms of other persons, or more commonly, animals. Then, leaving their skins on the forest floor, the disguised *soukwayans* sneak into the village. They enter the houses of their enemies and the people they envy, and they suck the peoples' blood. Alternatively, a *soukwayan* might go to an enemy's garden, suck the sap or juices from his crops, steal food, or "mash up the garden." A *soukwayan* might also suck the blood of his enemy's animals. For the most part, *soukwayans* stick to sucking on people. If a villager wakes up to find a mouth-shaped bruise in a place where she does not remember injuring herself, she knows that a witch has sucked her.

If the victim has not yet touched the suck-bruise, she can attempt to kill the witch. She can go to a lime tree and cut the bottom half off one ripe lime without pulling the lime off the tree. She must rub her suck-bruise with the bottom half of the lime, then throw the lime over her shoulder. Then, as the top half of the lime withers on the tree, so the *soukwayan*'s health declines. When the lime on the tree dies, so will the *soukwayan*. The trouble with this method is that a person naturally and without thinking touches or rubs a new bruise upon finding it. Another way one can kill a witch is to find its skin in the bush and pour salt on it. When the witch returns, its skin will be shrunken and dry. The witch will not be able to wear its skin, and without skin, it dies. There is no account of this happening in the village. If there were witch skins on the forest floor at night, Bwa Mawegans would not find them. Bwa Mawegans rarely dare to go into the witch-filled bush at night. When they do, they stay on the tracks.

There are several illnesses that Bwa Mawegans blame on witches. The most common one is "low blood," or not enough blood. This makes people feel tired, weak, and dizzy. A person with low blood will either have lost the blood through a severe cut, or he will be covered in the telltale bruises left by the *soukwayan* that sucked his blood out.

A *soukwayan* can also contaminate a victim's blood by biting with a dirty mouth. This leads to the local illness "dirty blood," where "dirts" in the blood stream pollute the body (discussed further in Chapter 7).

Bwa Mawegans blame *soukwayans* and *lougawous* for contagious diseases as well. Bwa Mawegans know that blood-to-blood contact can transfer diseases from one person to another. An AIDS intervention campaign recently undertaken by the Ministry of Health seems to have reinforced this idea. Logically, Bwa Mawegans assume that witches who have their last victim's blood on or around their mouth can spread not only AIDS, but other contagious diseases such as tuberculosis, measles, chicken pox, and hepatitis. Likewise, *soukwayans* can spread diseases from animal to human or from animal to animal. When one young village man became ill with an AIDS-like wasting disease (some say it was a liver disease), many villagers accused a nearby older woman of either slowly sucking the life out of the man, or giving him a strange disease that she spread to him by first sucking on a sick goat. The two neighbors allegedly had conflicts before the young man became ill. The conflicts increased as the young man's illness worsened. On several public occasions, he all but accused her of causing his illness. The woman denied practicing witchcraft. This did not help her case. All witches deny their abilities. The young man died after about seven years of illness. Though not every villager willingly blames the older woman, the dead young man and his allies planted a seed of doubt in all villagers' brains. Nearly everyone in the village is highly suspect of her and circumspect in her presence. Her status has changed from that of a respected catechism teacher and Village Councilwoman to a semi-outcast whom villagers generally ignore.

Bwa Mawegans have a few preventative measures that they use to ward off witches. They sleep with their windows and door closed to impede a witch's entry. After closing the door from the inside, they lean a broom in the upside-down position (bristles up) against the door. Upside-down brooms "disturb" witches. They place a pair of scissors in an open position above window and door frames to "cut the witch off" when he tries to enter. If a villager has some sort of conflict with a suspected witch, or feels that there is something "mysterious" happening with his or her body (e.g., he feels inexplicably tired, or he finds a suck bruise), he or she will eat additional garlic. Bwa Mawegans say that the garlic goes into the blood and makes it taste bad so the witches won't want it. Bwa Mawegans generally season with garlic, but in cases of suspected witchcraft extra garlic will be added to the family stew pot. In severe cases, a person will wear strong-smelling, garlic-infused oil to ward off witches. In addition to garlic, villagers use seven herbs (listed in Table 5.3) to ward off witches. They infuse all of these herbs, singly or blended together in any combination, in a pot of boiling water. When the liquid has cooled, they drink a cup of the infusion and bathe the entire body with the rest.

Anthropologists have observed that in societies where witchcraft is a concern, individuals use witchcraft accusation—or the threat of it—as a form of social control (Whiting 1950). It is the same in Bwa Mawego, where greed and jealousy are the only cited motives for witchcraft. Witches are "greedy" or "jealous" people. Witchcraft provides a way to express discontent over the balance of **reciprocity**. An important value of these villagers, as with many **peasants**, is that no one should

TABLE 5.3   HERBS USED IN INFUSIONS TO WARD OFF WITCHES

Common Names: *Patwa* and English	Plant Species Name	Plant Family
estwa fwajil	*Polygala paniculata* L.	Polygalaceae
lespwi lom	*Alternanthera flavescens* Kunth	Amaranthaceae
male garlic	*Mansoa alliacea* (Lam.) A. Gentry	Bignoniaceae
sime kontwá, worm bush, worm grass	*Chenopodium ambrosioides* L.	Chenopodiaceae
ti fwige blan, ti fwige jeun, silver fern, gold fern	*Pityrogramma chrysophylla* (Sw.) Link.	Pteridophytes
tombe-leve	*Centella asiatica* (L.) Urb.	Apiaceae

display a noticeable interest in the accumulation of material goods. This attitude is tied to a notion or **image of limited good** (Foster 1965) within the community. A villager can (perhaps unconsciously) strategically claim witchcraft against another person. The insinuation of sorcery damages the accused witch's reputation, thereby leveling social imbalances. Witchcraft, then, is a cultural notion closely tied to the perceived cause of some illnesses.

Cross-culturally, accusations of witchcraft increase when a community is in times of social change and conflict as competing factions blame misfortunes on each other (Helman 1994:125). This may account for some of the current preoccupation with *soukwayan* in Bwa Mawego, as the village is starting to undergo changes in technology (recent electricity, radios, etc.) and social structure. More young people are leaving the village to work in Roseau or on other islands, and bringing more cash and goods back to the village. The division of wealth must be more apparent than it was in the previous generation, when all villagers were subsistence farmers.

Obeah and Personalistic Illness

There are three kinds of illnesses that Bwa Mawegans tend to attribute to obeah. These are (1) any illnesses with convulsions or tremors, (2) illnesses not diagnosable or curable with biomedicine, and (3) an illness with symbolic import (e.g., a man who cheats on his mate developing a sore on his penis, or a thief injuring the hand). Obeah illnesses are "sent" illnesses. That is, they originate because someone goes to an obeahman and requests the obeahman's help to "send" an illness (i.e., a curse) on someone else. A Roman Catholic priest can help rid a person of a sent illness; however, in many cases, the only way to fight obeah is *with* obeah. Since there are not many obeahmen on the island, it is likely that people who seek cures from the nearest obeahman suspect that this same man helped send their illnesses in the first place. The locals don't blame the obeahman for the curse, however, and obeahmen don't blame themselves. He is a neutral agent with talents equally for sale to wicked and righteous villagers. Thus, in cases of obeah, the villager who sends an illness using the obeahman is thought to be an "evil" person, not the obeahman himself.

Personalistic medicine in Bwa Mawego contains a moral component that allegedly serves as a deterrent to sorcery (Brodwin 1996 observed a similar pattern in Haiti). Once a villager employs obeah, his intended victim will indeed become affected. However, obeah can backfire, causing pain to the purveyor of the illness. Repercussions to obeah can happen in two ways. First, the victim of a sent illness can visit an obeahman; the obeahman can divine who sent the illness; and the victim can choose to send the illness back on to the original sender. Second, an illness will automatically either rebound to the sender or backfire if the reason for the curse is unfounded.

For example, there is an obeah hex that a parent can send on her daughter and the daughter's mate to ensure that the couple stays together. However, if the couple's relationship was not one ordained by Jah (God), the couple will always stay together but they will always fight.

As an example of obeah rebounding to the sender, one villager, Mistress (Mrs.) Wellington, recounted her own experience with obeah backlash. Mistress Wellington and her mother both own rum shops. Mistress Wellington buys her rum by the gallon from her mother, who keeps a large rum cask at her shop. Another villager, Mr. Penny, regularly drank his rum at Mistress Wellington's shop. Mistress Penny resented the time that Mr. Penny spent at Mistress Wellington's shop. Mistress Penny used to announce publicly that Mistress Wellington was in love with her husband and trying to steal him. Mistress Wellington explained that Mistress Penny "put something for my foot to spoil so I would stay in one place and I couldn't walk through the village or to my mother's shop." One day, Mistress Wellington stepped down, and for no apparent reason, sprained her foot. She said:

> I couldn't walk on that foot. For more than a week I was resting the foot and just rubbing it with sea moss and caster oil. Then, one day, Mistress Penny's foot hurting her. The doctor cut her foot to inspect it. He saw puss. And it was smelling and a lot of puss leaking out. Everyday the foot worse. It started bleeding and stinking. Her pressure went up. So happened she had diabetes so the foot wouldn't cure.

Mr. Penny explained to Mistress Wellington's mother that he used to tell his wife that Mistress Wellington was innocent of loving him. He also told his wife that if she sent something, the evil would fall back on her. But Mistress Penny did not heed her husband's advice. As a result, Mistress Penny's foot was in worse condition than Mistress Wellington's. Bwa Mawegans hesitate to "send" illnesses on their neighbors for fear of this sort of backlash.

Jah and Personalistic Illness

Whether Dominican villagers are nominally Rastafarian, Protestant, or Roman Catholic they believe in one God (alternately called *Jah* in English and *Diò* in Patwa) and they fear (and also hope for) his retribution. Bwa Mawegans accept that Jah punishes people for their sins with illness. The worse the sin, the worse the illness punishment is. Illness in this case is a form of penance and a reminder to repent for past sins and to seek Jah's guidance to live a better life in the future. Anthropologists have found similar views of illness as divine retribution in the United States both among low-income African-Americans (Snow 1978), and middle-income suburban Americans (Helman 1994). Bwa Mawegans sometimes welcome their chance to "purify the soul" with a sickness. They fear Jah's vengeance too. It can be swift and harsh, as in the case of a "greedy" village woman whose late-term pregnancy was taken away from her. The backfiring of Obeah spells is another kind of divine retribution. Bwa Mawegans fear their own punishment from God, yet they are glad for it to keep other villagers on the straight and narrow.

Naturalistic Illnesses in Bwa Mawego

The majority of possible ailments that Bwa Mawegans recognize are what medical anthropologists characterize as naturalistic illnesses. In Bwa Mawego naturalistic illnesses are the result of exposure to one of three insults. The first kind of insult is exposure to an environmental health risk that throws the body's system out of equilibrium and puts the body at risk. The second is exposure to a person with a contagious, or "running" sickness; though Bwa Mawegans generally attribute catching a "running sickness" to exposure to the sickness combined with body-system imbalance. The third type of naturalistic insult is an injury.

The most common illness explanation involves disrespect of naturally occurring risks in the environment. To Dominicans, maintaining a balanced body "system" is the first rule of health maintenance. Staying healthy primarily entails (1) eating a balanced diet (according to local nutritional and **humoral** theory), (2) not letting one's body become deeply chilled or overheated, (3) sleeping enough without being lazy, (4) exercising without working to the point of exhaustion, (5) keeping the blood clean. I discuss all of these points in detail when I present Dominican ethnophysiology in Chapter 7.

For lack of a better fit, I include illness that results from a breach of **taboo** with naturalistic illnesses. Breaking a taboo involves disrespect of what is reckoned as a law of nature, much like letting oneself become chilled results in illness by not observing nature's law to remain at a suitable temperature. In Bwa Mawego, some birth defects are blamed on breaking a pregnancy taboo. For example, while a woman is pregnant, both parents avoid killing or butchering any animal. Locals say that a breach of this taboo can result in a birth defect in which the child is born with some attribute of the dead animal. For example, if a parent kills a pig, the child may have deformed hands or feet, said to look like cloven hooves (taboo is discussed further in Chapter 7).

Occasionally witchcraft is suspected in injuries that result from falls and falling object (such as a fruit from a tree, or a mudslide); however, for the most part, injuries are naturalistic illnesses. Naturalistic injuries might be caused by an accident or by the purposeful actions of another person. Although other people cause some injuries on purpose, these are not personalistic illnesses. The difference between injuries resulting from a naturalistic (i.e., punching another person) and a personalistic illness is that the naturalistic punch is overt and does not involve supernatural forces.

Understanding the naturalistic illnesses in Bwa Mawego requires one to comprehend local concepts of how the body works. This ethnophysiology is the subject of Chapter 7, which details Dominican views on the human body.

6/Bwa Mawego's Sectors of Health Care

Where, when, and how people get medical treatment is a component of many medical anthropological studies. Anthropologists want to know who their subjects turn to for medical help, how often, and under what circumstances. Basic information on "healthcare-seeking behavior" can shed light on many medical issues. It reveals a community's prevalent health problems, for instance. This information also helps in assessing the user-friendliness of local healthcare delivery. Perhaps most importantly, knowledge of local patterns of healthcare-seeking behavior can be invaluable for designing **public health** programs and for evaluating the effectiveness of existing public health outreach.

Healthcare seeking is an issue because most societies have some degree of **medical pluralism**. That is, people have multiple treatment options open to them, including self-treatment. For example, an American with bad back pain might try taking some over-the-counter pain medication, stretching, and soaking in a hot tub. He might also, while praying for relief, make an appointment to see a massage therapist, a chiropractor, or an orthopedic surgeon, depending on the type and severity of his back pain. These options reflect the medical pluralism in the United States and tell us something about U.S. medical culture. In contrast, a man from a tribal culture who has a bad back might try to rest in the semitraction of his hammock for a few days and take some medicinal herbs. Next he might go to a shaman who would talk to the patient about the problems in his life, perform a type of exorcism on the evil spirit blamed for the back pain, and give the patient additional herbal medications. The options open to this tribal patient, and how and when he employs them, would give us insight into his culture of medicine.

Medical systems are a complicated aspect of culture. To reduce complexity, anthropologists break healthcare options into three broad divisions: (1) popular, (2) folk, and (3) professional care (Kleinman 1980). The three sectors of health care can be analyzed by considering two criteria—specialization and professionalization. The popular sector is distinct from the folk and professional sectors in that it lacks specialization. The popular sector consists of regular people caring for themselves and for their families. Specialists in the folk and professional sectors require training, talents, or experience beyond those available to the population at large. One can distinguish between the two specialist sectors because "professional" care requires formal, standardized training, and certification (e.g., medical school and a medical license) not required for a "folk" practitioner.

Regardless of cultural context, the popular sector is the first and most often used area of health care (Kleinman 1980). Whether a person lives in a tribal band, a chiefdom, or a state level society, it seems natural and pragmatic for a person to treat his or her children and his or her own ailments immediately and privately before seeking help from some medical specialist. In contemporary North America, the popular sector includes Mom's chicken soup and Tylenol.

The folk sector of health care tends to be large in non–Western and non-industrialized societies, and it was a large sector of Western health care into the 1900s. This sector includes all of the people who, rather than going through formal schooling for their medical training, learn through self-teaching and exploration, unofficial apprenticeships, and knowledge passed down through kin. Folk healers include (among others) midwives, herbalists, bonesetters, and shamans.

The professional sector of health care includes all licensed or legally sanctioned healthcare workers. The professional sector includes doctors, dentists, chiropractors, nurses, physical therapists, psychotherapists, dieticians, paramedics, and numerous types of medical technicians. In industrialized countries with large government bureaucracies and active, often used legal systems, many jobs that used to be part of the folk sector now require rigorous schooling and certification. This is the case with registered nurse midwives, for example. Masseuses are giving way to certified massage therapists. The Hindu Ayurvedic system of medicine has medical philosophies and practices that differ from those of Western biomedicine. Ayurveda used to be India's primary folk medicine. Now there are several established Ayurvedic medical schools, and since 1970 Ayurveda has been a legal and complimentary alternative to Western biomedicine in India (Fulder 1988).

The three healthcare sectors can overlap to varying degrees, depending on the culture. Also, the relative size and importance of each sector varies across societies. For example, some industrial societies may not recognize a folk sector, while small-scale groups have no professional sector. Nevertheless, Kleinman's system provides a useful framework to analyze and discuss medical systems. I employ it here to discuss health care in Bwa Mawego.

BWA MAWEGO'S POPULAR SECTOR: BUSH MEDICINE

The popular sector of medicine involves no payment. It includes self-treatment, and treatment from family and friends. It is the milieu in which people first identify and explain the cause and severity of illness, and in most cases where the first treatment should take place.

In Bwa Mawego people refer to the popular sector of medicine as "bush medicine." Bush medicine is a major preoccupation of many Bwa Mawegans. This fixation is somewhat predictable as cross-culturally the vast majority of health care takes place within the popular sector (Kleinman 1980). The popular sector of medicine is very important in poor, Third World areas because economic and social barriers restrict use of the other sectors (vom Eigan 1992). The people of Bwa Mawego need to rely on popular sector medicine (bush medicine) even more than average Third World villagers do because Bwa Mawego is so remote (the nearest doctor is 45 minutes away; and the nearest pharmacy is two hours away when one can find or afford a ride). Home treatment with bush medicine is immediate and free (see Figure 6.1), and the remedies (mostly wild plants and some over-the-counter medicines and household goods) tend to be less expensive than specialist-prescribed ones.

The term "bush medicine" is common throughout the Caribbean (Laguerre 1987). In some places, "bush medicine" refers to the practice of specialized herbalists in the folk sector called "bush doctors." There is a large range of curative knowledge within Bwa Mawego's lay population (detailed in Chapter 8). There are no specialized "bush doctors," however. People use the term "bush doctor" as a joke or an exaggerated compliment, much the way Americans use the terms "movie star" or "rocket scientist." Modesty is an important virtue among Bwa Mawegans. Certainly, no one would presume to call himself a "bush doctor" as it would be tantamount to calling himself an "expert." It would be bragging. Calling someone else a "bush doctor" would be impolite as it might bring jealousy (a major village preoccupation). I asked over half of the adults in Bwa Mawego who the bush doctors in the village were. Most responses were similar to that of the woman who told me, "It haven't any bush doctors here in Bwa Mawego, but my brother Benjamin know plenty bush medicine, you know. People always asking him for suggestions." Bwa Mawegans say that everyone in the village is his own bush doctor. At the same time, they assert that a *true* "bush doctor" would not only have more specialized knowledge than the average Bwa Mawegan, but would charge for both advice and bush remedies, as do a few people in Roseau and elsewhere on the island. Hence, in Bwa Mawego bush medicine is in the realm of the popular sector. Everyone knows some bush medicine. It is the first and most frequently used form of treatment.

THE PROFESSIONAL SECTOR: BIOMEDICINE

If bush medical treatments prove ineffective, or if a person's injury or pain is severe enough to require a specialist, Bwa Mawegans seek biomedical help from the nurses and doctors of the island's professional sector. Clinic access is a recent and undependable phenomenon in this remote village, however. Bwa Mawego shares a small health center (clinic) with its neighboring village (see Figure 6.2). The health center is within walking distance. However, the often slippery and steep walk to the clinic makes it inaccessible to sick patients. The health center's main function is as a dispensary for first aid and immunizations. During my first two trips to Dominica, a nurse was only at the village health center on Thursdays. In 1997, a Guayanese nurse came to live in the village and work in the clinic every weekday. Villagers now complain that although the clinic is open more often, the stock has not increased (enough), so the clinic is frequently out of supplies. For many people, a visit to the nurse is not worth the walk when they feel sick or are injured.

Self-transport to a larger clinic is rarely an option for Bwa Mawego residents. Villagers do not own cars (or animals to ride) and the buses only leave the village at 5:30 AM, unless special, private arrangements are made. For emergencies, villagers can call an "ambulance" (actually a pick-up truck) to come from a larger clinic about 45 minutes away. The ambulance carries the patient back to the clinic in the truck-bed.

Figure 6.1 A young woman cuts some pwev jine *(Costus sp.). The leaves are steeped and drunk as a digestive aid.*

Figure 6.2 Villagers waiting to see the nurse at the Bwa Mawego–St. Pierre Health Center

Villagers say that although this larger clinic is better stocked than the village clinic, it too frequently lacks supplies. Often the patient continues onto Roseau in the ambulance-truck.

According to people in Bwa Mawego, the hospital in Roseau is overcrowded and understaffed. Further, it is difficult to get to the hospital from Bwa Mawego. If there is an ambulance-truck available at the closest clinic, a patient from Bwa Mawego will not arrive at the hospital for over two hours. It takes that long for the ambulance to wind through the mountainous route to Roseau. And an ambulance is not always immediately available. After suffering a late-term miscarriage, and while still bleeding heavily, one mother in our study spent three hours waiting by the village's "big road" for the ambulance-truck.

If people have a serious medical condition that requires surgery, but not necessarily immediate surgery, they attempt to find means to go to Guadeloupe or Martinique. Most people have family on one island or the other. These French islands are larger and considerably more developed and prosperous than Dominica. Reportedly, they have larger hospitals, better doctors, and better medical equipment.

Most Bwa Mawegans have misgivings about dealing with biomedical professionals. In general, Bwa Mawegans are reluctant to deal with officials and authority figures, especially those from outside the community. They avoid and deride politicians, policemen, visiting preachers, and even uniformed telephone repairmen. When government surveyors came to the village to measure the lot for a new Village Council building, villagers chided them and threw stones at them until they left. In Roseau there is reportedly a welfare office where people can sign up for free medical care. One informant, who lost a tooth rather than seek help from the welfare office, said that no one from the village would go to that office, "because they asking you questions about where you live and everything. No one wants to tell them strangers all their business." Basically, this is a rapport issue—until a villager has built an understanding relationship with an outsider, the outsider usually is distrusted or disliked. When a nurse worked at the village health center only once a week, and that nurse was not always the same person, villagers mocked the service at the village health center. Now that the person who staffs the health center is "a nice nurse" who lives in their village, most people only complain about the lack of clinic supplies—not about the clinic in general.

While Bwa Mawegans readily seek biomedical attention for their ills, they do so with reservation. Villagers with the most liberal attitude about biomedicine have no particular fear of physicians. They view doctors simply as educated individuals who help their patients as best they can. Yet, even people with this view are uncomfortable going to doctors because of (1) the privacy issue (not liking to show their body to or answer questions from a stranger), and (2) the loss of control that biomedicine entails. Whereas in bush medicine a patient is in complete control over the treatment of his own body, the biomedical patient must submit entirely to the will of the physician and the power of his medications. For example, most villagers assume that all biomedical pharmaceuticals are concentrated "bush" (herbs). However, when a doctor prescribes medication, the bush is concentrated into tablet or injection form so one can not identify what he is taking or how strong it is. For example, a village woman took prescription birth control pills for a couple of years. The pills were allegedly so strong that they made her sterile for life. There are perhaps hundreds of stories of how a doctor helped or saved the lives of villagers. However, I have documented over 30 legends of people who took prescribed medications that poisoned them, caused a bad reaction, or made a condition worse.

Some people in Bwa Mawego say that doctors are greedy. Villagers maintain that doctors view "bush medicines" as competition for their own prescriptions. If people had no bush medicines they would have to go to the doctor more often. They thus fear that if the doctors found out about local treatments, they would do their best to get rid of the local remedies, thereby drumming up more business for themselves. Physicians allegedly connived to eradicate two once popular bush medicines. The first loss was the leech, which Dominicans used to clean infected wounds. In this case, the medical doctors allegedly poisoned all of the ponds and rivers where leeches once lived. In another case, doctors supposedly cut down all the plants of a certain kind of bush medicine. It is difficult for villagers to trust men who they regard with such covetous, selfish motives.

To many villagers, medical science, or "doctor science" is secret, dangerous, and mysterious—particularly where anesthesia and surgery are concerned. Some associate it with "High Science"—a "wicked" religious alternative to Christianity, whose philosophy centers on attaining secret knowledge to make oneself wealthy.[1] There is thus some ambivalence concerning biomedicine. Bwa Mawegans might fear a doctor's power, but they are often glad for his help.

THE FOLK SECTOR

Midwives, Priests,[2] and Obeahmen

Bwa Mawego's folk sector of medicine is the least-used sector of the local health-care system. Medicine of this sector is a last resort. In a survey of African-Caribbean Medicine, Laguerre (1987) notes that there are three classifications of Caribbean folk healer: (1) the curers—those who practice medicine without any magical or religious component, (2) faith healers—whose power comes from God and can only be applied for good purposes, and (3) magical doctors—who can use their powers for both good and evil. Traditionally, Bwa Mawegans used all three types of these folk practitioners in the form of midwife/herbalist, priests, and obeahmen (sorcerers). Now only priests and obeahmen remain in this sector. There is no midwife/herbalist.

The last village midwife died around 1980. Since then, no one filled her niche. The standard rationale for the absence of a midwife is that the government now requires all new births to be registered at the hospital or one of the larger government clinics. This makes midwives unnecessary for birthing. In addition, villagers feel that there is risk in becoming an expert whose knowledge competes with that of biomedical doctors. As mentioned previously, villagers simultaneously respect and mistrust physicians. Indeed, older villagers say that it was a doctor who killed Ma Jean, the last midwife/herbalist. They say that Ma Jean was a very powerful healer. Villagers preferred to seek her treatment over the doctor's. Near the end of Ma Jean's life, there was a sick woman who the doctor "condemned" as not treatable. Then, proving the

---

[1] Bwa Mawegans say that one can buy books on how to practice High Science (the religion) in town. The books are reportedly similar to books like *The Farmer's Almanac* (the local version is somewhat occult), dream interpretation books, books on spells, and so forth. I have never seen a High Science book.

[2] Although priests are undoubtedly professionals, they are professional clergy, not professional medical providers *per se*. Following Kleinman (1980), I include them in the folk sector of health care.

doctor wrong, Ma Jean cured the woman. A while after that, Ma Jean came down with a condition that she could not cure herself. She sought the doctor's help. The jealous doctor allegedly seized this opportunity to give Ma Jean poison tablets. Since then, there have been no midwives or other specialist-curers within the village's folk sector.

Villagers still seek religious and magical healing within the folk sector, however. They primarily seek out the healing powers of the Roman Catholic priest. In the last 20 years fundamentalist Protestant missionaries came to the village and inspired three villagers to become ministers. Although this weakened the Roman Catholic Church's influence on the village in general, the priest remains a stronger figure in terms of healing than the familiar, and relatively untrained, village ministers. In recent years, there has not been a parish priest in residence in Saint Pierre, the neighboring village where the Catholic church is located. This makes religious healing less accessible than it used to be.

The priest helps villagers pray for protection from sickness and evil. The preventative solace his prayers offer may be the priest's primary anti-illness function in the community. Of course, in cases of severe illness, villagers go to the priest in hopes of divine intervention for themselves or their loved one. In addition, when people consider themselves victims of "evil" (sorcery), they go to the priest. As one informant said, "If you have pain that won't cure, first go to a doctor. If the doctor can't detect anything, or if he gave you a remedy that doesn't help, maybe you keep returning, but you start to sospec' it's evil and you go to the priest."

Not everyone (especially the new fundamentalist Protestants) trusts the priest completely. He is, however, more trustworthy than a physician or an obeahman for two reasons. First, the priest is a mere conduit for the power of God. He has no actual power himself, so he cannot be too dangerous. Second, unlike the doctor or the obeahman, people assert that a priest must keep people's business a secret between God and himself, or else go straight to hell. God's power is not necessarily as potent as the power of Satan, however. Visits with the priest may prove ineffective, forcing one to seek help from an obeahman.

The obeahman or "guarder" (*kimbwaser* or *gadé*) both inflicts and heals supernatural illness.[3] He is the only practitioner who can cast a hex. He is also the practitioner best able to remove a hex. When neither a doctor nor a priest can ease an affliction, a patient will seek out an obeahman.

Some people never bother to seek a priest's help, but after the doctor go directly to the obeahman. They say the obeahman can be stronger than a priest. An obeahman has the power to tell a patient (1) whether or not "someone did him something [hexed him] for true," and (2) the identity of the evildoer. Then, the obeahman attempts to undo the spell—or, if the patient wishes, turns the curse back on to the original hexer. Finally, he tells the patient what he or she needs to do to cure herself. Patients usually have to ingest and rub themselves with a foul-smelling herbal mixture (available in the pharmacies in town and from the obeahman). They also must repeat affirmations and prayers, especially Psalm 23.[4] There is an obeahman in a village about 45

---

[3] If an obeahman falls stricken with a supernatural illness, he cannot cure himself.

[4] They particularly repeat the verse, "Yea though I walk through the valley of the shadow of death, I shall fear no evil: for thou art with me" (verse 4).

minutes away from Bwa Mawego (the same village with the larger clinic with the ambulance). For particularly tenacious cases, people go to Guadeloupe where there is a very powerful obeahman.[5]

PATH OF TREATMENT SEEKING

Compared with Dominicans, Haitian villagers have similar medical beliefs and practices and similar economic difficulties (see Brodwin 1996). Haitian and Dominican healthcare-seeking behavior is comparable, although Haiti's denser population offers more healthcare options than exist in Dominica. In Haiti, the first specialists that rural people seek out are dispensary nurses, herbalists, midwives, injectionists,[6] and occasionally town pharmacists (Coreil 1983). Of these specialists, the only corresponding option in Bwa Mawego is the health center nurse. And, indeed, she is usually the first outsider that Bwa Mawegans go to for medical aid or consult. As a second step, rural Haitians seek care from shamans, physicians, and municipal hospitals. Generally, the second group of specialists differs from the first specialists seen in that they (1) treat different conditions, (2) use more technology (or shamanic paraphernalia), (3) have more formal training, and (4) charge more for treatment. In Haiti, another stage of care can be sought from certain *vodou* shamans and large metropolitan (Port-au-Prince) medical centers. These options are rare for rural Haitians, however (Coreil 1983). Once a rural Dominican feels that he or she needs expertise beyond the health center nurse, his or her healthcare-seeking approach largely mirrors the rural Haitian pattern.

Here, in summary, I present the path that Bwa Mawegans follow for health care treatments, including all three sectors of health care (see Figure 6.3). Villagers of Bwa Mawego treat the vast majority of their ills within the popular sector of bush medicine. They treat most of those few illnesses that they cannot self-treat with some form of biomedicine. The type of biomedical care that a person uses depends on the availability of medical supplies at the various health centers and the severity of one's condition. Villagers do not usually seek help from the folk sector until the popular and biomedical sectors fail to help their illness.

POPULAR TREATMENT AND ACCULTURATION

Currently, self-treatment with over-the-counter pharmaceuticals, rather than bush medicine, is fairly infrequent for rural Dominicans. Buying over-the-counter medicines (other than epsom salts and antacid powder sold in village shops) requires getting to a pharmacy (2 hours away) and often speaking with a pharmacist, as pharmacists keep many common medications (such as ibuprofen) behind the counter. This process is generally uncomfortable and inconvenient for Bwa Mawegans. Residents obtain over-the-counter pills, such as Parasitamol (a brand of

---

[5] Occasionally one seeks other potent obeahmen in Haiti, or another French-speaking island.

[6] Injectionists may or may not be trained nurses, but have training/experience with hypodermic needles, and for a fee will inject patients with prescription serums or other potions (Coreil 1983. See Landy 1974 for the **syncretic** medical role of injectionists, and Outwater et al. 2001 for a recent case study).

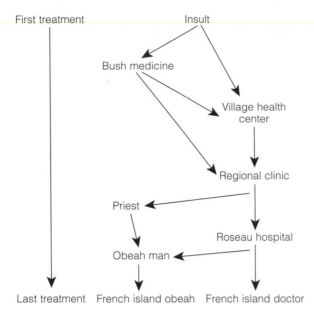

Figure 6.3 The path of healthcare seeking in Bwa Mawego

acetaminophen, like Tylenol) in two other ways: (1) health center nurses dispense them while supplies last, and (2) Bwa Mawegans traveling to neighboring islands (where one can buy medications without speaking with the pharmacist), kin who live elsewhere, and (to a lesser extent) we anthropologists bring bottles of analgesic tablets, first aid supplies, and so forth into the village. In most cases, villagers prefer to use bush. However, no bush is thought to help pain as much as over-the-counter drugs.

One man who had some Pepto-Bismol at home (his wife bought it in town months before) tried drinking the pink bismuth for a backache because it was "a pharmacy medicine like Parasitamol and them." In this case, the resident was willing to risk ingesting a medication with which he was relatively unfamiliar because he did not know a bush treatment that would sufficiently help his condition and he was unable to walk to the clinic. This man, who has a job outside the village, is more acculturated than most people in Bwa Mawego and thus has less intimidation about biomedicine.

As the village increasingly acculturates, and acceptance of biomedicine becomes widespread, over-the-counter drug use will likely increase. Over-the-counter drug use puts an element of biomedicine (now totally in the professional sector) within the popular sector of health care. Hopefully, as the rural parts of the country acculturate, health workers will impress on villagers the importance of following drug indications and directions.

7/Body Image
in Bwa Mawego

Around the world, people have different conceptions about the body that anthropologists refer to as **body image**. For instance, different cultures have various ideals of how a beautiful body should look. Cultures vary in attitudes about how much of the body should be clothed, and who can stand near or touch someone else's body under what circumstances. Culture also influences the way we picture and describe internal organs. For example, Americans often refer to their abdominal cavity as the "stomach." An American might claim to have pain in his "stomach" when the biological organ bothering him might be his small intestine or spleen, not his stomach. Ethnophysiology refers to cultural notions about body structure and function. Knowing local theories of anatomy and physiology is key to learning how people in a culture perceive and respond to illness.

This chapter describes rural Dominican body image in three sections. The first part of the chapter defines Dominican hot/cold humoral theory. This discussion includes local classification of human health conditions and other natural occurrences into perceived "hot," "cold," and "neutral" categories requiring constant balancing. The chapter's second section presents Dominican concepts of body maintenance in terms of two obvious necessities—nourishment and sleep. The final section describes Dominican beliefs about the body and its processes, or ethnophysiology. It deals with four specific body systems: the digestive, circulatory, reproductive, and nervous systems.

HOT AND COLD

People in many societies—Western cultures included—believe that a well-balanced lifestyle yields a healthy mind and body. People strive for a "balanced" diet, and some harmony between work and play, sitting and exercise, and so forth. Humoral medicine is a similar concept in which wellness is maintained or restored by balancing opposite forces (or **humors**) such as heat and cold, or dryness and wetness.

The hot/cold humoral system has been documented throughout the New World, particularly in Latin America (for an overview, see Foster 1994). Foster claims that

"Humoral medicine in the Americas is the most completely described of all eth-nomedical systems" (1994:2). In the **hot/cold humoral** system, people group men-tal and physical states, food, medicine, and air and water temperature, into either "hot" or "cold" categories. With the exception of air and water temperature, "hot" and "cold" classification does not generally refer to a thermal state. "Hot" and "cold" instead often refer to a culturally ascribed symbolic value. The North American view of anger as hot-headedness and indifference as coldness reveals a glimpse of similar symbolic use of "heat" and "cold."

The Dominican hot/cold system appears to differ in focus from the majority of New World humoral systems. Latin Americans categorize nearly *all* foods, herbs and illnesses as either "hot" or "cold," with perhaps a few "neutral" exceptions. Dominicans view only *certain* plants and illnesses as having "hot" or "cold" quali-ties. The humoral system remains important in Dominica because those "hot" and "cold" illnesses are some of the most common ailments.

RURAL DOMINICAN HUMORAL SYSTEM

The foundation of humoral theory in rural Dominica is that humans are made of meat. Human body tissues and blood therefore behave similarly to meat and gravy. Like meat and gravy, human flesh and fluids become thin or supple when warm, and thick or hard when cool. Cold and heat affect the viscosity of all bodily fluids except saliva and urine. Blood is really the most important bodily fluid in Dominican eth-nomedicine. The discussion of the circulatory system deals with the humoral attrib-utes of blood in more detail.

Temperatures of water and air in the physical environment can have heating or cooling effects on the internal and external body. In the Dominican view, every liv-ing thing has its own inherent humoral temperature. The humoral status of animals is about the same as that of humans. Each plant species has its own degree of "heat" or "cold." Most plants are "neutral" (in the same basic range as humans and other animals). Some plants, however, have a "cold" quality. If a person ingests one of these "cold" plants, either as food or medicine, the plant will cool the body. Other plants are particularly "hot." Ingesting them will heat the body. Emotions also have hot/cold humoral qualities. For example, fear is cold while anger is hot. If tempera-ture, food/drink, or emotions create too much "cold" inside a person's body, his or her bodily fluids and tissues thicken or harden. This thickening of fluids causes a "cold" illness. Conversely, when temperature, food/drink, or emotions result in too much bodily heat, a person's insides soften and thin, or (in extreme cases) cook.

The body can regulate its own temperature to some degree. If a person needs to cool down, the pores will allow some heat to escape from the body and the person will perspire to cool the skin. Because the air temperature in Bwa Mawego is typi-cally hot, sweating and open pores do not cool the body well. Usually, cooling requires external forces such as shade, breeze, bathing, and ingestion of humorally cool foods and fluids. In contrast, the body is good at heating itself up. When one contracts a "cold" illness, the body often heats up on its own to "melt out" the cold. Sometimes, "melting out" a tenacious "cold" overheats the body. In the Dominican view, a fever (a hot condition) comes from overheating in response to a cold illness. The body can thus transform a cold condition into a hot one. However, a hot condition will never turn cold without taking some action such as taking a medicine with "cold" properties.

The remedy for a human or animal suffering from internal heat or cold is to medicate with a plant product with the opposite hot/cold property. People with a "hot" illness use a "cooling" herbal remedy made from a "cold" plant. People with "cold" illnesses use "warm" or "hot" remedies.

Ascription of Plant Humoral Quality in Bwa Mawego

To understand how Dominicans think of herbal cures, it helps to know how they justify assigning "hot" or "cold" essences to plant species. Tradition provides the basic guidelines for deciding whether a plant is hot or cold. Medicinal plant use is so common in Bwa Mawego that children observe their mothers, fathers, aunties, and neighbors preparing "bush teas" on an almost daily basis from the time the children are old enough to get near a cooking fire or stove. Indeed, one of my first teachers of bush cures was a five-year-old girl, who taught me about a dozen medicinal plants used for "bush teas." Children know the humoral qualities of many plants through traditional rote learning. Through casual observation and conversation, children memorize the names, uses, and humoral qualities of the plants their family and neighbors use. Besides tradition (learned essentials), other considerations for deciding if a plant is hot or cold include: (1) a plant's perceived sensory effect, (2) where the plant grows, and (3) direct observance of the plant's effect on people.

A Dominican's first justification for ascribing a plant's hot or cold quality might be a person's immediate sensory response to the plant. How does the plant's sap feel to the skin or mouth? Does exposure to the plant make one's skin burn as with *zoutí* (stinging nettle)? Or, does it feel cool and soothing like *aloz or l' aluwé* (aloe). After one ingests the plant, does it feel refreshing (i.e., "cool"), or piquant (i.e., "hot") on one's mouth/throat?

Dominicans sometimes justify a plant's use by referring to the plant's "burning" or "cooling" properties. **Organoleptic qualities**, such as taste, appearance, and odor may be helpful memory aids in Dominica as elsewhere (Leonti et al. 2002). And references to sensory qualities may be passed down as mythical explanations of plants that work. It is doubtful that Dominicans assign hot, cold, or neutral values to plants solely because of the plant's sensory or organoleptic properties.

Messer (1981) and Brown (1976) found that people in their research areas (Oaxaca, Mexico and Highland Ecuador, respectively) classified some foods according to their sensory qualities (e.g., spicy foods are "warming"). However, both studies found that a plant's perceived physiological effect on people was more important in assigning it a hot or cold value than the immediate organoleptic sensation a plant produced. People in both populations reasoned that, ultimately, their experience and observations of what the plant did was their highest priority in classifying a plant's humoral quality. I suspect that this is the same phenomenon at work in Bwa Mawego.

If sensory effects were the main evidence of a plant's healing power, then one might expect plants with strong organoleptic signs to be the most popular remedies. This is not always the case. Actually, organoleptic indicators are present in a quarter of the most salient "hot" or "cold" herbal treatments. Of the six common illnesses that Dominicans classify as "cold," three of the most popular treatments produce a potentially "heating" organoleptic quality.[1] Of the six "hot" common illnesses, only one salient treatment might be considered "cool" to the senses.[2] The other cold treatments have no "cooling" sensory effect.[3] Furthermore, most medicinal plants that Bwa Mawegans use produce no skin or mouth sensory reaction, other than a bitter or sour taste.

Next, people might also ascribe a plant's humoral quality based on where the plant grows. This kind of ascription does not appear to occur in Bwa Mawego. The ambient temperature or sun conditions of a plant's growth environment does not dictate a plant's humoral status. Neither does the plant's humoral growth environment (i.e., the humoral quality of other herbs growing near an individual plant).

Similar to the findings of Brown (1976) and Messer (1981), the most important factor that Bwa Mawegans use to determine a plant's "hot," "cold," or "neutral" value is the effect that the plant has on the human body. People explain the plant's use (and ascribe a hot/cold/neutral quality) in terms of the internal logic of the ethnomedical system. For example, in Dominica, constipation is a hot condition. Dominicans would thus refer to a plant with laxative results as a cold plant, as it alleviates a hot condition.

In some societies, hot/cold assignment of plant humoral quality appears to have nothing to do with a human's physiological use or reaction to the plant. For example, New York Puerto Ricans classify lima beans and white beans as "cold" and kidney beans as "hot" (Harwood 1971). However, the Dominican humoral system is not one in which people know the "hot" or "cold" quality of a plant solely through tradition or memorization of that plant's quality. Rather people appear to assign a humoral quality as an afterthought based on what the plant does. When I asked informants if a plant had a hot or cold value, they generally answered with a reason. For example, one might say, "That herb make you refresh. It's a cooling plant." Or, "That's a hot plant. It melt arthritis in your joints so they moving easily."

The literature points to some other factors that some people use to assign "hot" versus "cold" values. For example, Nahuatl Indians in the Valley of Mexico make humoral distinctions between certain foods in their raw versus cooked state (Madsen 1955). This is not the case in Bwa Mawego where, for example, a humorally hot "bush tea" remains hot, even if it cools completely. Likewise cold food remains cold (like *pawpaw* [papaya] in goat stew) even if it is hot or cooked. In some populations (e.g., Guatemala (Logan 1973)), color is an ascription factor, but not in Bwa Mawego. The Central American Quichés' humoral definition of meat is tied to the animal's wild or domestic status (Neuenswander and Souder 1977). Meat is "neutral" in Dominica, so this distinction contrasting natural to human-altered food is not an issue. However, Dominicans do make a similar type of distinction: processed vs.

---

[1]Here, I identify *pachuri* (for colds and coughs) and bay oil (for rheumatism) as organoleptically "heating," and *kali* (for asthma), *kouton nue* (for fright), and *kul bwa* (for if "something hurts") as sensory neutrals.

[2]"Cold" treatments are *koukouli* (for "inflammation" and "buttons"), *malestomak* (for boils), Pawpaw (for "pressure"), lime (for fevers), and *tomatoz* (for sore throats). Pawpaw (or papaya) fruit remains protected from the sun's heat because the tree's large leaves shade the fruit, and the fruit's skin protects the flesh from the heat. Hence, fresh, moist pawpaw fruit might seem "cool" to Dominicans. Burning sensation from acid in lime and *tomatoz*, though potentially "hot" to the senses, does not effect the Dominican classification of these fruits as "cold" treatments.

[3]This is according to my personal assessment of the plants' sensory qualities. An emic investigation into this phenomenon might be interesting.

unprocessed staples. Dominicans view processed starches (e.g., wheat flour, *farín* [manioc flour], and corn meal) as "hot" foods. Whole carbohydrate foods that—other than peeling or cooking—do not require processing (plantain, dasheen, potatoes, yams, and breadfruit) are "neutral" staples.

Humoral Neutrality

The "neutral" concept exists in most Latin American humoral systems that anthropologists have studied. However, it is rare in Latin America for an item to be "neutral in its own right" (Foster 1994:120). For example in Tzintzutzan, Mexico, items can only be regarded as "neutral" as a statistical average because some informants list them as "hot," while others list them as "cold" (Foster 1994:120). Most but not all reports from Latin America that deal with the "neutral" humoral value follow the Tzintzutzan pattern. Infrequent examples of true humoral "neutrals" are basic staple foods, most commonly beef, chicken, maize, potatoes, and beans (Foster 1994). Like these Latin Americans, Dominicans classify their basic staples (tubers and beans) as well as all meat except a few "cold" fish species as humorally "neutral"—that is having the same humoral quality as the balanced human body.

Dominicans differ from their Hispanic neighbors in that their staple foods do not stand alone as "neutrals." Indeed, to Dominicans, most plants and animals have a "neutral" quality. Many illnesses are also "neutral" in humoral terms, in that the bodily insult was caused by a condition outside of the hot/cold continuum. For example, to a Dominican, a cut is neither hot nor cold. The wound is the same humoral quality as the rest of the body. Treatments for cuts are thus "neutral." If, however, the wound becomes infected (by some sort of "heat" entering the cut), the *infection*—not the cut itself—becomes a "hot" condition (a type of "inflammation") that requires "cold" treatments.

In Dominica, "hot" and "cold" foods and medicines are the exceptions. They are, nevertheless, important exceptions in medicine because "hot" and "cold" substances have the power to cause or cure illnesses.

Of the 22 most salient illnesses that the community listed (see Chapter 8), villagers consider six of the illnesses (27%) as "hot," and six as "cold" (Table 7.1). One illness, diarrhea, has hot and cold variants (thus, following Foster 1994, averages as "neutral"). The remaining nine (41%) illnesses are "neutral" because their fundamental etiologies (and treatments) focus on insults or imbalances outside of the heat/cold continuum.

THE BODY'S BASIC REQUIREMENTS

Sleep

On most evenings, adults in Bwa Mawego go to sleep between 9 and 11:00 PM (earlier for children), and wake between 5 and 7 AM. Locals say that sleep is necessary for body rejuvenation. Without sleep, neither the body nor the mind can be strong. While one sleeps through the night, the body undergoes two processes in addition to rejuvenation. First, while the outer body rests, the organs can put energy into digestion. Digestion, while building up the body tissues, also yields gas. Hence, gas collects in the sleeper's belly.

TABLE 7.1   HUMORAL QUALITY
OF COMMON ILLNESSES

Hot	Neutral	Cold
prickle-heat	diarrhea	colds
buttons	worms	cough
boils	upset stomach	asthma
sore throat	vomiting	fright
inflammation	cut	something "hurts"
fever	headache	rheumatism
	pressure	
	sprain	

Second, residents assert that as one sleeps, the body takes in cool night air through the pores and the lungs. The body can thus "ease off" any heat build-up it accumulated through work or play on the previous day. First, the sleeping body cools down to an optimal temperature. Then, depending on how cool the night is, or how much cooling the sleeper's body needed, the body begins to accumulate excess cold, especially toward the earliest morning hours. This cold thickens the "goits" (flesh that amasses around joints, especially in older people) so that older people wake up stiffer than younger ones. Cold in the body also thickens the blood and mucus so that people often wake up sluggish or congested.

Nutrition

There is a lot of variation in what, when, and how much people eat in Bwa Mawego. There are, however, three general dietary rules. First, everyone's food and drink intake attempts to follow the basic guidelines of local hot/cold humoral theory. Second, every villager starts the day with "tea." Finally, everyone eats lunch, the main meal of the day, between noon and 2:00.

The hot/cold humoral qualities inherent in things people eat correspond with the local **explanatory models** of nutrition. Animal products (meat, milk, and eggs), like the healthy human body, are humorally neutral; after all, our own bodies contain these same elements. Bwa Mawegans regard these protein foods as essential, at least in small amounts, as the body can transform them easily into human blood and tissue. "True food" (staples like boiled tubers and starchy fruits) and legumes are also neutral. The neutral status of "food" surprised me somewhat. I expected tubers and legume foods to have complimentary hot/cold values, as they are fundamental in the Dominican diet, **protein compliments**,[4] and almost always eaten together. Processed starch foods are "hot" (and cause constipation) while fruits and greens are "cool" (and alleviate constipation). These notions make sense in terms of two opposing Dominican food preoccupations: keeping the belly full, and keeping the belly and "boweel" (bowels, or intestines) free.

Dominicans use the word "tea" to refer to any hot, non-meat beverage. It is rarely store-bought "green tea" (i.e., cured leaves of Asian tea shrubs (*Camellia sinensis*

[4]Approximating the essential amino acids present in animal foods.

(L.) Ktze.)—green, oolong, or otherwise). Rather, people drink some kind of plant-based **infusion** from materials that they harvest themselves. These "teas"[5] include coffee, or "cocoa tea" (hot chocolate), or "bush tea" (any herbal tea, such as mint and orange leaf tea). People drink morning "tea" to "ease off" two bodily accumulations that occur during sleep in the cool air: (1) the gas that accumulates in the belly overnight, and (2) the cold that builds in the body overnight (i.e., "tea" loosens up mucus and joints). In addition to their regular morning "tea," about half of the families drink a partial cup (depending on the size of the drinker) of *sime kontwá* (*Chenopdium ambrosioides* L.) "bush tea" (a vermifuge) every morning before ingesting anything else.

Another important beverage is rum, or *won* in Patwa. With the exceptions of a few strict Seventh Day Adventists, all villagers, from teenagers through the elderly, engage in drinking on occasion. Middle-aged and older men drink the most. At least 25% of adult males are routinely publicly inebriated. Alcohol doubtless comprises a large proportion of the calories that these men consume. Beer, brandy, ginger wine, and bottled rum is usually available at most village shops; but the typical (and most economical) drink is a "shoot" of cask rum followed by a chaser of water. Villagers conceive of all alcohol and illnesses relating to alcohol as humorally "hot." Drinkers try to balance their humoral intake by eating "cold" fruits.

Lunch, the main meal, is "food," complimented with "peas" (any kind of bean) and usually meat or bouillon-based gravy. Bwa Mawegans only use the word "food" to refer to the starchy provisions that form the base of their diet. Dominicans especially refer to their principle subsistence crop, dasheen (taro) as food; however, plantains, breadfruit, sweet and Irish potatoes, and yams are also "food." Processed starches: manioc flour (*kasava, or farín*), arrowroot starch (*tuloma*), rice, cornmeal, and anything made with wheat flour (e.g., bread, pasta, dumplings) is "like food" but is not "true food." Food "fills your belly," and "stays with you" without causing constipation. Edibles "like food" fill the belly, but only for a short time. Further, these processed starches are humorally hot. Eaten alone they cause "inflammation," which swells up the inner body, causing constipation by blocking the bowels. Bwa Mawegans occasionally eat "hot things" (e.g., dumplings) as a "food" replacement. They must then accompany "hot" starches with fruit juice, greens, cucumber, or another humorally "cold" item to "keep the system free of blockage."

"Food" (or things "like food") does not "build" the body. Rather, it provides simple sustenance—gives energy and fills hungry bellies. Fruits and vegetables build the body, especially digesting into components of body fluids (blood, breast milk, and semen). Meat, milk, eggs, and (to a lesser extent) legumes digest directly into body components, such as muscles and blood. People discuss these edibles as the essence for strength, growth, and wound healing.

---

[5]Ethnobotanists usually refrain from using the term "tea." "Tea" is problematic because for Westerners, it refers to the drinks we call "hot tea" and "iced tea", and for individuals familiar with places like Dominica where "tea" is a general term, other words can be more descriptive. Ethnobotanists favor the specific words, "solution" or "infusion." I use the words "tea" and "bush tea" as Dominicans do, but with quotation marks to remind the reader that these are local terms referring to solutions.

Rural Dominican Ethnophysiology

Balance and cleanliness are the two main principals of Dominican ethnophysiology. A healthy body has three requirements. First, it should remain in a neutral, warm state of equilibrium regarding humoral heat and cold. Second, the body requires equilibrium regarding intake of food and drink and elimination of waste. Third, it must be pollutant-free, internally and on the surface.

Dominicans visualize the body as maintaining its balance through filtration and exchange of air and fluids that may carry "dirts" or other harmful substances. Filtration occurs because the skin and internal organs are semipermeable. Similar ideas are evident elsewhere in the Caribbean (e.g., in Jamaica; see Sobo 1993). Pores throughout the body allow heat and toxins to escape. Yet the body remains vulnerable to risk because porous skin does not completely protect a person against illness-causing agents. Bodily insults—dirt, poisons, heat and cold—can enter a person's system via skin pores. Veins and organs associated with blood circulation and digestion are also semipermeable and act as filters that help the body rid itself of "dirts" in food and blood. "Dirts" filtered through the skin and internal organs are eliminated in bodily wastes (urine, feces, pus, etc.).

The Digestive/Urinary System

After swallowing, food and drink passes from the mouth to the "troat" and runs behind the lungs through the "troat pipe," and down into the "belly." The belly is not an organ, but the general term for the abdominal cavity; or, as one informant put it, "The belly like a bag. It hold everything under your lungs until your ass." In the belly, the "troat pipe" channels the food into the stomach. The stomach is a bag that "pound up all what you eat," then bit by bit squeezes a portion of the food into the "worm bag."

Though Dominicans say that all animals have worms, humans are the only animals with an organ specifically for the worms. This organ, the "worm bag" is a worm holding station. All people have some worms, and for the most part, worms live in harmony with their human hosts. Some villagers resent all worms as continual menaces—parasites that rob the body of nutrition. Others feel that (as long as the worm bag is not overpopulated) worms are beneficial. They function in the digestive process to refine the food, turning it into rich blood, much the way that earthworms convert composting material to rich soil. The rich blood that the worms expel passes through the walls of the worm bag and into the belly. Worms, like humans, produce gas as a by-product of digestion. This gas, like blood, also passes through the worm bag walls and into the belly. From the worm bag, semidigested solids, waste, blood, and nutrients travel into the intestines or "tripes."

The intestines further break the food down, separating the food's body and blood-building components from waste. The intestines pass gas, good blood and "things that building blood" out through their semiporous walls and into the belly, while they push waste downward into the bowels.

Thus far, two organs (the worm bag and the intestines, or tripes) have leeched blood, or blood-building components out into the belly. This happens because, in addition to the belly's function as an organ container, it is also a blood collection device. All of the blood and blood-building material flows out of the organs, into the belly and down to the bottom of the belly. One informant explained to me that, "At the bottom of the belly it have a thing like a funnel. Ya, and that thing collecting all the blood an' run it up a tube to the 'leevah' [liver]."

The liver cleans the blood. Then it sends the good, clean blood up a big vein that leads directly to the heart. Meanwhile, the liver sends all the bad things from the blood out a waste tube and into the bowel (locally pronounced "boweel").

The top of the bowel contains all the waste of the liver's blood filtration, the waste from digestion, blood, and almost all the water that the person has ingested. The blood needs to be harvested, as does the water. The body needs the water for two reasons: (1) it can go into making blood, and (2) it can wash away "dirts" and poisons. Part of the "boweel's" job is to suck blood and water from the waste, leaving just enough moisture to "help the manure slide out." The boweel then diverts the water and blood into a tube that leads to the kidney.

The kidney has one entrance tube (for the dirty bowel water) and two exit tubes. The kidney takes the liquid and blood and regulates its hot/cold nature (to a point) and cleans the blood by filtering out toxins. The toxins get mixed with the leftover water resulting in urine. The urine passes through one of the kidney's exit tubes and directly into the bladder. The clean blood exits the kidney through the other exit tube—a vein that goes directly to the heart.

Once the bowel removes the bloody water, all that remains in the bowel is "shit" or "manure." A healthy person should evacuate this manure within one day. The longer the excrement remains in the "boweel," the more toxins are leeched into the body. Once absorbed, these toxins give a person headaches and "gripes" in the belly, and introduce "dirts" and "nastiness" into the whole body. The bottom of the bowel leads directly to the "ass muscle" where "the shit leave the body."

Just above the "ass muscle" there is a gas tube that joins with the "boweel." This is one of the exit tubes for gas that accumulates in the belly. The other gas exit tube joins with the "troat tube" just above the lungs. Gas that collects in the belly can exit upward or downward, depending on which part of the belly it was nearer to begin with.

The Circulatory System

Bwa Mawegans describe the heart as a muscular pump that receives blood from two blood entrance tubes. Informants explain that the bottom in-tube gets clean, new blood coming from the kidneys and liver, while the top one takes in old blood from the body for recirculation. The heart pumps, squeezing the blood from the entrance veins into one big exit vein (presumably the aorta) that divides three ways. The left vein division fuels the left side of the body with blood, the middle division goes up to the head, and the right division delivers blood to the right side of the body.[6]

Sobo notes that in rural Jamaica, "blood is the primary and most thought about bodily component" (1993:38). Laguerre (1987) points to the importance of blood to illness and well being throughout Afro-Caribbean folk medicine. Dominicans likewise emphasize blood quality as a primary cause and indicator of health or illness.

---

[6]None of my informants mentioned the lungs or breathing in conjunction with circulation. Unfortunately, I never probed about the function or importance of air intake. This will be interesting to look into in future research.

Bwa Mawegans judge the quality of one's blood by three basic criteria: viscosity, quantity, and purity.[7]

BLOOD THICKNESS   Bwa Mawegans assert that blood viscosity varies with temperature. Blood, like gravy, congeals when it is cool and thins when it is hot. Warm blood is too thin. It does not scab quickly, and flows through cuts or menstruating women too fast. The ambient temperature, humoral "heat" in food or "teas," or overexertion can cause warm blood.

Bwa Mawegans "working the bay leaf" are at particular risk for hot, thinned blood. The work involved in bay oil production is strenuous (chopping and carrying 100 pound bails of leaves), and hot (harvested in the open sun and distilled using fire), and the bay leaves themselves are one of the most humorally "hot" of all the "bushes." Bay work is a common cause of overheating.

Warm blood usually goes away on its own as the body cools and rests. Prolonged warm, thin blood leads to weakness or may make some "anemic." Villagers say that "anemic" people are thin and always tired, and have poor color and tired eyes. According to locals, anemics have thin, weak, pale blood. Folk diagnosis involves checking the color and texture of the veins on the underside of a person's arms. Anemics can "cure" themselves with rest and eating "plenty peas" (beans), especially wild "pigeon peas," or *pwa angol* (*Cajanus cajan*). Anemics also need to eat "plenty meat," especially wild *manikou* (opossum) and agouti, but goat or beef is also good. In addition, villagers proscribe the reddest, ripe tomatoes and deep red *mube* bark "tea" (species unidentified) help to "build" or restore thin, hot anemic blood. This example is typical of organoleptic medication.

Cold blood is thick. It clots too easily, potentially causing a "mass" that blocks circulation. If a mass blocks circulation to the "brains" or heart, a person could drop dead suddenly. Otherwise, cold blood might just slow a person down. It also might cause one's mucus to thicken and one's joints to stiffen.

A person's blood can become "cold" through prolonged exposure to cold, or sudden exposure to cold when one is feeling hot. The former, exposure to cold temperatures (locals describe air below about 68°F as "cold"), is a relatively rare experience for Dominicans. It does occur, however, during tropical depressions, at higher elevations, and near the cool shade of springs. If a person experiences these conditions in addition to being wet (e.g., if he is out at sea, caught in the rain, or swims in cold water for too long) the effects of the cold air will be amplified, increasing his risk for developing chilled blood.

A person whose body is at a neutral, warm temperature need not fear cool air or water. However, one who is hot from sun or work risks shock if he or she is exposed to cool air or water. Shock, like prolonged exposure, can thicken blood viscosity.

Although the Dominican humoral system recognizes food and herbs that are cold enough to cause vomiting or "loose boweel" (diarrhea), there is no food or herb whose humoral quality is so cold that it can effect blood viscosity.

The emotions fright and shock cause the most severely "cold blood." When one suffers a near-death experience, sees a witch or a spirit, receives news that a loved one is severely injured or dead, or suffers a similar emotional trauma, one's blood

---

[7]Viscosity, quantity, and purity are my terms, not Dominican ones.

instantly becomes very cold. The cold blood forms clots and cannot flow properly. The blood in one's heart might start "getting into a mass" causing one to be sick. If a frightened person's mass of cold blood blocks blood flow to the heart, or if a clot blocks blood flow to the "brains," the person will die.

BLOOD "PRESSURE"   Residents describe "pressure" as a hot condition in the blood and the veins that can be caused by (1) diet, (2) digestion, or (3) stress, or emotional "pressure." The body of someone suffering from pressure is internally "hot" or inflamed. Inflammation causes the veins to swell, making the tubes for blood circulation narrower. A large gas build-up can also push against veins, restricting the amount of blood that can pass through the veins. A person with pressure also has hot blood. Hot blood generally becomes thin and weak. However, hot blood under "pressure" goes one step further and actually begins to cook, as if boiling off the water in the blood. This makes the blood too concentrated, or too "rich." Because this blood is extra rich and thick, the body has a hard time pushing it through the already compromised veins. Hence, pressure builds up in the veins. The illness is thus named for both its perceived cause (emotional pressure) and its perceived effect (vascular pressure).

"Pressure" results from the stress of worrying, studying too hard, and having strained relationships. These stressors cause the mind to work overtime, which generates heat in the blood.

Dietary "pressure" can result from eating too many processed starches, the "hottest" foods. Drinking too much rum (also very hot) exacerbates the possibility of developing "pressure."

Some people with otherwise healthy diets have bodies that digest too efficiently. If people are particularly good digesters, or have a diet particularly rich in foods that "build the blood," their blood will be too thick and rich. The local ethnophysiology of the digestive and circulation systems provides for "building" blood, but not for thinning blood or taking blood away. Menstruation rids females of some extra blood, or extra blood richness, but this might just be "a temporary ease-up" before the blood again becomes too rich. One informant stated:

> Pressure troubling me. My blood too rich. I can't have no alcohol, no tonic—that drunking me. I get this from foods. You can see in my veins (looks at wrist), it too dark, too rich. The doctor says I should make another baby to use the blood up, make it thinner. I don't want to have another baby now. I had to beg the doctor to cut me. Finally he took some of my blood, but it wasn't enough you know.

BLOOD PURITY   Blood may be polluted by "dirts" that get inside the body. As dirty blood flows through the body, "dirts" in the blood irritate and abrade body tissues. The result is what Dominicans call "inflammation" (internal humoral heat and occasional swelling). "Inflammation" can be in a specific body part, but more often it is generalized. General inflammation eventually moves outward to the limbs and the head, and finally to, or through, the skin. Dirt enters the body via food, air pollution, or an open wound.

"Dirts" from food might escape through the walls of the "worm bag," stomach, or intestines into the "belly," and through the "belly" walls where it pollutes the outer body and blood as it circulates through the body.

"Dirts" also enter the body system by one breathing it in. Smoke carries small "dirts." Smoke is all around the village. Villagers use fire to cook, clear gardens, distill bay oil, and burn rubbish. People also breathe in "dirts" in dusty air. Bwa Mawego is on the wet, eastern side of the island, so dust is uncommon. People might breathe in dust and ashes while cleaning out their hearth or while planting in a newly cleared garden on a dry day. If one goes to "town" (Roseau, the capital), he will certainly breathe in some dust. Roseau is on the island's drier side, and the relative bustle of its 15,000 inhabitants results in airborne dust. Villagers always complain about feeling dirty and run down after a trip to town.

Lastly, "dirts" can enter the body through a wound. Bwa Mawegans claim that cuts (especially cuts on feet) and bites (especially dog and witch bites) are the wounds that put people most at risk for dirty blood. The most common way villagers cut their feet is by stepping on broken glass. The village is at an acculturation or economic stage in which several factors concur: (1) shops in the village sell glass-bottled drinks, (2) most people can afford to buy an occasional bottled-drink, yet (3) many villagers cannot afford shoes for daily wear (though they might have a pair of dress shoes for church and town).[8] Those who do wear shoes in the village typically have either flip-flops or rubber sandals—neither of which offers much foot protection. Since village tracks are dirt and since it rains often, feet are usually muddy. "Dirts" can enter the foot wound at the time the cut occurs or anytime before the wound heals. It is nearly impossible to keep a foot wound clean and dry. Although dirt could enter the body via any cut, and village life offers myriad of ways to cut oneself, foot cuts are at a particular risk for dirtying the blood.

Bite wounds lead to "dirty blood" because "dirts" on the teeth of the biter get injected under the victim's skin and into the blood stream. Dog bites are relatively common in the village. According to villagers, bites from blood-sucking "witches," *soukwayan* and *lougawou* (see discussion in Chapter 6), are also common. As the *soukwayan* and *lougawou* roam, disguised as animals, throughout the sleeping humans and animals of the village, they suck blood and act as **vectors** for blood "dirts." This is one of the few instances where a personalistic cause of illness (see Chapter 6) enters the realm of bush medicine. Here, the concept and treatment of the wound and blood "dirts" are the same, regardless if the biter is an actual animal or a wicked person in animal form.

The liver, kidneys and blood veins filter "dirts" from blood. This dirt then needs to be flushed through the body system. Drinking enough water helps one's body to flush out small, normal amounts of pollution. Otherwise, a "washout," or purgative, is necessary. In Bwa Mawego, people take "washouts" as both a cure and a prevention for dirty blood.[9]

OTHER BODY FLUIDS   People in Bwa Mawego contend that perspiration, urine, mucus, breast milk, and semen, like blood, can contain "dirts." Indeed, perspiration,

---

[8] The shoe situation is changing rapidly as the village acculturates. I estimate that in 1993, at least 60% of the village went barefoot daily, about 30% wore rubber sandals or flip-flops, and about 10% wore boots or shoes on any given day. By 1998 it seemed that about 30% of the village wore shoes or boots, over half wore rubber sandals or flip-flops, and only 10–15% regularly walked around the village barefoot.

[9] Perhaps the alleged necessity to maintain clean blood (and having herbals to rid the blood of impurities) accounts for the village's relative disregard (Sobo 1992) for menstrual blood pollution (see "Reproductive System" subheading).

urine and mucus ought to contain "dirts" as the function of these fluids is to carry "dirts" out of the body. Again, it is important to drink enough water, as water helps wash the body, preventing too much "dirts" from entering or staying in the blood stream, breast milk, or semen. A man with dirty semen can pass those "dirts" on to his mate. A woman with dirty breast milk can pass "dirts" to her nursing child. Bwa Mawegans commonly identify dirty milk as the reason for babies' rashes, including infant acne, which people dub a kind of prickle heat. A baby's father must therefore be careful to keep himself internally clean (via nutrition and sexual fidelity) because, through dirty semen, he can pass "dirts" to his mate, who in turn passes the pollutants to his nursing child.

"Heat" and "cold" effect the viscosity of the white body fluids (mucus, breast milk and semen) in a similar way that "heat" and "cold" affect blood. A "cold" shock turns regular, runny mucus into thick, white mucus in the nose or chest, and turns tears into mucus in the eyes. Untreated, white mucus turns into yellow or green mucus, which is much colder and thicker than the white kind. The response to these conditions involves bringing heat into the body's mucus-producing areas. This includes drinking humorally "hot" "bush teas" and breathing in steam to thin the mucus, allowing it to escape. This is a clear example of how Bwa Mawegan treatment procedures and vocabulary fit with the culture's explanatory model of illness.

As with the mucus example, Bwa Mawegans say that a "cold" shock might "freeze" or thicken a woman's breast milk so that she can no longer nurse. Men who have suffered from a "cold" shock, especially from "fright," can likewise experience impotence attributed to frozen sperm.

The Reproductive Systems

Bwa Mawegans recognize that a female has eggs that she stores in the ovaries, that a man makes sperm in his testicles, and that babies come from the joining and "germination" of sperm and egg inside the woman's womb.

Cross-culturally, a ubiquitous body image exists in which the uterus is thought to open and close monthly in a notion, which Hanson (1975) coined as the "mechanical uterus." People reckon that the uterus remains closed-off during most of the month. Then it opens for menstruation, ridding itself of old, polluted blood (MacCormack 1982). In this model, people assume that conception can only occur while the uterus is open, right before and right after menstruation (MacCormack 1982). Bwa Mawegans too regard the uterus as an opening and closing organ. In Bwa Mawego, however, the people imagine the uterus is almost always open to some degree, closing only briefly in the middle of a woman's menstrual cycle. The best time for a woman to get pregnant is sometime in the middle of the month, right before or right after the organ has closed completely. In their model, the sperm, being liquid, can usually get up through the small opening to the nearly closed uterus, but the nearly closed uterine state helps to keep the "germinating" baby in the womb till it can "take root." One informant explained that if a woman becomes pregnant when the uterus is open, near menstruation, she would probably not stay pregnant because nothing is there to hold the baby in: "Most probably she would shake the baby loose if she fall, or when she walking downhill."

Many societies view a woman's menstrual period as a time when the woman is extremely physically or spiritually weak (Strassmann 1992). A menstruating woman is therefore thought to be susceptible to illnesses, sorcery, and other supernatural afflictions. Dominicans partially ascribe to this notion in the sense that they see a menstruating woman as slightly more vulnerable to illness but not to sorcery.

As in most places with humoral hot/cold theory, Dominicans view menstruation as a "hot" condition. It is not, however, an extremely "hot" condition (like inflammation or a fever). As she is humorally "hot," a menstruating woman should avoid extremely cold temperatures because she could shock herself with cold. Likewise, she should avoid drinking "plenty juice" since fruit juices are "cold." A chill inside her body would cause a cold, "gripes" (stomach pains), or "might make the period flow clear." She can work, but should not work too hard, as her "hot" condition makes her susceptible to overheating. She should not drink rum (a very "hot" drink) as it will make her drunk easily and perhaps result in "pressure" from dehydration.

For the most part, a menstruating woman can continue with her daily routine. There are dietary guidelines and activity restraints, but no prohibitions (i.e. she can moderate rather than totally avoid). At the same time, people expect a woman to be tired and somewhat weaker than normal while she menstruates. Sometimes older daughters, sisters and mothers will take over some of a menstruating woman's work and cooking duties for a day or two. Female kin help out of sympathy, not because of any cooking or working taboos on menstruating women. In fact, Bwa Mawegans have no apparent **menstrual taboos**. Menstruating women practice no food restrictions, seclusion, or segregation; her touch is not dangerous. And although Bwa Mawegans certainly regard menstrual blood as dirty, it is not dangerously polluting to plants, animals, other humans, or the woman herself. This lack of restrictions is unusual for a horticultural community (Quinlan and Quinlan n.d.). In my own experience, and from conversations with other field workers at the site, women appeared relaxed about others seeing their menstrual blood on skirts, sleepwear, panties, or rags. The casual attitude about menstruation fits with the village's relaxed attitude toward body functions and body image.

Though there are no menstrual taboos to speak of, there are several pregnancy rules and restrictions. Pregnant women should try to eat "plenty greens and carrots" but should not eat "plenty hot foods [processed starches] so she won't get *shugá* [i.e., sugar-diabetes]." Pregnant women should not eat hot pepper, or do excessive hot work. These will cause "inflammation in the crotch" (yeast infections). The pregnant woman should avoid hard work and carrying heavy loads or else she risks miscarriage.

The pregnant woman may not attend a funeral. She must not worry, "stay lonely," or think about problems, lest the child be born with an unpleasant personality. She may not kill or butcher any animal lest the baby be born with some attribute of the dead animal. If a woman kills a chicken hawk, for instance, the baby might be born with a long, loose neck. One who kills a cat might bear a child with a clubfoot or short, deformed fingers (i.e., with hands or feet like paws). Villagers report that killing, or even seeing, a dead snake can result in a child being born without full use of his arms or legs.

Dominicans have some degree of ritual *couvade* (see Munroe et al. 1973), as the baby's father must also restrict himself in certain ways. He must not work too hard. This could result in the child's mother having labor complications. Like the mother, he must not kill animals (chickens and fish excepted) or look at dead animals. His actions, like the mother's, put the baby at risk for birth defects.

Towards the end of a pregnancy, there are certain "bush teas" that a woman can drink to insure a safe delivery. One woman who was completing a full-term pregnancy explained that she had begun to drink "bush teas"[10] to protect her baby. "If someone [i.e., a sorcerer] is against you and trying to do something to the baby, you cannot make [give birth to] the baby. I don't think a baby will be normally overdue unless someone is doing you something."

The Nervous System

Bwa Mawegans regard individuals as being born with nerves that range from strong to weak. Someone with weak nerves is particularly vulnerable to the effects of emotions, alcohol and drugs.

As I mentioned earlier in this chapter, stressful emotions such as anger and worry are humorally "hot" and can result in "pressure." Fear and shock are humorally "cold" and can lead to "fright." Though all individuals experience these emotions from time to time, not everyone becomes ill. Those with weak nerves are the most likely to develop an illness, especially a long-lasting or chronic illness. People with the weakest nerves are in jeopardy of developing not only "fright" or "pressure," but madness, or craziness (Bwa Mawegans refer only to men as "mad," and only to women as "crazy"). In the case of madness, a person's prolonged exposure to strong emotions causes so much pressure that one "bursts his brains."

For example, Charles, a "natural mystic" (Rastafarian ascetic/prophet) was a kind, religious young man from the village who was always praying, singing reggae and thinking ("practicing the Rasta meditations"). He thought about the welfare of the village and his fellow villagers. For example, he predicted that if people continued to cut down the bush on the mountain above the village (to plant bay) that Jah would dry up the bathing waterfall. This and other "prophecies" he made came true. One time, Charles climbed to the top of Morne Soufriere (the highest village peak) to do his Rasta meditations. Villagers say that he meditated so hard that he "burst his brains." At this point, a dragon appeared to him. He fought the dragon from the top of the mountain all the way down to the sea. His fight caused rockslides and earth slides that people in the village saw that day. This was the day Charles' madness began. Since then, Charles has had episodes when this normally gentle man screams and breaks things, especially glass bottles and windows. The police have been called to the village to apprehend him on multiple occasions, and he has been hospitalized several times. Villagers nevertheless like and respect this man. One of the things they respect him for is his mind. The notion that his brain was weak (and now is "burst") is a separate issue from his inherent intelligence.

Much in the way that some people have the proclivity toward madness caused by thinking or emotions, other people have a weakness tolerating *ganja* and alcohol. Simple substance dependence is fairly common among village men.

In Bwa Mawego, public intoxication and alcohol abuse are evident every day. Behavior of intoxicated males follows a pattern. Drunks stagger up to any nearby person and argue a (usually senseless) point, preach, or repeat a personal drinking

---

[10] Herbs include mango leaves, comfrey, *go di te*, *sime kontwa*, and *japaná*.

expression.[11] If there is a woman within sight, a drunk man typically approaches her with absurd sexual gestures and propositions. Drunken behavior leads to conflicts; however, alcohol-related violence is rarely a problem as friends and kinfolk are quick to intervene. Several village men remain economically inviable due to their alcoholism. On the positive side, the popularity of rum accounts for the many rum shops which are neighborhood social centers and provide a living for 10% of the village. Nevertheless, conditions related to alcohol abuse (ranging from hangovers to mental illness and liver disease) pose predominant health problems for the community. According to locals, it is the "nerves" a person is born with that account for whether or not one becomes alcohol dependant. People with "strong nerves" can drink socially on occasions, while those with "weak nerves" become heavy, problematic drinkers.

Of all the people who are heavy marijuana smokers or rum drinkers, there are a few who suffer a severe mental break tied to their substance abuse. There are just a handful of these unstable ranters in the village—some make kind or humorous declamations, while some make vicious statements. Bwa Mawegans explain that these are people who never should have partaken in rum or marijuana because they had "weak nerves that giving them weak brains." In the case of these mentally ill people, it was the substance that "burst their brains." Other villagers question blaming the substance as the cause of mental illness. They point out that the sufferer of mental illness may have had a proclivity toward "weak nerves," and "weak emotions" that led to their misuse of drugs in the first place. Yet despite the "weak brains" of these "mad" men and "crazy" women residents, villagers appreciate some of them for their mental creativity.

SUMMARY

The purpose of this chapter was to introduce readers to the emic perspective that people in Bwa Mawego share regarding how the body works, and what it requires to function healthily. Dominicans observe a hot/cold humoral system in which "hot" and "cold" natural forces must be balanced to maintain or restore a person's health. In the Dominican humoral system, "cold" is imagined to stiffen body parts, while "heat" loosens them. Unlike most humoral systems, the Dominican one views most meats, plants, and body functions with a "neutral" value, neither hot or cold. A proper diet includes eating complimentary "hot" and "cold" substances along with "neutral" staples. In addition to balancing humoral forces, Dominicans attempt to balance food intake and waste evacuation, and work and sleep. Dominicans suspect that many health problems come from pollution in the body. Internal dirt irritates a body from the inside out and interferes with efficient circulation. In Bwa Mawego, the vast majority of health explanations reflect the above discussed body image and local priorities of balance and cleanliness. The next chapter demonstrates how Dominicans combine body image with existing health problems and plants to form diagnoses and treatments.

---

[11]These particular repeated phrases are usually idiosyncratic. They may be nonsensical such as, "*Cabwit, mouton*" (Goat, sheep), fantastical such as, "I marry a Russian girl," or truthful such as "*Mwen sou*" (I'm drunk), or "all dem chil'ren in my house."

8/Bush Medicine in Bwa Mawego

Illnesses and Their Treatments

People in every culture usually try to treat their ailments at home before seeking help from a medical specialist (Kleinman 1980). People in developing countries rely very heavily on home remedies because of common factors that deter them from getting biomedical treatment. Often medical facilities are far away from the people who need them. Biomedicine is relatively expensive. Finally, cultural and socioeconomic differences between physicians and patients hinder trust within the doctor-patient relationship. In contrast, home-based care with traditional remedies is free (or inexpensive), easily accessible in most cases (e.g., herbs in a garden near one's house door), familiar, and often private (see Figures 8.1 and 8.2).

In the case of Bwa Mawego, use of biomedicine is growing slowly. The government recently imposed laws requiring hospital births and the village acquired a resident nurse. These two factors alone resulted in increased village familiarity with biomedicine. Nevertheless, poverty, lack of available pharmaceuticals, isolation, and lack of transportation still dictate that the people of Bwa Mawego care for themselves with locally obtainable bush medicines whenever possible.

Within an ethnomedical system, remedies correspond to local ailments. Everybody recognizes the conditions he or she can treat. And everyone has culturally-influenced ideas about each illness—ideas that stem from notions about the body. A person's concepts of ethnophysiology influence the types of herbal remedies he or she selects for a condition. Consequently, there is a deep connection between ethnopharmacology and ethnophysiology.

This chapter discusses common illnesses and their herbal treatments in Bwa Mawego. Some of the common illnesses in Dominica are universal health problems; others are specific to that area. It is important to consider illnesses in emic terms because local concepts of illness affect treatment behavior. The approach here is to use the complementary perspectives of two areas of ethnobiology: ethnomedicine and ethnobotany. The dual approach allows us to examine the details of Dominican home-based bush medicine. Specifically, the local rationale for using certain plants to treat particular illnesses tells more about local ethnomedical models of illness than we would have learned by examining the illnesses separately from their treatments.

Figure 8.1 A mother crushes glorisida (Papilion glirisida) in her infant's bath water to treat "prickle heat."

Figure 8.2 A husband grinds set vil (Ambrosia hispida) to make a poultice for his wife's sprained ankle.

THE ILLNESSES

Before I could determine Bwa Mawego's most commonly used bush medicines, I had to find out which afflictions Bwa Mawegans treat themselves or at home. For this information I used freelist interviews (i.e., asked villagers to list conditions they could treat with bush medicine; see Chapter 4). I conferred with Bwa Mawegans on the wording of my freelist prompt so that the question would sound natural and acceptable to most villagers. The prompt ended up being, "Here in Bwa Mawego, what things they curing with bush medicine?" This prompt elicited a list of conditions commonly treated with bush "cures." It did not evoke mention of conditions that people treat with bush for "protection" or "build-up" (strengthening). The prompt also did not elicit gynecological conditions like menstrual pain, childbirth, and menopausal hot flashes. Villagers use bush medicines for several gynecological purposes, but these conditions are considered part of life's expected course, not sicknesses that require a "cure." Consequently, the freelist result is essentially a list of illnesses (Table 8.1).

Illnesses with a **salience score**[1] below 0.09 (see Table 8.1) are excluded from further consideration because less than five people mentioned them. Illnesses that had low salience in the freelists are either (1) not frequently treated with bush medicine when they occur, or (2) have low incidence in the population.

ILLNESS DOMAINS

The concept of **domains** is often used in anthropological linguistics. In Standard English usage, the word domain refers to ownership or control of a region, or a sphere of knowledge or influence. Linguistic anthropologists use the word similarly, but in reference to the way that spheres or clusters of terms and ideas belong together in people's minds. An English speaker naturally groups the terms "red," "blue," and "yellow" together in the domain of "colors," for instance, while "Austrian," "Chinese" and "Venezuelan" go in the "nationalities" domain. A domain is thus a clumping of words/concepts that share a core meaning that relates to one mental category. Sometimes a language does not have a specific word for a domain. For example, English speakers tend to mentally cluster "worms," "spiders" and "insects" though there is no one English term for this category (Brown 1979; Brown calls the domain "wugs"). By studying linguistic domains, anthropologists gain insight into the ways that people in a culture organize their thoughts. In my work, finding out about illness domains provided a way for me to organize my research questions so they would make the most intuitive sense to Bwa Mawegans. Knowing the illness domains also shed light on how locals conceive of the various conditions.

When asked to put the common illnesses into groups, Bwa Mawegans placed illnesses into four categories. **Pile sorts** (see Chapter 4) revealed that above all other criteria, people in Bwa Mawego classify the illnesses they treat as either hot illnesses, cold illnesses, stomach problems, or external problems (see Figure 8.3). As people sorted illnesses, they rationalized (often out loud) their assignment of an illness to a particular pile according to notions of the illness' cause, effect on the body, symptoms, and treatments. The resulting categorization thus reflects local explanatory models of these illnesses.

Joining illnesses into domains was not always a simple task for villagers. Some illnesses like "cough" and "cold," went together naturally. They often occur together, have similar local etiologies, and require the same bush treatments. Bwa Mawegans in the pile sorting groups[2] thus saw immediate similarities in some illnesses and sorted them without debate amongst the group. Three domains—"hot," "cold," and belly"—immerged immediately. Some common illnesses were difficult to place. For example, it was hard for villagers to decide whether "buttons," rashes

---

[1]A value indicating cognitive and cultural significance (see Chapter 4).
[2]The pile sorts were done with three groups of people from the village (see Chapter 4).

TABLE 8.1 FREELISTED ILLNESSES TREATABLE
WITH BUSH MEDICINE (N = 30)

Illnesses	Frequency of Mention	Percent of Total Mentions	Salience Score
Worms	26	87%	0.523
Head Colds	22	73%	0.457
"Inflammation"	21	70%	0.428
Cough	20	67%	0.326
Fever	19	63%	0.476
Gas	19	63%	0.309
"Loose boweel"	18	60%	0.305
Upset stomach	17	57%	0.397
"Something hurts"	15	50%	0.324
"Pressure"	15	50%	0.3
Prickle heat	15	50%	0.276
Sore throat	13	43%	0.262
"Buttons"	13	43%	0.246
Rheumatism	13	43%	0.197
Vomiting	12	40%	0.226
Boils	12	40%	0.209
Diarrhea	12	40%	0.166
"Fright"	11	37%	0.205
Sprain	10	33%	0.181
Asthma	10	33%	0.17
Headache	10	33%	0.166
Sores/cuts	9	30%	0.09
"Colic"[a]	3	10%	0.031
Sore eyes	2	7%	0.025
Diabetes	2	7%	0.024
Bles[b]	2	7%	0.022
"Washout"	2	7%	0.021
Menstrual delay	2	7%	0.019
Soukwayan	2	7%	0.016
Lota[c]	2	7%	0.011
Ulcer	2	7%	0.01
"Slow brains"	1	3%	0.02
Heart problems	1	3%	0.018
Vant dewange[d]	1	3%	0.016
Anemic	1	3%	0.011
Birthing	1	3%	0.008
Mawage[e]	1	3%	0.005
"Ground itch"[f]	1	3%	0.003
Toothache	1	3%	0.003

[a]Crankiness and diarrhea associated with a hangover or menstruation.
[b]A large, swollen bruised, as from a blow.
[c]Tinea versicolor, a fungal infection producing pale patches of skin.
[d]Collapsed uterus.
[e]A hex that makes one sleep all the time or lazy.
[f]Athlete's foot

supposedly caused by excess "heat" in the body, went with "cuts" in a category I termed "external illnesses," or with "inflammation" in the "hot" category. There were multiple illnesses that, like "buttons," potentially fit in more than one category. I include the names of these illnesses in the overlap of domains in Figure 8.3.

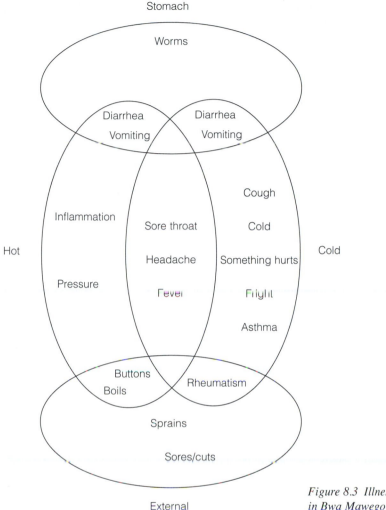

Figure 8.3 Illness domains in Bwa Mawego

Usually, when pressed, Dominicans used humoral qualities as the deciding criterion regarding where to place an illness.

In Bwa Mawegan ethnophysiology, cold (temperature or humoral exposure) is said to make body fluids and tissues congeal or stiffen, whereas heat thins or softens them (see Chapter 7). Much of Bwa Mawegan illness classification is based on humoral theory. Four conditions were humorally neutral, however. With neutral illnesses the locus of the symptoms (i.e., where the pain occurs) was the main criterion villagers used to group the illness. Consequently, the domains "belly illnesses," "external (skin and joint) illnesses,"[3] "hot illnesses" and "cold illnesses" emerged as the four important, yet somewhat overlapping, domains of illness for Dominicans. The extent to which illnesses in each domain share etiologies and treatments reflects local rationales for clumping the conditions into these four illness categories.

[3]"External" is a term that I, not Bwa Mawegans, employ for this domain.

The salient illnesses within each domain are described later in detail. Bwa Mawegans use specific remedies for each illness. Salience analysis of bush medicines revealed that for some illnesses, villagers clearly preferred one certain remedy to others. For other illnesses, villagers consistently listed a group of medicinals such that each one in the group had a high salience score, and each appears to be a popular alternative treatment for the condition. The most consensual treatments for the illnesses villagers often treat with bush medicine are presented in Table 8.2. The salient prescriptions form the core pharmacopoeia of Bwa Mawego.

To illustrate the relationship between Bwa Mawegan ethnophysiology and ethnopharmacology, I use the rest of this chapter to present the each salient illness together with its most salient remedy. These examples point to the linkage of plants (remedies) and culture in within a medical tradition.

COLD ILLNESSES AND THEIR TREATMENTS

Head Cold (Lawim)

Bwa Mawegans regard the common cold, or *lawim* in Patwa, as the result of exposure to cold ambient temperatures. This commonly occurs by (1) getting caught in the rain for an extended period, (2) prolonged swimming in cold water, or (3) by encountering cool temperatures or water when one is hot and one's pores are open, allowing the cold to penetrate the body quickly. This cold changes the viscosity of clear and runny mucus to white and thick mucus that congests the head and chest. If someone does not treat *lawim* immediately, or if the original cold exposure was particularly shocking, the white mucus turns yellow or green and becomes even thicker.

The treatments for a cold (i.e., *lawim*) involve bringing heat (humoral or thermal) into one's mucus-producing areas. People do this by breathing in steam and by drinking bush teas made with the "hot" herbs. I discuss *pachurí*, the most salient herbal treatment for *lawim*, after the section on the "cough" because the herb is the most salient treatment for both conditions. The head cold (*lawim*) and the cough share etiologies and treatments. Bwa Mawegans insist that "colds" and "coughs" are different illnesses because, though they often go together, one can have *lawim* with no cough or a cough without *lawim*, such as bronchitis. Nevertheless, as Table 8.2 shows, the set of herbs prescribed for coughs and *lawim* are similar. Not only are the most salient treatments the same, but they appear in the same order.

The Cough

The term "cough" is nebulous as it refers to both a verb and a noun; the noun in turn refers to both a condition (chest congestion) and its symptom. Bwa Mawegans listed "cough" as something people "curing with bush medicine." Here, they refer not to the sudden expulsion of air from the lungs, but to the respiratory illness that causes one to have a cough. This illness is a "cold" one. It often occurs simultaneously with a cold, or as the aftermath of a cold. Dominicans note that one can exacerbate a cold or develop a cough without a cold (e.g., bronchitis) by breathing cold air directly into the lungs (through the mouth) at night or in a cold spot. If one has a cold with a stuffy nose, it is difficult to avoid an eventual cough because one must sleep with his mouth open. A humoral cold shock via fright or something ingested might result in a cough by turning regular, runny mucus in the chest into thick, white mucus.

TABLE 8.2 PRINCIPAL PRESCRIPTIONS FOR COMMON ILLNESSES

Illness	Principal Remedy Content	Common Name	Salience Score (0-1)	Material Used
Head cold	*Hyptis pectinata*	*pachuri*	0.389	aerial plant
	Pluchea carolinensis	*tabak zombi*	0.237	aerial plant
	Sauvagesia erecta	*ti manyok, zeb mayok*	0.096	aerial plant
Cough	*Hyptis pectinata*	*pachuri*	0.389	aerial plant
	Pluchea carolinensis	*tabak zombi*	0.237	aerial plant
	Symphytum officinale	*konsout*, comfrey	0.076	aerial plant
Asthma	*Cannabis sativa*	*kali, zeb,* ganja	0.295	leaves
	Pluchea carolinensis	*tabak zombi*	0.099	aerial plant
	Hyptis pectinata	*pachuri*	0.062	aerial plant
"Something hurt"	Termite nest	woodant's nest, *koul bwa*	0.648	nest and termites
	Eryngium foetidum	*chado beni*	0.273	aerial plant
Fright	*Gossypium barbadense*	*kouton nué*, black cotton	0.413	leaves
	unidentified	*ti di te*	0.391	aerial plant
	Plectranthus amboinicus	*go djai, go di te*	0.312	aerial plant
Rheumatism	*Pimenta racemosa*	*bwa den*, bayleaf	0.554	oil
	Rincus communis	*kawapat, gwen*, caster	0.44	oil
	Boa constrictor oil	snake oil	0.201	oil
Headache	*Petiveria alliacea*	*kojourouk*	0.574	leaves
Fever	*Citrus aurantifolia*	lime, *sitwon*	0.52	leaves & root
Sore "troat"	*Lycopersicon esculentum*	tamatoz, *tomat*	0.363	green fruit
Inflammation	*Momordica charantia*	*koukouli*	0.437	aerial plant
	Aloe barbadensis	aloz, *lalue*	0.414	inner leaf
	Cocos nucifera	*koko*, jelly, coconut	0.374	endosperm
	Peperomia pellucida	*zeb kwes*, kouklaya	0.199	aerial plant
	Carica papaya	pawpaw, *papay*	0.104	fruit
	Gliricidia sepium	*glorisida, lesidra*, glory cedar	0.095	leaves
Pressure	*Carica papaya*	pawpaw, *papay*	0.889	fruit
	Stachytarphete jamaicensis	*veng-veng latjewat*	0.132	aerial plant
Buttons	*Momordica charantia*	*koukouli*	0.437	aerial plant
	Aloe barbadensis	aloz, *lalue*	0.414	inner leaf
	Cocos nucifera	*koko*, jelly, coconut	0.374	endosperm
	Peperomia pellucida	*zeb kwes*, kouklaya	0.199	aerial plant
	Carica papaya	pawpaw, *papay*	0.104	fruit
	Gliricidia sepium	*glorisida, lesidra*, glory cedar	0.095	leaves
Boils	*Lepianthes peltata*	*mal estomak*	0.294	leaves
	Plantago major	*plante*	0.283	leaves
	Tallow candle	soft candle	0.25	melted wax
Sprains	*Pimenta racemosa*	*bwa den*, bay	0.554	oil
	Rincus communis	*kawapat*, cast	0.44	oil
	Boa constrictor oil	snake oil	0.201	oil
	Cocos nucifera	*koko*, coconut	0.099	oil
Cuts, sores	*Cordyline terminalis*	*malvina, san dwagon*	0.32	leaf scrapings

(continued)

TABLE 8.2 *(continued)*

Illness	Principal Remedy Content	Common Name	Salience Score (0-1)	Material Used
Worms	*Chenopodium ambrosioides*	*sime kontwa*	0.912	aerial plant
	Aristolochia trilobata	*twef*	0.621	leaves
	Ambrosia hispida	*set vil*	0.44	aerial plant
	Portulaca oleracea	*koupiye*	0.265	aerial plant
	Artemissia absinthium	*lapsent, absinthe*	0.148	aerial plant
Diarrhea	*Psidium guajava*	*goiyav,* guava	0.93	leaves
	Zingiber officinale	*janjam,* ginger	0.182	rhizome
	Syzygium aromaticum	*klou giwav,* clove	0.169	flower
	Any starchy food staple	roast "food"	0.105	charred "food"
Upset Stomach	*Aristolochia trilobata*	*twef*	0.433	leaves
	Zingiber officinale	*janjam,* ginger	0.261	rhizome
	Ambrosia hispida	*set vil*	0.18	aerial plant
	Chenopodium ambrosioides	*sime kontwa*	0.167	aerial plant
	Psidium guajava	*goiyav,* guava	0.114	leaves

As with head colds, treatments for coughs involves bringing heat (humoral or temperature) into the lungs by breathing in steam and by drinking bush teas.

PACHURÍ—Voucher Specimen: MBQ20, UMO186348[4]   In Bwa Mawego the most salient treatment for a cough or a cold is *pachurí*, [5] or *Hyptis pectinata* (L.) Poiteau (see Figure 8.4). Forty-nine Bwa Mawegans (44%) named *pachurí* in their freelists. This pantropic weed is a member of the mint (Lamiaceae) family (Nicholson 1991). It is an aromatic herb, usually under a meter tall, but it grows to two meters when it is in bloom. People in Bwa Mawego cultivate this herb in partially shaded sections of their house gardens. One can generally smell a patch of *pachurí* from several meters away.

Like many members of the mint family, the plant's aromatic oils clear one's head when inhaled in steam. Bwa Mawegans say that *pachurí* tea eases the "full feeling" in the head and chest, relaxes a person, and warms the mucus in his chest, making it thin enough to cough.

Pachurí has a pleasant aroma and flavor. Some villagers make an infusion, or "bush tea" with it to drink as a tonic for a chill, to ease rheumatism, or for nonmedical reasons. For colds, they also use *pachurí* in tea form. They either (1) steep one fresh branch (about 45 cm long) containing approximately ten mature leaves (or the equivalent amount of plant matter) in approximately one liter of boiling hot water for five minutes, or (2) boil the same amounts of plant and water for one minute. A person with a cold can drink this tea four or five times a day.

---

[4]Voucher specimens are identified with two codes. The first, beginning with MBQ, is my collection number for the voucher. The second, starting with UMO, is the specimen's accession number at the University of Missouri Dunn-Palmer Herbarium where the collection is curated.

[5]This is the less common of two commercial herbs marketed as "patchouli" for their fragrant essential oils. (The two smell the same. The other is *Pogostemon patchouli* Pill.) This scent is popular among American hippies. Bwa Mawegans pronounce the word with a French "r" in both English and Patwa. This word is unusual as "r" normally shifts to a "w" in Patwa.

Figure 8.4 Pachurí *(Hyptis pectinata [L.] Poiteau)*

Humorally, this plant is extremely "hot" to Dominicans. If a person is not suffering from a cold, villagers say that one must be careful about when drinking *pachurí* because it is so "hot." Bwa Mawegans say that a healthy person should never drink *pachurí* during a full moon because the herb is too "hot" or "strong" then. Even when the moon is waxing or waning, a healthy person should avoid drinking *pachurí* during the heat of the day, in the morning before working, or on cold nights. Drinking *pachurí* during the heat of the day allegedly causes one to overheat immediately. Drinking it as a morning tea raises one's inner heat too quickly so the drinker would likely overheat during morning work. Moreover, if the drinker is already cold, the "heat" of *pachurí* bush tea will shock the system, throwing the body out of humoral equilibrium.

In laboratory animal testing, infusions of *Hyptis pectinata* were **analgesic** and prevented or relieved edema (Bispo, et al. 2001). Essential oil from *Hyptis pectinata* demonstrated **antimicrobial** activity and **cytotoxicity** against a variety of tumor cells (Pereda-Miranda et al. 1993). The plant is used for chest complaints in Africa (Dalziel 1937) and for colds in Jamaica (Ausprey and Thornton 1955).

Asthma

Much like cough, Bwa Mawegans attribute asthma to "cold" in the lungs. They explain that only certain people are susceptible to asthma because of a two-fold inherent "weakness." First, Bwa Mawegans assume that asthmatics have "thin lungs." This would make their lungs chill more quickly than normal, thick lungs. In the local humoral system, human flesh that is chilled is stiff. This perceived stiffness makes it laborious for asthmatics to breathe. In addition to thin lungs, asthmatics have "sensitivities" that non-asthmatics do not have.

One kind of sensitivity is an allergy. Individuals with allergies have "cold" reactions to plants and animals that are "neutral" for most people. A person with normal, thick lungs thus has allergic reactions similar to a common cold, whereas the thin-lunged allergy sufferer reacts with an asthmatic attack.

The other kind of sensitivity that asthmatics might possess is an emotional one that Bwa Mawegans refer to as "weak nerves." Individuals with weak nerves are susceptible to attacks of "fright." "Fright" is also a "cold" condition. In the case of the asthmatic, the cold from even a small fright might chill the thin lungs enough to make breathing difficult. A person with both thin lungs and weak nerves will thus have asthmatic attacks in circumstances when most people would simply cry, scream, or feel nervous or frightened. Similarly, biomedical studies find that, in patients with asthma, stress can be sufficient to induce breathlessness (Rietveld, van Beest, & Everaerd 1999).

Treatments for asthma include *kalí* (*Cannabis sativa* L.), the previously discussed *pachurí*, another herb called *tabak zombi*, and the tail of a type of a small lizard (species unidentified) that villagers call *zandolí*. These remedies share the reported properties of helping one to relax while bringing "warmth" into the lungs.

KALÍ—Sight Record, No Voucher Kalí, *Cannabis sativa* L., is by far the most salient asthma medicine in the village. Bwa Mawegans also call this plant *zeb* (in Patwa) and marihuana, ganja, herb, and sensi in English. These English names are used throughout the English-speaking Caribbean. *Kalí* is a robust, erect, bushy herb. The regional variety reaches a maximum height just over two meters. Its leaves are deeply veined and palmate in five thin, **lanceolate** (speartip-shaped) segments with serrated edges. Unlike most plant species, *kali* has separate male and female plants. Botanists surmise that the species is native to Central Asia and spread very early. It is one of the world's oldest cultivated varieties and now grows throughout the earth's temperate and tropical climates (Schultes and Hofmann 1992). It is illegal to grow *kalí* in Dominica.

Like most places in the Caribbean, some Bwa Mawegans (especially those born after about 1950) smoke *kalí* leaves and inflorescences to reach "spiritual heights" and to relax. Villagers also smoke *kalí* for nausea[6] and for acute asthma attacks. The most common way to administer medicinal *kalí* is in the form of "*kalí* tea." Villagers make this by boiling a handful of leaves (15–20) in one liter of water for around three minutes. Villagers drink "*kalí* tea" for colds, bronchitis, and pneumonia.[7] They drink one full cup of tea at the time of an asthma event, then ½ –¾ a cup every four hours for the rest of the day.

---

[6]Villagers mentioned smoking *kalí* for nausea during informal interviews. However, only one person listed this use in the nausea/vomiting freelist.

[7]I learned about these uses during informal interviews, participant-observation, and from doing health surveys. These uses were not salient in the freelist interviews, however. I suspect that, because of its illegal status, villagers omitted mentions of *kalí* in formal interviews because there were several alternative common remedies to mention. They apparently altered this attitude when asked about asthma treatments because *kalí* is a much preferred standard asthma treatment.

Jamaicans also use this herb as a tea for asthma, and for fevers and colds (Ausprey and Thornton 1955). Marijuana has some antibiotic activity (Lewis and Elvin-Lewis 1977). It is affective against inflammation and joint damage in arthritis, and exhibits a wide range of immune system activity in animal and human tests (Straus 2000). It is an **antiemetic** (Pertwee 2001). In trials with patients on chemotherapy, cannabinoids (chemical constituents of cannabis) reduce nausea, control vomiting, and are a patient-preferred treatment (Tramèr, et al. 2001). Cannabis is used effectively by patients with multiple sclerosis (MS) for muscle spasm and pain. In an experimental model of MS, low doses of cannabinoids alleviated tremor (Williamson and Evans 2000). *Kalí* smoke is a **bronchodilator** (Patrick 1980) and aerosolized THC (the plant's active chemical compound) works at the same rate as salbutamol, the common asthma pharmaceutical inhaler (Nahas, Sutin, and Bennett 2000). Cannabis is an analgesic. In randomized controlled clinical trials, cannabinoids give humans about the same level of pain relief as codeine in acute postoperative pain (Campbell et al. 2001). It is no wonder that a locally occurring plant with calming, **antispasmodic**, pain-relieving, anti-inflammatory, and bronchodilating effects is the village's most salient asthma treatment.

"Something Hurt You"

A Bwa Mawegan who is very hot—be it emotionally hot (angry or shamed), or physically hot (from sun or exercise)—must avoid ingesting extremely humorally cold foods, notably cold fruit (such as pineapple), or some reef fish (such as barracuda).[8] Locals say that very cold foods shock the hot body, and therefore "hurt" the person. Symptoms of "if something hurt you" are said to include nausea, vomiting, a generally sick, "poisoned" feeling, a severe headache, or breathing troubles. These symptoms are so general one might expect this illness to be a "neutral" one. To Bwa Mawegans, the initial cause is certainly humorally "cold," however. The condition "something hurts you" is therefore a "cold" illness.

WOODANTS' NEST   The most salient treatment for when "something hurt you" is a boiled chunk of "woodant" nest and its resident ants. Of the most salient treatments for illnesses, this remedy is the only non-herbal one. The "woodant" or *kul bwa*, in Patwa (unidentified termite species) makes large, black and brown, above-ground nests. Typically, these nests are in the 20–30 cm diameter range. I once saw a woodants' nest in the bush that had a diameter of around 90 cm. Termites appear to build these nests on the ground in any partially shaded area in the village or bush. There is usually some dead wood in their vicinity, however, this is true for almost any spot on the island's East Coast. I have seen woodants' nests in gardens, under forest, and protruding from rock cliffs.

The woodants' nest has no broader use in local medicine other than "if something hurt you." If someone needs a nest, and does not know where one is, he or she simply asks neighbors until someone remembers seeing a nest. The nests are fairly obvious and easy to find once one is pointed in the right direction.

---

[8]Bwa Mawegans view most fish as humorally neutral. Reef fish that Bwa Mawegans say are "sometimes" very cold can occasionally carry ciguatera—a food poisoning from large reef fish that have eaten smaller fish that consumed natural toxins, e.g. certain plankton. Toxins can concentrate as they move up the food chain, but their adverse effects appear limited to humans (Otwell 1989).

A Bwa Mawegan harvests the woodants' nest by cutting a twelve ounce can-sized chunk out of the nest with a cutlass. The person scoops the chunk of nest into a rag or plastic bag and ties it up (though these insects do not bite). In the kitchen, he or she places the piece of nest in a small (3 quart) pot. Any insects from the plastic bag or rag are shaken into the pot as well. Hot water is added into the pot to cover the chunk completely, and the pot is set to boil for five minutes. During this process, the termites, or "woodants" come out of the nest and float on the water. The preparer then pours the water and insects into another vessel and throws the nest away. The patient drinks the "tea"—complete with the insects—three times a day or until he or she feels complete relief or vomits (after which the stomach "gripes" usually stop).

Villagers say that, in addition to making one vomit, there is something about the "heat" from the woodant tea that cures the "hurt" from something shockingly cold. If one makes himself throw up by sticking his finger down his throat, they say he will get rid of the "cold poison" still in the stomach, but not the effects of the cold that already entered the patient's system.

Fright

Fright, the emotion, results in the illness that is also called "fright" (or *sésismá* in Patwa). One can think of the condition Dominicans call "fright" as a phenomenon that behavioral scientists call a culture-bound syndrome (Hughes 1990, Yap 1977), or a culturally unique pattern of mental illness.

There are several cultures that associate a particular illness with emotional fright (and even call the illness "fright"). Though there are various "fright" illnesses across the world, each of them has aspects that make the syndrome unique to (or bound within) the culture where it occurs.[9] The world's various "fright" illnesses share an etiology—they are all blamed on a fright or scare. The symptoms of "fright" illnesses vary from culture to culture and can include physical symptoms, psychological/behavioral symptoms, or a period of misfortune in the sufferer's life (Simons 1985). In several of the fright illnesses, the sufferer can develop the illness because of someone else's (e.g., a parent's) fright (Rubel, O'Nell, and Ardon 1984). In other fright instances, the illness onset can occur days, months, or years after the original frightening event. Some fright illnesses involve local etiologies involving soul (or vital force) loss (Rubel, O'Nell, and Ardon 1984, Simons 1985). For example, the Latin American illness *susto* (Spanish for "fright"), is a chronic illness in which the sufferer is supposed to have lost his or her soul because of a severe fright (Rubel, O'Nell, and Ardon 1984). *Susto* has diverse symptoms, including depression, agitation, anorexia, diarrhea, and fever, and shares biomedical diagnostic features with psychosomatic and other neurotic disorders (Finerman 1993).

In contrast with other fright illnesses, Dominican "fright" (or *sésismá*) does not involve soul loss. It usually occurs immediately or always within a month of the traumatic event. Further, Dominican "fright" only results from a direct and personal experience of extreme emotional trauma or if there is some kind of blood or body fluid exchange. For example, one mother explained:

---

[9]Other fright illnesses include *susto* (Latin America) (Rubel, O'Nell, and Ardon 1984), *saladera* (Peruvian Amazon) (Dobkin de Rios 1985), *lanti* (Philippines) (Hard 1985), *mogo laya* (New Guinea) (Frankel 1985), and *narahati* (Iran) (Good and Good 1982, Pliskin 1987).

Usually it *djombi* and thing [witches] causing fright. Or bad news—that giving you fright too. If you have fright and breastfeed the baby, it could cause the baby death. The blood go through your milk. I watched a dog die, and the same way the dog was dying so like did Rastina (infant daughter). Then, I drank *go dite* bush tea and I could feel the fright go back down from my toes, up my legs, and through my body. After that, I could breastfeed again.

The symptoms of a person with fright include frequent recollections or dreams about the traumatic event, persistent anxiety or arousal, difficulty concentrating, hypersensitivity (including exaggerated startle responses), and outbursts of anger or grief. In an etic sense, the symptoms that Dominicans associate with "fright" are highly comparable to the set of symptoms biomedicine associates with Posttraumatic Stress Disorder—which is also precipitated by an emotional trauma (American Psychiatric Association 1994).

In the emic sense, as discussed in Chapter 5, Bwa Mawegans maintain that a fright or shock causes one's blood to chill or freeze into clots or "masses." Frozen clots block proper blood flow through the body and thus impede "nerve" functioning. Medications that Bwa Mawegans use for "fright" are humorally warm. They help to "melt" the chilled blood masses. Bwa Mawegans say that a person often feels soothed after just one dose (usually a cup of "bush tea") of a fright treatment. However, in a severe case the cold in the blood will start to build up again after a few hours. Someone suffering from "fright" may "cure" within a couple days of his or her shock. However, if one's trauma was particularly horrible, or if one has weak nerves to begin with, he or she might suffer from "fright"—and continue taking bush treatments for it—for up to two solid years, and sometimes sporadically after that.

KOUTON NUÉ—Voucher Specimen: MBQ177, UMO186416   *Kouton nué* in Patwa, or "black cotton" in English (*Gossypium hirsutum* L., Malvaceae family) was Bwa Mawego's most salient treatment for "fright" (mentioned by 48% of informants). *Kouton nué* is a native tree of the Greater Antilles and naturalized in the Lesser Antilles (Nicholson 1991). Elsewhere this species is grown commercially (Nicholson 1991). Trees in the village grow to around three meters tall. The large, red-tinged leaves (40 cm) are **alternate**, on long **petioles** (at least 10 cm), and have five triangular lobes. The cotton around its seeds is gray. There are five or six of these trees growing in the village, near people's houses. As with all fright treatments, villagers say that bush tea made with *kouton nué* relaxes a person and "warms frozen blood."

If a Bwa Mawegan wants to make *kouton nué* tea, he or she asks one of his neighbors who has a *kouton nué* tree for some leaf. This is a small request, as the tree's leaves are so large. One can make at least three servings by boiling one lobe from one leaf (torn up) for around three minutes. Villagers with "fright" drink a cup of this tea once or twice a day until their "fright" subsides. People with lasting cases of "fright" typically vary their herbal treatments every few days.

Literature on the agricultural aspects of *kouton nué* abounds; however, little laboratory work has been done on its medicinal chemical properties. However, the xylem from the stems of G. Hirsutum is highly toxic to fungi that are **pathogenic** to animals and may be useful for treating fungal diseases (Mace, Stipanovic, and Bell 1993).

Ethnographic information on the medicinal use of this plant, aside from the cotton fiber, is also scanty. In Trinidad, cotton seeds (of various species) are a favored treatment for deworming dogs (Lans et al. 2000). In India and Pakistan, they use leaves of *G. herbaceum* (a related, Asian species) to make an extract for treating diarrhea, hemorrhoids, kidney stones and painful, reduced urination (Hutchens 1991). In North America, the Alabama and Koasati Indians used the roots of *Gossypium* ssp. to make a tea for women in childbirth. A **decoction** from the bark of cotton roots was an official U.S. drug used from 1863 to 1950 to stimulate menstrual flow and aid contractions during labor. South Carolinians also used the roots for asthma (Vogel 1970). Hodge and Taylor (1957) report that Island Caribs spun *kouton nué*'s cotton for cloth, and used the leaves to make a post-partum bath for women.

Rheumatism

Rheumatism in Bwa Mawego, as elsewhere, refers to pain and stiffness in the joints and the back. Bwa Mawegans say that this condition tends to move from the outside (extremities) to the inside, first appearing in the fingers and toes, then the wrists and ankles, the elbows and knees, the shoulders and hips, and finally the spine. They blame this condition on coldness. The further in (away from the extremities) one's rheumatism occurs, the "deeper" one's bodily coldness.

In Bwa Mawegan ethnophysiology, rheumatism is a potential outcome of cold in the blood (i.e., cold through one's entire system). This cold can enter one's system via humoral, emotional,[10] or thermal means. Joints become cold when chilled blood runs past them. Symptoms of rheumatism occur when "sinews" (tendons and ligaments) and "goits" (flesh around joints) cool and stiffen. "Goits" accumulate with age. Older individuals thus have larger joints than young people do. When an older person has a chill, he or she becomes more pained and disabled by the hardening of the "goits," because of the sheer size of the stiff goit. Further, older people are more susceptible to cold because Bwa Mawegans reckon that as the body ages it becomes less able to heat itself. Thus, the elderly are at greater risk for rheumatism than are the young.

Rheumatism is a cold illness, as Bwa Mawegans conceive that it is cold that makes one's joints stiffen. However, unlike other "cold" illnesses, rheumatism is not an illness of the "insides." Rheumatism affects the extremities. Thus, Bwa Mawegans view rheumatism as a cold illness that, because it does not involve internal organs, is similar to skin problems and injuries (cuts and sprains). Likewise, remedies for rheumatism involve both topical and internal treatments. Interestingly, only the topical treatments were salient in the freelist results. One villager suggested that these results show that when people think of treating rheumatism, they first think of how to bring warmth and movement to the specific joints that are troubling them. Only then can they worry about the systemic underlying cold.

BAY OIL—*Voucher Specimen*: MBQ17, UMO183834   Bay oil (see Figure 8.5) was the most salient treatment in the rheumatism freelist. Sixty-four percent of the people listed it. Bay oil, also called myrica oil, is the essential oil distilled from the leaves of a native West Indian tree, *Pimenta racemosa* (Miller) J. W.Moore (family Myrtaceae) (Brussell 1997). Bay oil is used to perfume various soaps and colognes, and is the primary ingredient in bay rum. Bay oil is *not* from the similar-looking

---

[10]Villagers recognize arthritis (which they call "a-fright-is") as a type of rheumatism. Several key informants told me that "a-fright-is" is the name for rheumatism from the cold of fright (a cold condition).

*Figure 8.5 A bottle of bay oil
held in front of a bay leaf
(*Pimenta racemosa *[Miller]
J. W. Moore) tree*

leaves of the laurel (*Laurus noblis*), that Europeans call "bay" and use to flavor soups. The bay, or bay leaf tree (*bwa den* in Patwa), is a cultivated tree with smooth, gray bark and leathery **elliptic** leaves on upward-growing branches that make the trees narrow. The trees can reach 10 meters in height (Honychurch 1986). In Bwa Mawego, people trim their bay trees at least every two years to distill the leaves. Thus, among the thousands of bay trees planted in and around Bwa Mawego, I have never seen one taller than three meters.

Bwa Mawegans use bay leaves to flavor gravy, and to make "a nice tasting tea" that is good for chills. They apply bay oil for sprains and strains in addition to rheumatism. Bay oil is very "strong." Before applying it to their skin, villagers mix the bay oil with another kind of oil (caster oil, coconut oil, snake oil, or cooking oil). They massage the affected area with the bay oil mixture. They can repeat this twice daily. More frequent applications would irritate (or "burn") the skin because the bay oil is so "hot."

In laboratory tests, the compound lupeol isolated from *Pimenta racemosa* leaves is effective against acute inflammation by oral route and when topically applied (Fernandez, Alvarez, et al. 2001). Abietic acid isolated from *Pimenta racemosa* is also anti-inflammatory after oral or topical administration, and has some preventative effect on swelling (Fernandez, Tornos et al. 2001).

Island Caribs drink bay leaf tea for stomach aches (Hodge and Taylor 1957). Haitians also drink the leaf tea for abdominal pain (Weniger et al. 1986). Trinidadians drink bay leaf tea for flues and coughs. It is effective for coughs as the leaves' volatile oil contains the lung expectorants eugenol and chavicol (Wong 1976).

Headache

For Bwa Mawegans, a headache is a humorally "neutral" condition. This is because headaches can be a symptom of "hot" conditions as well as of "cold" conditions. Headaches exist as a singular condition. In general, Bwa Mawegans regard headaches as the way that a person's body warns his or her mind that the metabolism is somehow out of balance. The headache sufferer is either sick already or doing something that could cause sickness. A person with a headache needs to stop breathing "dirts," or get out of the sun if hot, drink a warm tea if cold, stop working if tired, or stop drinking rum (if this person has not done so already). Unlike most Bwa Mawegan remedies, treatments for headaches (primarily *kojourouk* and aspirin) do not function to return balance to the body. They are simply painkillers.

KOJOUROUK—*Voucher Specimens*: MBQ50; UMO183848 The plant that Dominicans call *kojourouk* (*Petiveria alliacea* L.) (see Figure 8.6) is Bwa Mawego's only truly salient bush medicine for headaches. This member of the Phytolaccaceae is native to tropical America and is common in lower elevations (Hodge and Taylor 1957). The herb reaches 70 cm in height. It has alternate elliptic leaves up to 10 cm long, and spikes of small white flowers. The whole plant smells like garlic, especially when crushed. This plant grows throughout Bwa Mawego in house gardens, along the "big road" and footpaths, and as a weed under tree-planted areas. It appears to thrive in partial shade.

Some villagers gargle with kojourouk tea for sore throats. However, most Bwa Mawegans only use kojourouk for headaches. It is one of the few bush medicines that Bwa Mawegans do not drink as tea. For headaches they simply crush the leaves in their hands then sniff the fumes from crushed leaves. The duration of sniffing depends on the strength of one's headache. Villagers say that for some headaches kojourouk is better than aspirin because it works faster. Yet, for certain headaches, such as one from a hangover, aspirin is more effective. Laboratory tests found that *Petiveria alliacea* has an analgesic effect on animals (de Lima, et al. 1991).

Throughout tropical America, people use the leaf and stem of this species to make an infusion with gynecological applications as an abortifacient, to treat amenorrhea, and to aid childbirth (Joly, et.al. 1987). It is a folk medicine in Brazil where hot water infusions of the plant's leaves or roots are used as an analgesic, sedative, and diuretic and to reduce spasms, rheumatism, and fevers (de Lima et al. 1991). Island Caribs on Dominica used *kojourouk* to make a tea that they gave as an antidote for poison and for women during labor (Hodge and Taylor 1957). Miskitu and Sumu Indians of Nicaragua use *kojourouk* for aches and pains (Coe and Anderson 1999). Trinidadians use this herb to make a poultice for head colds (Wong 1976). People in the Virgin Islands use it for headaches. Rather than smelling the leaves, they make an infusion of *kojourouk* roots (Oakes and Morris 1958). In the northwest Amazon, Tikunas treat headaches by washing their heads with a decoction they make from *kojourouk* leaves (Schultes and Raffauf 1990). Haitians, like Bwa Mawegans,

Figure 8.6 Kojourouk
*(*Petiveria alliacea *L.)*

treat headaches by inhaling the fumes of crushed *kojourouk* leaves (Weniger et.al. 1986). Despite little pharmacological testing on this plant, the degree of its salience in Bwa Mawego, combined with ethnographic evidence of its similar use elsewhere, indicate that this plant is an effective headache treatment.

Conclusion to Cold Illnesses and Their Treatments

All of the illnesses discussed in the past pages, conditions that Dominicans view as "cold," require treatments that Dominicans think of as "hot" medicines. There is some overlap between "cold" conditions and their respective treatments. Dominicans do not use any "hot" bush medicine for any "cold" condition, however. In general, the purely "cold" illnesses have something to do with respiratory problems or are stress induced. Asthma involves both. Asthma remedies both relax a sufferer and ease breathing. Cough and cold remedies (and "something hurt you" to a lesser extent) target breathing, while remedies for "fright" are largely calming.

HOT ILLNESSES AND THEIR TREATMENTS

Fever

Since a fever is a rise in body temperature, it is, in one sense, the typical "hot" illness. Yet Bwa Mawegans say that fevers belong in both the "hot" and "cold" illness domains. This is because Bwa Mawegans believe fever is caused by exposure to either "hot" or "cold" conditions. In the first case, one's body temperature might rise from heat of sun, fire, or exertion, a "burning" love or anger, or from a "hot" "running [contagious] sickness." In the second case, a fever can immerge from a "cold" illness, making the fever a "cold" one, in a sense.

As we have seen previously, Bwa Mawegans classify common colds, coughs, and asthma as "cold" illnesses because they associate these sicknesses with a cold cause, and thick mucus is a cold symptom. When a person is suffering from a cold condition, the body heats up in an attempt to regulate its internal temperature. Sometimes, the body overheats while fighting a cold respiratory illness and a fever develops. Because of the rise in body temperature, a fever is clearly a "hot" illness.

However, in some cases, the fever's cause is "cold." Bwa Mawegans hence view a fever as a symptom that overlaps hot and cold illness categories.

Bwa Mawegans specifically treat the fever symptom, not the body system affected by the larger illness (i.e., when a fever coincides with diarrhea, fever treatment does not target the digestive system, but body temperature). All Bwa Mawegan fever remedies cool the body surface with evaporation. Villagers say that the herbal fever treatments cause one to perspire, and the sweat cools the body. Alternately, one could bathe with cool water, or rub rum on one's skin to cool the fever.

LIME—*Voucher Specimen*: MBQ15, UMO183840   Two parts of the lime tree—its leaves and roots—are Bwa Mawego's two most salient fever treatments. The lime (*Citrus aurantiifolia* Swingle), or *sitwon* in Patwa, originates in Southeast Asia (Honychurch 1986). English colonists brought it to Dominica early in its colonial history. Lime production is one of Dominica's principal industries (Honychurch 1995), though no one in Bwa Mawego grows limes for market. The lime tree is small, reaching perhaps four meters in height. Its leaves are alternate but paired, elliptic and leathery, with spines at the leaf axils (where the leaf petioles meet the stem/branch). White flowers precede green lime fruits. Lime trees abound in Bwa Mawego. I estimate that there are 30–40 trees in the village (one tree to every 3–4 households).

Bwa Mawegans use limes on an everyday basis for marinating meat and for making limeade. About ten percent of villagers use lime fruit juice for coughs and colds and about half as many use the fruit juice for fevers. "Lime leaf tea" is a popular bush tea for nonmedicinal purposes. It is also a medicine that Bwa Mawegans use to help "break" a fever. To make the "tea" they boil around 12 leaves, or a 30–40 cm twig with its leaves, in one and a half liters of water for two or three minutes. Lime root is "more powerful than the leaf" so less plant matter is necessary to make the decoction. Bwa Mawegans make "lime root tea" by boiling lime roots about the size of two pencils in one and a half liters of water for approximately ten minutes. An adult with a fever should drink about a cup and a half to two cups of either of these decoctions (less for children, depending on their size). Bwa Mawegans say that drinking lime "teas" causes a person to perspire profusely, after which the fever drops.

People in Jamaica and Montserrat use lime leaf infusions for colds (Ausprey and Thornton 1954, Brussell 1997). In West Africa, people make a decoction for fevers with lime twigs (Lewis and Elvin-Lewis 1977). Haitians treat fevers with a decoction made with only leaves from the lime tree (Weniger et.al. 1986). "Tea" made with lime tree roots is the treatment for venereal diseases in Trinidad (Wong 1976). In Jamaica, like Dominica, lime root "tea" is a fever medication (Ausprey and Thornton 1954).

Sore Throat

Bwa Mawegans frequently refer to a sore throat as simply "troat" (as in, "He have troat today"). Generally speaking, Bwa Mawegans regard red and inflamed conditions as "hot" illnesses. However, as shown in Figure 8.3, Bwa Mawegans hesitate to classify sore throats entirely within the "hot illness" domain. Like headaches, sore throats can occur with both hot illnesses (like flus) and cold illness (like colds). They thus fall into the overlap between "hot" and "cold" illnesses. Nevertheless, the sore throat itself (not the illness but the affected body part) is certainly inflamed, and therefore "hot." Sore throat treatments are gargled to bring coolness to the affected area. By gargling, one avoids swallowing a "cold" remedy, in case one's body is already in an overly cold state.

TOMATOZ—*Sight Record, No Voucher*   Though it was only mentioned by 41% of the villagers, the "tomatoz," (always pronounced as plural) or *tomat* in Patwa, is by far the most popular sore throat treatment in Bwa Mawego. The tomato (*Lycopersicon esculentum* Miller) is native to tropical America from Mexico to Brazil, and probably indigenous to the island of Dominica (Grisebach 1864). Like the U.S. commercial varieties, the Dominican tomato herb has alternate, compound, irregularly lobed leafs, yellow flowers, and round orange to red berries (i.e., tomatoes). The local tomato variety has fruit with a 2½–4 cm diameter. The plant grows in full sun and partial shade. Perhaps half of village households have one tomato plant growing in a 1–1½ meter-wide mound (Bwa Mawegans do not stake the plants). In the village, I have seen a couple of tomato plants that were not growing in gardens. These may be **escapes** (e.g., someone threw a rotten tomato from her house garden and a new plant grew where the fruit landed). I have never seen a tomato plant growing wild in the bush, though they may exist there.[11]

Dominicans eat fresh and cooked ripe tomatoes. Sore throats are the only ailment that Bwa Mawegans treat with tomatoes (or any other part of the tomato plant). They make a gargling solution with "young" (green) tomatoes. They smash or chop up three immature fruits, and boil them for several minutes in 2–3 cups of water. They gargle with the strained liquid. They repeat this as often as they want—usually every two hours. Bwa Mawegans say that this treatment both numbs the throat and makes the sickness go away faster. It is a treatment for children as well as adults.

A laboratory evaluation of tomato leaves found them to work as a local anaesthetic (Chandra, Singhal, and Gupta 1969). Tomatoes produce antiviral activity (Spinu et al. 1996). Further, a complex of organic acids in tomato pulp produces a wide-spectrum antibiotic effect on Gram-positive and Gram-negative bacteria and is antifungal on the genus Candida (Vorob'ev, et al. 1998).

Inflammation

The term "inflammation," as Bwa Mawegans use it, refers to a condition of internal heat and swelling. In Bwa Mawego, inflammation is not just a symptom, but an illness on its own. It is also a fundamental, underlying condition for two other illness categories (pressure and buttons/prickle heat). Bwa Mawegans use "inflammation" as somewhat of a catch-all that encompasses biomedical conditions including heat prostration, infection, constipation, dehydration, and stress reactions. In rare cases, inflammation can occur in a specific, isolated body part (i.e., an infection). However, most inflammation is spread throughout the inner body. Inflammation can come from "dirts" inside the body that are "scratching," thereby irritating and inflaming, one's insides. A diet high in processed carbohydrates (e.g., flour) can give one inflammation, as processed starch products are humorally "hot." Inflammation can also result from "pressure," a hot condition described later in this chapter. Most commonly, a

---

[11]Nicholson did not collect them for his *Flora of Dominica, Part 2: Dicotyledoneae* (1991).

person gets inflammation by becoming too hot through exertion in the heat (from the sun, or fire), perhaps combined with dehydration.

Inflammation, according to Bwa Mawegans, heats and swells the inner body. This swelling can restrict blood flow, which might make one feel faint. Internal swelling also blocks the "boweel" (bowels). Constipation is thus one symptom of inflammation (constipation can also be a *cause* of inflammation as constipation is dirt blocked inside the body). The heat caused by inflammation is supposed to escape the body through a person's skin. This causes skin eruptions (discussed with the "buttons and prickle heat" illness category)—another symptom of inflammation.

Treatments for inflammation accomplish two basic functions. First, they are "refreshments" or "coolings." This means that they make one feel cool, or quench one's thirst. Second, they are laxatives. This helps clean out excess "dirts" from one's "system."

KOUKOULÍ—Voucher Specimen: MBQ2, UMO183935   Of the many bush medicines for inflammation that Bwa Mawegans gave in their freelists, *koukoulí* (*Momordica charantia* L.) was the most salient. Fifty-eight percent of the village adults mentioned it. *Koukoulí* is called "cerasse," "maiden apple," or "balsam apple" elsewhere in the English-speaking Caribbean (Honychurch 1986). Bwa Mawegans only use the Patwa term *koukoulí*, which may come from a Carib term. It might also come from *pomme coolie*, this plant's name in other parts of the French-speaking Caribbean (Honychurch 1986) and elsewhere (e.g. Montserrat; see Brussell 1997). The species is native to the Old World tropics (Brussell 1997) but is now pantropical (Nicholson 1991). *Koukoulí* is a thin vine with simple tendrils and alternate, deeply lobed leaves. It has yellow flowers and orange, ovoid, nub-covered fruits. *Koukoulí* is a common weed in Bwa Mawego. It grows along paths and in bushes, and is one of the first plants to take hold in slopes that have been newly washed-out by mudslides.

The bright orange ripe *koukoulí* fruits are easy to see at a distance. As they walk through the village, Bwa Mawegans, especially children, pick these fruits off trailside vines, break them open, and chew on the sweet, red arils that cover the fruit's seeds. Bwa Mawegans make a bath with *koukoulí* to soak skin erruptions (see "buttons and prickle heat" subheading). For inflammation, they make a "bush tea" by steeping six to ten leaves (depending on leaf size) in about one liter of boiled water. They drink this infusion one to three times in one day, depending their assessment of the severity of the inflammation. Usually, within 12 hours after drinking "one big cup" of the *koukoulí* "bush tea," the drink cleans not only one's "boweel," but all the "dirts" from one's belly, organs, and blood. Afterwards one feels "refreshed," "like your system working well." One knows that his or her system is clean because the pores are clean, so the sweat flows freely. Further, one's sweat either has no odor, or smells "clean."

Momordica charantia is rich in antioxidants (Scartezzini and Speroni 2000). Momordin Ic, a constituent component in *koukoulí*, has been pharmacologically demonstrated to "accelerate gastrointestinal transit," making it effective as a laxative (Li et al. 2000).

According to Hodge and Taylor (1957), Caribs on Dominica use *koukoulí* for colds. This is interesting because in neighboring Bwa Mawego (where several residents are even *from* Carib reserve), the plant is a "cooling" plant used to induce cold. It would *never* be used to treat a cold, which would require a hot plant. I cannot help but wonder if Hodge and Taylor were the victims of a language misunderstanding in this case. Trinidadians and the Miskitu of Nicaragua use *koukoulí* for malaria, diabetes and hypertension (Wong 1976, Coe and Anderson 1999). Miskitu also use it for aches and pains, infections, skin rashes and sores (ibid.) In Haiti, *koukoulí* is a treatment for fevers and "liver troubles" (Weniger et al. 1986). Brussell reports that in Montserrat, *koukoulí* is a **purgative** (cleanses the digestive tract) and a means of "cooling the blood"(1997:54). Jamaicans use it to make a laxative tea (Ausprey and Thornton 1953). Though these other Caribbean uses may seem disparate, all but the Carib example are concurrent with Dominican use of the plant as a general "cooling" for "inflammation," in that all of the conditions treated with this plant elsewhere in the Caribbean would be termed "hot" conditions in Dominica.

Pressure

As discussed previously, inflammation is internal heat. The condition that Bwa Mawegans call "pressure" is a condition where emotional "pressure" caused by "a hot feeling"—a stressful emotion such as lust, jealousy, anger, and worry—leads to extreme internal heat. This strong heat includes very hot blood and leads to tightened veins, thickened (cooked-off) blood, and compromised blood flow. Pressure is a specific, severe form of inflammation. One can have inflammation without having pressure, but one cannot, to my understanding, have pressure without inflammation.

A body suffering from pressure is internally "hot" or inflamed. Inflammation, combined with emotional pressure causes the sufferer's veins to swell. Sometimes one can see the veins swell and throb in someone's temples or neck. Swollen veins result in narrower tubes for blood circulation.

In addition, in some people, emotional pressure causes gastrointestinal distress. Here, a person might generate extra gas. A gas build-up can also push against veins, crimping them, or restricting the amount of blood that can pass through the veins.

As discussed previously, the blood of individuals with inflammation becomes dangerously warm in a humoral sense, yet those with pressure have even hotter blood. The "forcing" of blood under pressure makes the pressure sufferer's blood so hot that the blood thickens (rather than becoming thin and runny, as with most "hot" conditions), as if the water in the blood were cooking off. It then becomes too concentrated, or too "rich," forcing the body to push it through the already compromised veins and causing a build-up. Hence, pressure builds up in the veins. The illness is thus named for both its perceived cause (emotional pressure) and its perceived effect (vein pressure).

Pressure is a type of inflammation. So there is some of overlap of cures that Bwa Mawegans listed for pressure and those they gave for inflammation. Most of the more salient pressure treatments deal with the acute pressure condition, rather than the underlying inflammation. These medicines are said to unblock and open up blood veins. With pressure, the obstruction of blood flow is the dangerous state that might lead to a stroke or heart attack.[12] One's first concern must be to free blood flow before

---

[12]The perceived physical *effects* of pressure (obstructed blood) almost mirror those of fright. And both syndromes are said to cause strokes and heart attacks. But the perceived *cause* is opposite. Fright is a cold syndrome in which the blood chills into clots after experiencing a cold emotion. Pressure is a hot syndrome where hot emotions result in poor blood-flow.

treating the underlying inflammation. The freelists reflect these priorities. Pawpaw, or papaya, is the most salient remedy because it is alleged to unblock both the veins and the bowels.

PAWPAW—*Sight Record, No Voucher*   "Pawpaw" in English, and *papay* in Patwa, are the names that Dominicans use for the "papaya" fruit and tree (Carica papaya L., *Caricaceae* family). This species is native to Dominica (Honychurch 1995). It is an herbacious tree, usually less than four meters tall, with no branches. It has large (over 40 cm wide) palmately lobed leaves on long petioles and large yellow flowers that give rise to large, edible green to yellow fruits with many black seeds and yellow to orange flesh. Dominicans cultivate paw-paws for their fruit. They grow these trees in their bush gardens, where they eat ripe fruits as "cooling," thirst-quenching snacks. More commonly, people grow pawpaws near their homes.

Dominicans frequently add diced green pawpaw to stews. It has little flavor, but tenderizes meat. People eat the ripe fruit, and blend it into juice. The "cooling" effects of pawpaw make it an essential part of a humorally balanced meal, especially if one serves some particularly "hot" food as well. Medicinally, villagers chew pawpaw seeds to get rid of intestinal parasites. They eat large portions of pawpaw fruit or drink the juice for inflammation, including reducing "buttons" or "pressure." For pressure, some people make a hole in a ripe fruit, remove the seeds, and pour boiling water into it. They let it steep until the water cools, then drink the pawpaw "tea."

In laboratory testing, unripe papaya fruit inhibits the growth and the reproduction of several pathogenic bacteria, including E.coli, salmonella, and staphylococcus. It contains concentrations of Vitamin C, glucose, malic acid, and citric acid. It contains free radical scavengers and shows antioxidative activity (Osato et al.1993). In clinical trials, application of the fruit proved effective in reducing swelling from edema and ecchymosis (water retention and bruising) (Vallis and Lund 1969). Papaya fruit juice reduces hypertension in laboratory rats (Eno et al. 2000). Pawpaw seeds exibit antiamoebic activity (Tona et al. 1998).

The Maya used papaya fruit for sores and eruptions (Ausprey and Thornton 1953), as do Caribs (Hodge and Taylor 1957) and people of the study village in Dominica. Trinidadians use the fruit to treat constipation and "heat" (Wong 1976). Jamaicans say that the fruit is "good for the blood" (Ausprey and Thornton 1953). Green papaya fruit is widely used among registered nurses in Jamaican hospitals as a topical dressing for chronic skin ulcers (Hewitt, et al. 2000). Pawpaw is reportedly used for hypertension in Trinidad (Wong 1976) and in Haiti (Weniger et al.1986). People of Montserrat mix grated pawpaw with milk to "quickly reduce blood pressure" (Brussel 1997:50). It seems possible that the concept of "pressure" (the folk illness) might exist among populations of other Caribbean islands. Though other Caribbean people may well use pawpaw for "high blood pressure" or "hypertension," they may also (or instead) use pawpaw for "pressure" as in Dominica. In Dominica, there is some overlap between the illness "pressure" and the biomedical condition "hypertension."

BUTTONS AND PRICKLE HEAT

Bwa Mawegans refer to small boils, such as those caused by localized **staphylo-coccal** (bacterial) infection—together with hives, pox, acne pimples, and any other small, inflamed spots—as "buttons." "Prickle heat" (prickly heat) is this tropical village's most common type of rash. Some Bwa Mawegans use the term "prickle heat," or simply "prickles" generically for any rash. To others, "prickles" is a synonym for "rash," of which "prickle heat" is one type. "Prickle heat" was a salient illness term in the freelist of "things they curing with bush medicine," whereas no one mentioned the terms "prickles" or "rash."

Though people recognize "buttons" and rashes such as "prickle heat" as separate entities, they are similar. Locals claim that both result from excess heat and dirty blood in the body. Furthermore, buttons and prickle heat require identical treatments. "Prickle heat" (rashes) and "buttons" are two of the terms that I collapsed into one freelist category after hearing Bwa Mawegans give three reasons for doing so during the pile sorting exercise. First, "buttons" and "prickle heat" share an etiology. Both result from excess heat and/or dirt inside the body. Secondly, buttons and prickle heat are both generalized presentations of inner dirt or heat because they pop up over large swaths of skin or the whole body (as opposed to boils, which appear in one concentrated lump). Finally, people treat buttons and prickle heat with the same remedies and procedures.

The first line of treatment for "buttons" or "prickle heat" is to consider what caused the patient's internal heat. Was it "dirts" inside the body, irritating it and causing "inflammation"? If this is the case, treatment may start with a "washout," or purgative treatment to clean out the body. Alternatively, did the patient's internal heat come from overexertion, or humoral heat from food or emotions? In this case, the patient drinks some "cooling" (*refrechmant* in Patwa). The difference between a "washout" and a "cooling" is mostly a matter of degree. "Coolings," like all Dominican humorally "cold" treatments, have some laxative action. The effect is mild however, as in consuming *pawpaw* (papaya). The primary function of "coolings" however is to either make one feel "cooler" or to quench one's thirst. For example, coconut water is extremely thirst quenching, and drinks made with *koukouli* (the most salient cooling) and *glorisida* make one feel cooler while reducing sweat output. "Washouts," on the other hand, function primarily as purgatives and emetics. These treatments allegedly have prompt, dramatic results. "Washouts" or "coolings" are not cures for "buttons" or "prickle heat" per se; rather, they are procedures to make one's body a worse host for the conditions. Due to the unpleasant nature of "washouts," villagers appear to prefer "coolings."[13] If villagers do not remember a specific incident in which they had a dirty cut or inhaled or ingested a lot of "dirts," they try a simple "cooling" or "refreshment" before taking a "washout." After "cleaning" or "cooling" the system, the next course of treatment for buttons or prickle heat is a topical application. Villagers freelisted "coolings" (drinks) along

---

[13]There are, however, certain villagers who take one of the more mild "washouts" (such as castor oil) once a month on a preventative basis.

with topical remedies, offering further evidence that this illness category overlaps the domains of "hot" illnesses and external illnesses.

Since inflammation is an underlying condition of people troubled with buttons or prickle heat, there is some overlap between treatments for buttons and inflammation, specifically the "cooling" drinks. Many of the bush cures for buttons and prickle heat have dual applications: one as a "cooling" drink and one as a topical treatment. For example, Bwa Mawegans crush *glorisida* leaves to make a bath or soak for prickle heat and buttons (as in Figure 8.1). This treatment is especially popular to alleviate infant rashes. However, as the infant soaks in the *glorisida* bath, the mother drips some of the bathwater into the baby's mouth. Most of the buttons/prickle heat treatments that people first identified during their freelists were not "cooling" drinks aimed at the internal inflammation, but preparations aimed at soothing dermatological symptoms (i.e., the skin eruptions). Even in cases like the *glorisida* example, people would generally list the topical application first, saying something like, "You bathe with *glorisida*, and you can drink it too."

The results for the buttons and prickle heat freelist are nearly identical to those for inflammation. This outcome occurred despite (1) the tendency to use topical remedies for skin eruptions, (2) tendency to use ingested palliatives for inflammation, and (3) Bwa Mawegan classification of inflammation as "hot," but buttons and prickle heat as overlapping the "hot" and "external" illness categories. As with inflammation, *koukoulí* is the most salient plant for buttons and prickle heat treatment.

Boils

In Bwa Mawego, the term "boil" generally refers to a large, swollen lump (over 1 inch in diameter), such as a cyst caused by a parasitic or bacterial infection. The term does not refer to small boils, such as those from infected hair follicles or staphylococcal infections (those are "buttons"). Boils can occur anywhere on the body. However, these large swellings tend to occur about the face, neck, and underarms. Like "buttons," boils are attributed to excess heat and dirt inside the body. Boils, like "buttons" and "prickle heat" are topical, or external manifestations of "heat." Thus, like "buttons," locals conceive of boils as part of both the "hot" and "external" illness domains. The treatments for boils are different from "buttons"/"prickle heat" treatments. Compared to "buttons" or rashes, Dominicans consider boils a concentrated (less generalized) manifestation of heat. Hence, they require strong remedies that "break the boils down" or "open up the boil."

MALESTOMAK—*Voucher Specimens*: MBQ178, UMO186417   Thirty-five percent of Bwa Mawegan adults listed *malestomak* as a treatment for boils, making *malestomak* this freelist's most salient response. The species (*Lepianthes peltata* (L.) Rafinesque[14]) is native to the American tropics. It is an herb with very large (35 cm) cordate, peltate leaves (see Figure 8.7) and pronounced nodes. The inflorescence is an **umbel** of five spikes. The shape of this inflorescence is no doubt the reason that

---

[14]There are five accepted scientific names for this species. The other four names are *Piper peltatum* L., *Pothomorphe peltata* (L.) Miq., *Heckeria peltatum* (L.) Kunth, and *Peperomia peltata* (L.) A.Dietr.

Figure 8.7 Malestomak
*(*Lepianthes peltata *(L.)*
Rafinesque)

Dominicans call *malestomak* "monkey's hand" elsewhere on the island (Honychurch 1986, Nicholson 1991). *Malestomak* grows in especially wet conditions such as ditches and by springs. Nicholson (1991) says the plant reaches two meters. I have never seen a malestomak much taller than one meter in or around Bwa Mawego.

Some Bwa Mawegans use *malestomak* as a headache treatment. For headaches, they warm one of the large leaves over a fire, put the leaf over their head, then wrap it around the scalp with a large scarf as a "hair tie." I have seen several people do this when they have a headache in conjunction with a head cold. The most common use for *malestomak* is as a plaster for boils. Bwa Mawegans either drip tallow candle wax on a boil-sized piece of the leaf, or cover the leaf piece with oil. They say any oil will work for this, but castor oil is best. They warm the greased or waxy leaf over a fire, then place the hot leaf over the boil. They repeat this process two to four times a day. They say that this treatment decreases pain in the boil and either brings the boil to a head so one can "burst it," or helps dissipate the "dirts" in the boil so that one can simply take a "washout" to get rid of the toxins.

In bioassays, several types of extracts of *malestomak* show antioxidant activity (Desmarchelier, Mongelli, et al. 1997). A chemical in *malestomak* leaf extract also scavenges **free radicals** and inhibits some cell damage (Desmarchelier, Barros, et al.1997). Extract of from *malestomak* leaves administered orally showed significant anti-inflammatory activity against **edema** (fluid accumulation) in rats (Desmarchelier, Slowing, and Ciccia 2000).

The Tikuna Indians of the Northwest Amazon make a tea with *malestomak* to induce abortions (Schultes and Raffauf 1990) and it is used in several parts of the Peruvian, Bolivian, and Brazilian Amazon region as anti-inflammatory, a fever reducer, and to treat external ulcers and local infections (Desmarchelier et al. 1997). Jamaicans (Ayensu 1981) and Caribs (Hodge and Taylor 1957) tie the plant around the head for headaches, as do Bwa Mawegans. The plant's Patwa name means "bad stomach." Neither Caribs nor Bwa Mawegans use *malestomak* for stomach problems. However, Haitians use the plant for stomach pain (Weniger et al. 1986). This use may occur on other French Creole speaking islands.

Conclusion to Hot Illnesses and Their Treatments

Any illness that involves warm, inflamed or swollen body tissue is reckoned a "hot" illness in Bwa Mawego. Hot illnesses also have to do with restricted internal movement due to swelling of veins or body tissues or clogs caused by dirt or feces. Constipation was not a salient illness in Bwa Mawegans' freelist of "things they curing with bush." Perhaps Bwa Mawegans do not regard constipation as an illness on its own. However, Bwa Mawegans clearly consider constipation to be a "hot" condition associated with several of the "hot" illnesses (especially boils, buttons, prickle heat, and inflammation). Treatments for "hot" illnesses are "cold." "Cold" bush medicines primarily involve either topical soothing or internal "free-ups" that noticeably reestablish internal flow by loosening the bowels or making one perspire.

EXTERNAL CONDITIONS AND THEIR TREATMENTS

Sprains

According to Bwa Mawegans, villagers sometimes sprain their wrists or shoulders while chopping wood or grabbing something (like a tree branch) to avoid a fall. From time to time men sprain their backs during agricultural labor. Still, when discussing sprains, most people bring up an ankle episode. Walking is Bwa Mawego's principal (and nearly only) form of transportation. A sprained ankle is thus particularly vexing. Sprains almost always take place on village paths or "tracks." Some of the village tracks are dangerous to negotiate because of root and rock obstacles. Even though villagers know almost every step of the local tracks, the tracks change after mudslides (small mudslides are common). Sometimes the outside edge of a track gives way while one is walking. Men carrying heavy bails of bay leaves or bananas are particularly at risk.

Sprains are humorally "neutral" injuries. It is thus interesting that treatments for sprains tend to be "hot." The most common treatments are topical rubs, the same treatments that Bwa Mawegans listed for rheumatism. People use the same rubs for rheumatism and sprains even though they regard sprains as "neutral" and rheumatism as "cold" (though the external/cold domains overlap). Bwa Mawegans note that a sprain, though "neutral" mirrors a "cold" condition because it leads to stiffness. "Hot" treatments in this case are also **prophylactic** in that they prevent any "cold" from entering and exacerbating the injury. In addition to using bush treatments, villagers immobilize the affected site by wrapping it in bindings or carrying it in a sling for a few days.

Descriptions and illustrations of bay oil, the most salient treatment for sprains, mentioned by 64% of village adults, is under the preceding rheumatism subheading.

Cuts and Sores

Though Bwa Mawegans recognize cuts and sores as two separate conditions, they constantly refer to them together when discussing bush medicine. Hence, I treated them as one wound category.

Bwa Mawegans listed cuts and sores as problems they "curing with bush medicine." However, wounds are one condition that Bwa Mawegans seem to avoid treating with bush medicine, if at all possible—especially if the cut is of considerable size or depth. Villagers value Western first-aid supplies such as topical antiseptics, antibiotic ointments, and bandages. They frequently seek first aid treatment from the local nurse, and from us anthropologists when we are in the village. Knowledge of bush treatments for cuts appears to be fading, or perhaps bush use for cuts was never prevalent. Over half of the village adults were unable to name a bush treatment for cuts or sores.

MALVINA, SAN DWAGÓ—*Voucher Specimens*: MBQ115, MBQ151, UMO185573, UMO185572   This plant (*Cordyline fruticosa* (L.) A. Chev.,[15] see Figure 8.8) that Bwa Mawegans call *malvina* and *san dwagó* in Patwa, and "malvina" in English was, by far, the most salient bush treatment that Bwa Mawegans listed for cuts and sores. In many cases, it was the only cut treatment that people could recall. This shrub has a single, narrow stem and reaches three meters (though the plants in Bwa Mawego are pruned back to two meters or less). The stem is textured with scars from earlier leaves. The leaves are linear-oblong (30–70 cm long, by 5–12 cm wide) and red to purple, or green to purple. Flowers are pale violet to pink and on terminal panicles. The species is native to Central Asia, India and Australia, but is now widely cultivated as an ornamental (Hoyos 1985). This plant propagates easily from cuttings. In Bwa Mawego, people plant *malvina* in their house gardens and around their yards as part of a hedge.

Malvina's only medicinal use in Bwa Mawego is for treating cuts and sores. For this, villagers first cut one leaf off the shrub. The undersides of *malvina* leaves contain minute gray specks of resin. Bwa Mawegans scrape the gray specks from the leaf with a knife, producing a sticky powder that they apply to cuts and sores. The treatment stops bleeding or oozing almost immediately and helps a scab to form.

There is little literature on medicinal use of this particular species. Trinidadians use the leaf to make a tea with which they treat amenorrhea (Wong 1976). Lewis and Elvin-Lewis (1977) report that species of the related *Dracaena* genus are the sources of "dragon's blood" resin which is used throughout the world, especially in Asia, to stop hemorrhages.

STOMACH CONDITIONS AND THEIR TREATMENTS

Worms[16]

According to local ethnophysiology, after one swallows food or drink, the substance passes from the mouth to the "troat," behind the lungs through the "troat pipe," and down into the "belly." The belly is not an organ, but the general term for the abdominal cavity, or as one informant put it, "The belly like a bag. It hold everything under your lungs until your ass." In the belly, the troat pipe channels the food into the stomach. The stomach is a bag that "pound up all what you eat," which then, bit by bit, squeezes portions of the food into the "worm bag."

All humans have a "worm bag," an organ specifically for worms. When infants are born, their worm bags are empty. However, besides living inside animals, worms live in—and lay invisible eggs in—the dirt. Babies acquire their initial worms by

---

[15]*Cordyline (Dracaena) terminalis* (L.) Kunth is a synonym for this species.

[16]For a more detailed description of Dominican and cross-cultural ethnophysiology and ethnopharmacology of worms, see Quinlan et al. 2002.

Figure 8.8 Malvina, *or* san dwagó *(Cordyline fruticosa (L.) A. Chev.)*

ingesting worm eggs when they inevitably suck and chew on their own dirty hands or other dirty objects. By the time a baby is a year old, worm eggs have hatched in his worm bag. Even a person who takes regular worm treatments maintains a worm supply by inadvertently ingesting small amounts of dirt (when gardening, on food, etc.) throughout his or her life.

All people have some worms, and for the most part, worms live in harmony with their human hosts. Many villagers feel that (as long as the worm bag is not overpopulated) worms are beneficial. They function in the digestive process to refine the food, turning it into rich blood, much the way that earthworms convert composting material to rich soil. Others, however, resent all worms as continual menaces—parasites that, despite creating some blood, mostly rob the body of nutrition.

The rich blood that the worms expel passes through the porous walls of the worm bag and into the belly. Blood collects at the bottom of the belly in a funnel-like organ and then filters through the liver. From the liver good, clean blood goes to the heart, and waste goes to the bowel.

Worms, like humans, produce gas as a by-product of digestion. This gas, like blood, passes through the worm bag walls and into the belly. Gas that collects in the belly can exit upward, through the "troat tube" (throat) or downward, through the anus, depending on which part of the belly it is nearer to begin with.

From a Dominican viewpoint, humans and worms have a symbiotic relationship. Humans should expect to have some internal worms at all times. Locals assert that worms, for the most part, are only dangerous or painful if they grow or multiply beyond the capacity of their worm bag. Outside of the worm bag, they steal nutrients from the host and begin to feed on other organs, primarily the stomach and "tripe" (intestines).

People attribute several symptoms to worm infestation. One symptom is excessive gas. A plethora of worms simultaneously digesting human food generates excess gas in the belly. "Gripes" or abdominal cramps are another symptom of worm infestation. Gripes result from too many worms stretching the worm bag, or worms outside of the worm bag feeding on other organs. Finally, seizures are sometimes attributed to extreme cases of worm infestation. Villagers call such a seizure a "fit" or "fix" of worms.

Ingestion of certain substances causes an overabundance of worms. Villagers suggest that milk and milk products, in particular, cause worms to thrive. They point to two phenomena as evidence for this claim. First, adults frequently experience stomach discomfort after eating dairy products.[17] Second, worms most often trouble young children who ingest more milk, and babies (under two) who drink (human) milk almost exclusively. Sweet foods may augment worm growth resulting in "fits" of worms.[18] Finally, eating dirt can introduce more worms and cause existing worms to grow and multiply. Hence, young children are at highest risk for worm infestation because they ingest more milk and tend to put dirty, possibly wormy things in their mouths.

Treatments for worms are humorally neutral. Dominicans allege that intestinal worms, like most other animals (including humans) share the neutral humoral status. This is one reason that humans make good hosts for the worms, as do their dogs, cats, and livestock. Bwa Mawegans take worm medications to either kill the worms or make them sleep. It is easier, they say, for the body to pass dead or sleeping worms.

SIME KONTWÁ—Voucher Specimens: MBQ23, UMO183860 *Sime knotwá* (*Chenopodium ambrosioides* L., Chenopodiaceae) (Figure 8.9) was the worm treatment with the highest salience value in this study.[19] Every informant included it in his or her freelist, and most people (73%) mentioned *sime kontwá* first. Some English common names for this species are "worm grass," "Mexican tea," and "fit weed" (Simpson 1962). In the French-speaking Caribbean, it is called *herbe à vers*, or *simén contra*. Dominicans refer to it as *sime kontwá* in Patois and English. *Sime kontwá* is a member of the Chenopodiaceae, the same family as spinach. *Sime kontwá* is a pantropical (Nicholson 1991), aromatic herb that is usually about 60 cm tall. Its leaves have short petioles, are lanceolate, and develop toothed edges with age. The flowers are globular, minute, and grow clustered on spikes. The stems become woody with age. *Sime kontwá* occurs in the forest and in cultivated zones throughout

---

[17]This is probably related to high levels of lactose intolerance within the population.

[18]Fits of worms I have observed may actually be diabetic seizures.

[19]Unlike the other illness sections in which freelist interviews were attempted with all resident adults, worm freelists were conducted with a quota sample of 30 (about one-quarter of village adults), stratified by age, sex and village location (see Quinlan et al. 2002)

Figure 8.9 Sime kontwá
*(*Chenopodium ambrosioides
L.)

the study area. However, in Bwa Mawego, people often transplant bushes to their yard or house garden.

Villagers drink a "bush tea" of *sime kontwá* fairly regularly. They make the decoction by breaking and dropping a branch about 25 cm long (this typically contains about 15–20 leaves), complete with twig, leaves and flowers, into approximately one liter of boiling water. They boil the herb for about one minute, until the water has a chartreuse tint to it. Half of the mothers in the study gave a small cup of *sime kontwá* "tea" to their children every morning (the amount of liquid depends on the body size of the child). Others prefer to give it once a week or so. More than half of the informants could not say exactly how often they drink a decoction of *sime kontwá*. They say they drink it from time to time, sometimes in the morning, sometimes to relax in the afternoon. If they feel a little stomach discomfort, or if they suspect that their worms are troubling them, they make themselves a cup of *sime kontwá* "bush tea." A number of people related that they drink *sime kontwá* "tea" until the bush by their house is nearly branchless. Then they drink other "bush teas" while their plant rejuvenates. People who drink the decoction regularly say that they never (or rarely) have worms in their stool because the drink "keeps the worms down" constantly. People who only drink *sime kontwá* when they feel worm symptoms say that dead and "sleeping" worms come out with their feces after one or two days.

Oil of chenopodium, which is distilled from *Chenopodium ambrosioides* is a pharmaceutical product used against tapeworms, roundworms, and hookworms. The active component, terpene ascaridole, makes up about 65% of the oil (Lewis and Elvin-Lewis, 1977). Extract from this plant is also active against the snail that transmits schistosomiasis (*Bulinus truncatus*) (Hmamouchi, Lahlou, and Agoumi 2000). The whole plant (Kapadia, et al. 1978) and the extracted oil of chenopodium (El-Mofty, et al. 1992) are carcinogenic to animals.

This species, *Chenopodium ambrosioides*, is used to treat intestinal worms throughout the Caribbean (Honychurch 1986). It is also a vermifuge in Mexico (Berlin and Berlin 1996), Guatemala (Booth, Johns, and Lopez-Palacois1993) and South America (Kainer and Duryea 1992, Schultes and Raffauf 1990).

Loose "Boweel" and Diarrhea

During the initial freelist of illnesses curable with bush medicine, Bwa Mawegans listed 'loose boweel' and diarrhea as two separate conditions. At that point, they indicated that diarrhea was "serious"—an intestinal flu that includes fevers and can lead to dehydration. "Loose boweel" is a condition that more often comes from eating something "a little bad," eating too many "cold" things, or from taking a washout. As one informant explained, "If you have a 'loose boweel,' then you go more often than you used to; but, diarrhea is sickness already." Later, when I conducted pile sorts with groups of informants, Bwa Mawegans insisted that I should treat "loose boweel" and diarrhea as one illness because the two conditions differ in degree, but not in kind. Further, the treatments for the two conditions are the same, only differing in the number of treatments that one might have to take.

Diarrhea can be either "hot" or "cold." For example, an intestinal flu with a fever is "hot" diarrhea. Diarrhea concurrent with pregnancy, menstruation, worry, or a hangover is also "hot," as these are hot conditions. People who come down with diarrhea after getting sunburned, laboring in a hot garden, or working with "hot" bay leaf have hot diarrhea. Conversely, people whose intestinal distress might result from a cold cause, such as a deep chill, fright, or ingesting "cold" substances have cold diarrhea.

Whether a person's diarrhea is of hot or cold origin is not important in terms of medication. All of the most salient diarrhea treatments are humorally neutral. Bwa Mawegans say that these treatments deal with the symptoms of diarrhea and by the time one already has diarrhea, the original cause is of secondary concern. If the first 3–4 common remedies are not enough, however, there are lesser-known treatments that people use specifically for hot or cold diarrheas. Only eight villagers (out of 108) listed more than one of the specific "hot" or "cold" treatments. Most people make guava leaf tea immediately (this herb is discussed in the following section). Many residents add cloves or slices of ginger rhizome with the guava leaf tea.

Goiyav—*Voucher Specimen*: MBQ62, UMO183852   Tea made from the leaves of the "guava" tree, or *goiyav* in Patwa (*Psidium guajava* L., Myrtaceae family), is the village's most salient diarrhea treatment (see Figure 8.10). Seventy-nine adults (73%) mentioned it in their freelists. This small tree is native to the American tropics (Brussell 1997). The tree has opposite rough oblong leaves. The flowers are large (2 cm wide) and white with five petals. The ripe fruit is yellow and round, 4–5 cm

Figure 8.10 Goiyav *or Guava (*Psidium guajava *L.)*

wide, and contains pink pulp and numerous seeds. In the village, these trees are widely cultivated for their fruit. They also grow in the nearby Littoral Forest.

Bwa Mawegans say that they plant and keep guava trees for their fruit. However, they use the leaves for diarrhea, vomiting, and nausea. Some people say that the tea is best made with new, young leaves.

Villagers boil about three guava leaves per cup of boiling water for a couple of minutes. They drink a cup of this decoction as often as they feel is necessary. This may be every hour for a severe case of diarrhea, or just once for a slight case of "loose boweel."

An infusion made with guava leaves reduces gastrointestinal propulsion in mice and increases intestinal water absorption in rats (Almeida et al. 1995). Guava leaf infusion also exhibits anti-microbial activity (Malcolm and Sofowora 1969).

A number of tropical American peoples use guava leaves to treat stomach ailments. In addition to Bwa Mawegans and Caribs (Hodge and Taylor 1957) on Dominica, Trinidadians (Wong 1976), Belizeans (Arvigo and Balick 1998), Haitians (Weniger et al. 1986), Mexican Yucatec Mayans (Eugene Anderson, personal communication) and Highland Mayans (Berlin and Berlin 1996), the Miskitu and Sumu in Central America (Coe and Anderson 1999), and the Amazonian Tikuna (Schultes and Raffauf 1990) all use infusions of guava leaves for diarrhea. Public health workers throughout the developing world advise treatment with guava leaves. For example, while doing ethnographic research with healers, Barbara Anderson (Loma Linda University Department of International Public Health) learned that public health workers routinely recommend guava leaves for diarrhea in Honduras, Jamaica, Thailand, and Cambodia (personal communication).

Vomiting and Upset Stomach

Vomiting and upset stomach is another category that I combined at villagers insistence. Originally Bwa Mawegans listed "upset stomach" (nausea) and "vomiting" as two things they could cure with bush medicine. As with diarrhea and loose boweel, villagers explained that vomiting and an upset stomach are different in degree, not in kind. These conditions might be triggered by a "hot" or "cold" event, or by something neutral, such as rotten food or worms. The treatments are all "neutral."

All of the salient remedies for upset stomachs and vomiting are also common for alleviating either worms or diarrhea and "loose boweel". I asked Bwa Mawegans if the inclusions of *twef* and *sime kontwa* (both worm medications) were because the upset stomach was a symptom of 'worm troubles'. They indicated that in addition to deworming, *twef*, and *sime kontwa* have stomach-settling effects.

TWEF—*Voucher Specimen*: MBQ14, UMO183936   *Aristolochia trilobata* L., or *twef* in Patois (see Figure 8.11) is the highest ranked upset stomach treatment, and the second-most salient worm remedy in Bwa Mawego. *Twef* is a vine that grows in bushy coastal areas and secondary forests throughout the Caribbean and southern Central America (Honychurch 1986). It has dark green, glossy, leathery leaves that are in three lobes and tubular ivory to pale green flowers. The vine climbs up trees in the Littoral Forest around the study site. Residents of Bwa Mawego transplant the vines to their yards where they typically grow up the sides of homes and outhouses.

Villagers use *twef* to settle upset stomachs and for worms, in the form of a leaf infusion. Village rum shops also sell shots (or "shoots") of "twef rum" (a **tincture** of approximately four *twef* leaves soaked in a fifth of cask rum). Many men in the village say they prefer to take their *twef* with rum. For the "tea," or decoction, villagers boil about half a *twef* leaf per cup of water for a few minutes (until the water changes color), then they let the leaves steep in the water while the tea cools. Adults drink one cup of the decoction. Children take less, according to their body size. Villagers say that a single dose of *twef* (cup of the infusion or shot of the rum decoction) calms upset stomachs immediately. They also say that one dose of *twef* usually kills all worms that are "outside" of one's worm bag, although people who suspect they have a particularly bad infestation may take a second dose on the following day. Worms are said to appear in the feces within one and a half days of the first dose. Children under five years rarely drink *twef* because parents prefer to give them something milder. Villagers say that one "must add plenty of sugar" to this tea and let it cool for a long time. This way one can drink it quickly, "like a shoot of rum." They say that even this way, *twef* tastes terrible. Indeed, *twef* "bush tea" is so awful that parents force their children to drink it as a punishment for speaking rudely.

Several villagers noted that, as a worm remedy, *twef* worked at least as well—in fact more quickly—than other medications. However, they prefer not to use it because of its bitter taste. In addition, they say that something that tastes so bad and works so quickly is obviously very strong. They believe *twef* might make one weak if taken often.

Aristolochic acids in this species are renal toxins in animals and humans (Lajide, Escoubas, and Mizutani 1993). Aristolochic acids extracted from *Aristolochi albida* (a Nigerian species) shows "extremely strong" feeding-deterrent and larval growth-inhibition activity in bioassays (Lajide et al. 1993). This lends credence to their potential efficacy against parasites. However, aristolochic acids are carcinogenic, causing stomach cancers, and atrophy in the lymph glands (DeSmet 1992). For that reason, *Aristolochia* species are banned in European medicines because of the dangers associated with aristolochic acids (Zhu and Phillipson 1996).

Nicaraguan Miskitu and Ulwa Indians use this species for digestive problems, as well as for bites, respiratory disorders, and as a general tonic (Coe and Anderson 1999). On the island of Marie Galante, *twef* is used as an emetic in case of poisoning (Honychurch 1986). In Trinidad, this vine is used for diabetes, hypertension,

Figure 8.11 Twef
*(*Aristolochia trilobata *L.)*

dysmenorrhea, as an abortifacient, and for snakebites (Wong 1976). It is also used for snakebites in tropical South America (Millspaugh 1974). In fact, almost all of the species in this genus are used in the countries in which they grow as remedies for poisonous snakebites. There are no poisonous snakes in Dominica, however (Coborn 1991).

9/Applications
and Conclusions

Sick residents of Bwa Mawego have a multilayered system of healthcare options available to them from the professional, folk, and popular sectors of their society. They can seek professional-sector, biomedical care from a nurse at the local health center, from nurses and physicians at a clinic in a larger village (a 45 minute drive away), or they can travel to a hospital and pharmacies in the capital.

Studies of medical systems often find that individuals (especially in the developing world) use traditional folk or popular medicine over biomedicine because traditional medicine is more convenient, familiar, and trusted. That is, traditional medicine is accessible and acceptable whereas biomedicine may not be (Anyinam 1987). As a conclusion, I apply information about Bwa Mawego's ethnomedical system to public health issues. In this process the sectors of healthcare are considered in terms of (1) barriers to accessibility and acceptability that deter villagers from using the healthcare sector, and (2) unique health benefits that the sector offers. These conclusions come from detailed data gathered in one Dominican village. They are, however, inductions that are generalizable to rural populations throughout the Caribbean and Latin America, and applicable to many of the world's rustic communities.

The assumption underlying this chapter is that individuals in Bwa Mawego (or anywhere) make rational healthcare decisions by analyzing the costs and benefits of using (or not using) the various medical options in their surroundings. When people decide how to deal with a health problem, they assess their health risk against the risk involved in their treatment alternatives. For example, if an individual, Tom, cuts himself and assesses his laceration as particularly "bad" or risky, he is willing to undergo costs in time, money, and additional pain to get sutures. If Tom does not assess the laceration as "bad," he might bandage it on his own. Health issues and people's reactions to them, however, are influenced by numerous social and economic influences besides the particular injury or illness (Gabe 1998). For instance, if Tom has little job security, he might not risk missing work to get sutures on a laceration that he probably would have sutured had he cut himself on his day off. Or, if Tom cuts himself in a particularly embarrassing or foolish way, he might (especially if he lives in a small town) forgo getting sutures (that he would have otherwise obtained) simply because he doesn't want to discuss his injury. Here, Tom's perceived risk to his reputation outweighs the risk of his injury. People make rational decisions about their health care based on their knowledge of the illness and possible treatments, their assessment of risk, and factors that compensate for risk, such as accessibility and acceptability of treatment options.

Cross-culturally, people evaluate their need for specialist care based on their perceived ability to self-treat. Hence, if a home treatment is reckoned effective *and* it is accessible and acceptable, people will always choose it. When there is little risk, then home medicine is the most acceptable option. If a home treatment is reckoned insufficient, however, people will bother to seek out a specialist's attention, in spite of physical, economic and social inconveniences. Tom, in the above example, may be well-equipped to treat a deep cut with first aid at home; however, if he has a finger dangling by a fleshy thread, he will probably seek surgery regardless of social and economic risks or inconvenience. In a Dominican example, there are common herbs growing around Bwa Mawego that are very effective against intestinal worms (Quinlan et al. 2002). It is extremely rare for a Bwa Mawegan to seek biomedical care for worms; bush medicine is the most accessible and acceptable healthcare option. In contrast, people in Bwa Mawego say that no bush medicine is as excellent a painkiller as the common biomedical tablets: aspirin, acetaminophen, and ibuprofen.[1] Although some residents are aware of bush headache treatments, for instance, knowledge of these medicines is dwindling. Even people who know bush headache remedies use bush treatments only when they cannot obtain "pain tablets," or they use bush medicine in addition to the tablets. In this example, biomedical pharmaceuticals are not the most accessible treatment, but their use is the most acceptable therapy.

PROFESSIONAL BIOMEDICAL CARE

Healthcare delivery programs, such as Project HOPE (Health Opportunities for People Everywhere), the World Health Organization, and the Dominican Ministry of Health seek to make biomedicine increasingly accessible and acceptable to people who would benefit from biomedical advantages (such as inoculations, or treatment and control of contagious or chronic diseases). An effective way to assess local healthcare delivery is to use a two-pronged approach that addresses (1) sociomedical factors such as cost and logistics (i.e. accessibility), and (2) ethnomedical factors such as etiological concepts and curing roles. Together, these issues indicate culture-wide areas of acceptability (or possible rejection) of biomedicine delivery (Kroeger 1983).

Several barriers to professional biomedical care present themselves in Bwa Mawego. First, it is often difficult for sick people to walk or find a ride to a clinic. Second, even though office visits are free of charge, "transport" fare from the village to a medical facility is expensive. Third, biomedical examination compromises residents' sense of privacy. Fourth, Bwa Mawegans are suspicious of village outsiders. Moreover, many villagers fear a doctor's power. Apparently, the perceived effective-

---

[1]Aspirin, acetaminophen, and ibuprofen are sold over-the-counter at Roseau pharmacies. However, customers must approach the pharmacist and specify the name and quantity of the medication they want to buy. It may happen, but I have never heard of a Bwa Mawego resident obtaining analgesics by talking with a pharmacist. Rather, they get the pills from the health center and from family and friends.

ness and ease of home treatment with bush medicine usually outweighs the costs of seeking professional medical consultation in most cases.

The aforementioned barriers to biomedicine fall into two categories in rural Dominica: transportation and trust. Travel across the terrain is difficult, which is a major reason the country is as poor as it is in the first place. Improvements in public transportation would doubtless make a large impact on healthcare availability. However, this development is easier said than done in economically disadvantaged regions. Bringing a nurse into the community has certainly increased the availability of biomedical care. It was, however, not a giant step. The village nurse has scant equipment and supplies and limited ability to deal with serious medical cases. However, she has done much in the way of public health outreach/education, and preventative medicine (e.g., vaccinations and contraceptives for women with health risks).

Perhaps the most important benefit the local nurse has offered has been to put a kind face on biomedicine. As mentioned before, lack of trust in clinicians impedes Bwa Mawegan use of biomedical services. This is an area where healthcare delivery might be improved with very little cost. With a small amount of outreach to the medical community, the social environment of health centers and hospitals might be improved. Healthcare providers might adjust their bedside manner when dealing with rural people, thereby making biomedicine a more acceptable option to them. Nurses, the practitioners with whom Dominicans usually interact, are in positions of power in Dominica. Often nurses grow up in rural villages themselves, then, with hard work, rise to become some of the most educated people in the population. Some nurses regularly display curt, condescending, intolerant, and generally impolite attitudes to "country people" who come to them for help. Their attitudes probably stem in part from frustrations with villagers' medical beliefs and health-related behaviors. However, a nurse who alienates rural residents from medical services only perpetuates the very system that frustrates the nurse. Nurses must strive to treat every patient (even alcoholics, mothers who refuse to vaccinate their children, etc.) with respect, or else these people defiantly reject biomedical advice altogether.

Nurses and physicians alike should expect patients to have ideas about health that are different from biomedical ones, and they should adjust the way they explain things so that the patient feels comfortable with his treatment (see pages 124–126 for specific suggestions under the subheading Bush Medicine's Influence on Biomedical Care later in this chapter). Clinicians who could maintain a demeanor that is professional, yet welcoming, flexible, and trustworthy could go a long way toward improving practitioner-patient relations and easing patients' intimidation to use biomedicine.

FOLK HEALING

Within Bwa Mawego's folk sector, villagers can seek out magicoreligious healing from priests and obeah men. Bwa Mawegans view this type of healing as most appropriate for illnesses attributed to sorcery (i.e., obeah or "witches"). Folk sector medicine is thus a last resort in this village. Although people in Bwa Mawego perpetually express concern about the *possibility* of sorcery, actually *accusing* a friend or neighbor of employing sorcery is a serious matter. Hence, Bwa Mawegans always self-treat with bush medicines and seek professional biomedical help before they concede that a fellow villager employed "evil" to cause the condition.

From an applied medical anthropological view, Bwa Mawegans are fortunate to have supportive healers in the folk sector who do not detract from villagers' interaction with the biomedical community. Across the world, many poor, remote communities, much like Bwa Mawego, have resident folk healers. In villages with folk healers, people tend to visit their healer-neighbors after determining that they need expert therapy. They thereby delay biomedical intervention at sometimes-crucial points in an illness. Bwa Mawego has no resident folk healer. Thus, folk medical practitioners offer Bwa Mawegans no logistic advantage. They are no closer to Bwa Mawego than professional biomedical services. Residents typically do not go to a priest or obeah man until they have already received biomedical attention.

Bwa Mawegans dislike having to seek any expert medical care; however, they seek care from the professional sector more readily than from the folk sector. Even though Bwa Mawegans are leery of physicians, they are even more hesitant to concede that their illness is a personalistic one (caused by obeah or "witches"). Because personalistic illness involves intravillage blaming and conflict, a resident always hopes that a physician will be able to identify a (naturalistic) cause of a discomfort, making folk treatment unnecessary. Only when "doctor science" fails or works incompletely or too slowly, do Bwa Mawegans seek magicoreligious healing.

Above all, folk healers' rituals increase a Bwa Mawegan supplicant's confidence that God, Jah, is on his or her side. If nothing else, healers of this sector must offer the sufferer a psychological advantage.

BUSH MEDICINE

Within the popular sector, Bwa Mawegans treat health complaints at home with bush medicine. Here, in conclusion, I discuss two implications of bush medicine for the people of Bwa Mawego. First, I address how knowledge of bush medicine (i.e., bush medical theory) affects local acceptance of and adherence to biomedical courses of therapy. I offer some related suggestions for West Indian biomedical healthcare providers. Secondly, I address the implications of bush medical knowledge for the general health of the study community.

Bush Medicine's Influence on Biomedical Care

The way that Bwa Mawegans conceive of body functions and malfunctions determines their course of illness treatment. Local ethnophysiology also influences patients' understanding of biomedical treatments. The bush medical view of the body does not always coincide with biomedical understanding of the body. When dealing with medical professionals, deeply held cultural notions surrounding bush medicine may cause a patient misunderstandings and poor adherence to prescribed biomedical treatment regimens.

From a patient's perspective, medicine is more effectual and reliable with some understanding and assurance of the treatment's purpose. For patients to be satisfied with a biomedical experience, comply with a treatment regimen, and return for follow-up examination, they require knowledge about the basics of their diagnosis and the reason for using a treatment in the prescribed manner. As was demonstrated in Trinidad, clinicians must present information so that the patient comprehends what his diagnosis and treatment are; otherwise, patients are dissatisfied and alienated from their own treatment (Phillips 1996). Patient understanding is especially important where biomedical care is seen as foreign and somewhat suspect, as in rural Dominica. It is therefore advisable that West Indian healthcare providers learn about their patients' concepts and ways of talking about the body in order to better communicate with patients. Clinicians who explain therapies in ways that make sense to their patients, can increase their patients' trust and compliance. I condense Dominican body image below and offer some suggestions.

Dominicans regard cleanliness and balance as the foundations of proper body function and health maintenance. Locals assert that "dirts" enter the body through body pores and orifices. The "dirts" clog veins and body organs and pollute the inner body. Likewise, feces that rests in the bowel for too long blocks body functions and poisons a person's body. Internal "dirts" create irritation and an overall humorally "hot" body condition Bwa Mawegans call "inflammation." To avoid inflammation, Bwa Mawegans keep their skin clean so that "dirts" can escape through unhampered perspiration. They also keep their insides "clean" by ingesting herbal laxatives and emetics. A clinician who finds that the treated patient is suffering from "heat," "dirts," or "inflammation" may want to inquire about the type and amount of laxative or "cold" bush medicines a patient is using. Further, the joined concepts of "dirts" and "inflammation" are not far from the biomedical notion of "infection." Health care providers might explain infections and antibiotic use in these terms. A Bwa Mawegan woman named Jeanette once visited me after seeing a physician at the regional health center for a painful, red, swollen ankle. Jeanette urged me, "Look in your books there and see what these tablets he gave me do." I looked at her medicine's label and at my books. I told her that she had antibiotics. She asked what that meant. I (awkwardly) tried to explain bacterial infection and antibiotic use. Jeanette stared at me blankly until suddenly she raised her eyebrows and said, "So, these tablets are to clean my blood to make the inflammation in my leg pass?" "Exactly!" I said.

Bwa Mawegans emphasize the importance of maintaining a balanced body "system." Balance is necessary regarding how much blood one has; how often one eats, drinks and eliminates waste; the size of one's intestinal parasite load; and the hot/cold humoral state of one's body.

The local hot/cold humoral system is particularly important to health maintenance because "hot" and "cold" ailments constitute some of the most common health complaints. In addition, some conditions are humorally neutral. Likewise, Bwa Mawegans regard bush medicines as humorally "hot," "cold," and neutral. The Dominican system is not a humoral system in which people know the "hot" or "cold" quality of a plant through mere tradition or memorization of that plant's quality. Rather, people appear to assign a humoral quality based on the effect that the plant has on the human body. People explain the plant's effect (and ascribe a hot/cold/neutral quality) in terms of the internal logic of the ethnomedical system. Dominicans thus describe a plant with expectorant qualities as a "hot" plant, because it alleviates a cough, a "cold" condition. Rural Dominicans ascribe hot, cold, or neutral values to prescribed pharmaceuticals using the same logic, according to what illness the medication treats.

There are healthcare implications for peoples' assignment of hot/cold/neutral values to medicines. If a Dominican recognizes his illness as "hot," he or she will assume that his prescribed medication is "cold." One village woman, Mary, was given ampicillin for a very inflamed, infected dog bite on her calf. Mary told me that ampicillin must be "cold" because her wound was so "hot." The ampicillin was quickly effective against Mary's infection, which bolstered her belief that ampicillin was "very cold." Six weeks later, Mary took her son to the health center because of his bad cough, a humorally "cold" condition. Mary's son was diagnosed with pneumonia and, like his mother, received ampicillin. Mary was reluctant to give her child the supposedly "cold" medication for fear that ampicillin would worsen his already "cold" condition. She told me, "the doctor must have made a mistake." Such predicaments have been described in Latin America (Harwood 1971, Logan 1973). In this case, I intervened by telling Mary that I thought that doctors could listen with a stethoscope or look at X-rays and find dangerous concentrations of "inflammation" in the lungs even before the heat spreads to the outside parts of the body (Mary's son had no fever, which was why Mary regarded the illness as "cold" rather than "hot"). My explanation may not have been the best one; however, it worked in that Mary ended up following the doctor's directions with confidence.

Whereas most New World hot/cold humoral systems classify all illness and treatments as hot or cold, the Dominican medical system offers an escape from the hot/cold dichotomy: neutral conditions and neutral medications (i.e., reckoned "not hot or cold"). Healthcare workers may want to make use of this concept whenever possible. Neutral medications target areas that residents associate with a particular health problem. For example, Bwa Mawegans recognize two kinds of diarrhea: one with a "hot" etiology, and another caused by "cold." Bwa Mawegans drink guava leaf bush tea to treat both types of diarrhea. Guava leaf is neither "hot" nor "cold"— it simply calms the bowels. It might help a clinician to tell patients that he or she views the medication she is prescribing as neither hot nor cold, but that many doctors have seen it work well against the patient's particular ailment. Assignment of a neutral value may not work with all medications because residents, like Mary in the previous example, may have strong preconceived humoral notions about the medication or their condition. Nevertheless, healthcare workers might often use the local neutral concept successfully.

Anthropologist Michael Logan notes that it is improbable that a physician (or nurse), in the course of infrequent office visits, might change a patient's deeply engrained belief in humoral medicine. It is thus more pragmatic for health workers to (1) accept that their patients think in humoral terms, and (2) work within the humoral medical system (Logan 1973).

I follow Logan (1973) in recommending that physicians *briefly* interview each patient about the patient's preconceptions about the presenting illnesses. Asking a patient, for example, how he or she thinks the illness was contracted (to check for a hot, cold, or other folk etiology) likely adds a minute or less to a medical examination. However, this inquiry allows a medical caregiver to construct a regimen and explanation that satisfy the principles and goals of the practitioner and the patient.

Bush Medicine as Primary Care

There is no doubt that bush medicines are accessible and acceptable. Self-treatments are often immediately obtainable, free, and allow Bwa Mawegans to maintain privacy and regulate the strength of their own medicines. Anyone unsure about how to treat oneself or one's children can seek advice from a trusted neighbor or kinsperson.

Further, Bwa Mawegans are confident that bush medicines are helpful because the same medications have been used in Bwa Mawego for generations.

Do Bwa Mawegans sell themselves short by heavy reliance on bush medicine instead of biomedicine? The answer to that question depends on how well bush treatments work. There is ample reason to believe that bush medicine offers rural Dominicans a practical, functional, and curative form of primary care. Not only is bush medicine convenient, but there are two indications that bush treatments are biologically therapeutic. First of all, Bwa Mawego is the sort of community that typically uses pharmacologically active plants. Furthermore, the salient medicinal plants thus far identified in Bwa Mawego demonstrate possible efficacy.

Ethnobotanists have identified commonalties in places where people use medicinal plants with significant pharmacological activity. These settings share three features: (1) a cultural mechanism for generation-to-generation transmission of ethnopharmacological knowledge, (2) a floristically diverse environment, and (3) residence in an area over many generations (Balick and Cox 1996:39–40). These characteristics all exist in Bwa Mawego. First, the village is small and everyone has many kin ties and access to kin from all living generations. Many people live in extended family compounds where ethnopharmacological knowledge can pass easily across generations. Second, the village lies within a region of tremendous botanical diversity. And third, Bwa Mawegans have been in the same ecological zone for about nine generations (most can trace their ancestry back to descendents of the early nineteenth century village founders). Bwa Mawego is thus typical of a community where species used in popular medicine are pharmacologically active.

Bwa Mawego has thirty-two particularly salient bush medicines (in Table 8.2 listed by illness, and listed by species in Appendix C). These medicines all seem to be plausible bioactive therapies. Those bush remedies mentioned in the literature for their crosscultural use or their chemical constituents appear to be useful for the conditions or symptoms they treat in Bwa Mawego. Bush medicines, hence, form viable alternatives to biomedical pharmaceuticals in their own right.

Using bush medicine may provide a therapeutic bonus beyond its convenience and pharmacological value. Indeed, people who self-treat with bush medicine may, by maintaining control of their own treatments, have better functioning immune systems than people who directly seek professional treatment and people who do not use any treatment.

There is a relationship between one's sense of personal control and one's level of stress (Funch and Marshall 1984, Thoits 1995). For example, even though we know that travel by car is more dangerous than air travel, many of us feel much greater stress flying than driving because as an airplane passenger we feel no control over our trip. The degree of power or control one feels over one's life circumstances is termed a **locus of control** (Rotter 1966). A person who has an *external* locus of control feels that forces (people or luck) outside of the person's realm of control determine his fate, whereas a person with an *internal* locus of control feels that one's own actions largely determine one's circumstances. The more internalized one's locus of control is, the less stress one is likely to experience. This relationship has been demonstrated in various areas of life such as marriage (Barnet 1990) and work (Hartl 1996, Rahim and Psenicka 1996).

Several researchers have identified a relationship between stress and illness (Hamburg, Elliot, and Parron 1982, Steptoe 1991, Compas and Boyer 2001). Highly stressed undergraduate students, for instance, are more likely to seek treatment for physical complaints than less stressed students (Manuck, Hinrichsen, and Ross 1975). Individuals with preexisting diseases have relapses in response to stress (Trimble and Wilson-Barnet 1982). And stressed individuals are at increased risk of catching new diseases. A study that assessed healthy subjects for their degree of psychological stress then exposed each subject to a cold virus, identified an association between stress and decreased resistance to (i.e., increased risk of) respiratory illness (Cohen, Tyrrell, and Smith 1991). In older adults, negative (stressful) social interactions are associated with elevated stress hormones, increased cardiovascular activity, and depressed immune function, whereas supportive social interactions are associated with the opposite profile (Seeman 2000). Mark Flinn (1999), in his 14-year study of Bwa Mawegan children, finds ties between stress and illness. Stress influences children's immune response. Children that suffer from chronic stress due to long-term troubles in their family environment show suppressed immunity measured by various immune factors.

Research shows that a person who feels in control over his or her life or his or her situation is better able to fight off and resist illness than a person who feels that his fate is in someone else's hands (McCubbin 2001). The increased risk of illness that comes with lack of control is, in part, is tied to stress. A study of 35–55 year olds of one community found that people with external locus of control experienced more stress and had higher levels of reported illness than individuals with an internal locus of control (Horner 1996). On the job, for example, stressful, demanding work situations tend to lead to poor health; however, people with high control over their job or work tasks have significantly lower levels of illness than workers with less control (Karasek 1990, Schaubroeck 2001). Our bodies have an intricate network of neural and molecular connections that result in a feedback relationship between the brain and the immune system (i.e., stress leads to illness and illness leads to stress). The brain and immune system function such that psychological dimensions of a stressful situation, including a person's ability to control the stressor influence a person's biological stress response (Dantzer 2001). So, for example, Brosschot and colleagues (1998) find that men with a low perception of control in a stressful situation have reductions in their immune cells, while men perceiving high control have an increased number of immune cells.

If an external locus of control leads to stress, and stress leads to compromised immune function, then feeling marginalized and uncomfortable with the professional culture of biomedicine, as Bwa Mawegans do, must be unhealthy. When dealing with conditions that are beyond the scope of bush medical treatment, Bwa Mawegans doubtless have highly external locus of control over illness, as do other marginalized populations in Haiti and Appalachia, for example (Coreil and Marshall 1982). However, Bwa Mawegans use bush medicine, not biomedicine, to deal with the vast majority of their illnesses.Bush medicine must give Bwa Mawegans an internal locus of control.[2]

Health care using home remedies should serve as a booster to a person's immune system. Because of the feedback relationship between a person's psychological

---

[2]I assess Bwa Mawego's health locus of control from many ethnographic interviews, in which informants told me that they can take care of themselves, how well bush medicine works, that they hardly ever need to go to the doctor, and so on. Evaluation with a formal instrument such as the Multidimensional Health Locus of Control scale (Wallston, Wallston, and Devaellis 1978) would clarify this issue.

outlook and his immune function, the mere availability of bush medicine may render the population somewhat more resistant to disease. The bush medical tradition (1) gives individuals the ability to self-treat, (2) does not stress a Bwa Mawegan the way that reliance on "doctor science" does, and (3) may internalize Bwa Mawegan locus of control regarding most illness. For the most part, bush medicines appear to be biologically active for the illnesses Bwa Mawegans treat. It follows that, in cases in which bush medicines are as effective—or nearly as effective—as pharmaceutical medications obtainable through a clinic visit, a rural Dominican's choice to self-medicate with bush may be his or her most therapeutic option. Thus, a Bwa Mawegan (like any of us) only seeks professional biomedical help in cases when an illness appears beyond the scope of home treatment.

In terms of frequency, self-treatment within the popular sector must be the world's dominant domain of health care. Yet the sector remains poorly understood worldwide. Bwa Mawego's strong tendency and preference to self-administer bush medicines demonstrates the importance of more research on medicine of the popular sector. Studies of home remedies may yield discoveries of herbal medicines and philosophies that could benefit many. Data about the health-related views of "nonexperts" in a population gives a broader understanding and example of the constant human battle to control one's physical condition. Finally, learning a society's common views of the body and health care yields information that health-care workers can use to tailor their patients' treatments in the most mutually acceptable manner.

Bush Medicine's Future

How will the future impact Bwa Mawego's bush medicine? This society is undergoing rapid economic and cultural adjustments in the twenty-first century. There are several agents of change that might threaten or augment Bwa Mawegans' knowledge of bush medicine. First, villagers are beginning to rely on cash crops and chemical herbicides. Over time, these practices may reduce local biodiversity and access to medicinal plants that are currently extant near the village. Recently, Stepp and Moerman (2001) revealed that medicinal plants often come not from primary forests, but from secondary growth (e.g., weeds) in disturbed areas. Indeed, though Dominicans do forage medicinal plants from the primary forest, their 32 most *salient* medicinal plant species are all either weeds (50%) or cultivated species (50%). It makes sense that weeds and cultivated plants would be very salient because these are the plants that villagers come across repeatedly in their daily lives. The question is, will ethnobotanical weeds become scarce in the village if use of chemical herbicides becomes the norm? If medicinal species become inaccessible, villagers' memories of the plants' uses will surely also diminish. Furthermore, villagers may become less focused on (and familiar with) weed species (now used for medicine) as they adopt a chemical weeding practice involving standing and spraying and drop the practice of bending down close to plants and actually touching them to weed.

There are also religious issues that may affect local medical practice. Catholicism is becoming less important due to the loss of a resident priest in the neighboring village (traditionally priests have a curing role). Meanwhile other religions are gaining acceptance. One of those religions, Rastafarianism—which is particularly popular with young adults in Bwa Mawego—emphasizes self-sufficiency via reliance on nature. Rastafarianism may revitalize the community's old traditions and general knowledge of bush medicine.

Some other aspects of acculturation may counter use of bush medicine. Already the last midwife is dead, leaving no bush medical specialist in Bwa Mawego. The village now has a full-time nurse for its local health center. Will increased exposure to biomedical practice change villagers' use of bush medicine? The village is gaining plumbing, a resurfaced road, and a new, more accessible secondary school in a larger village 45 minutes away. How will these major changes effect the village in general and bush medicine in particular? Will Bwa Mawegans abandon their traditional medicine as alternative forms of health care become increasingly available? Or will they adopt a syncretic medical model? The consequences of acculturation on bush medicine will make for interesting long-term observation.

Appendix A

TABLE A   PLANTS MENTIONED IN FREELISTS

Species Taxon	Common Name*	Medicinal Use	Plant Part	Preparation	Hum**	ID#***
Algae, marine spp.	sea moss (E), limu dou mer (P)	sprain	whole plant	poultice	N	
Aloe vera	aloz, haloz (E), lalue (P)	inflammation, constipation	leaf	crush and drink	C	sight record
Ambrosia hispida	wormbush (E)/set vil (P)	worms, gripes	all but root	"tea"	N	183862
Ambrosia hispida	wormbush (E)/set vil (P)	swelling	whole plant	poultice	N	183946
Annona muricata	soursop (E)/kouasol (P)	inflammation, stops overheating, gas, helps you sleep	leaf	"tea"	C	183835
Aristolochia trilobata	three-leaf (E)/twef (P)	worms, upset stomach	leaf	"tea"	N	183936
Begonia hirtella	losei (P)	cold	leaf	"tea"	H	186373
Cannabis sativa	kali, ganja, marihuana, sensi (E) kali, zeb (P)	asthma, cough	leaf	"tea"	H	sight record
Capraria biflora	island tea (E)/di te payi (P)	pressure	all but root	"tea"	C	186359
Cardiospermum microcarpum	bata pesi (P)	red eyes, prickle heat, cooling	all but root	"tea," wash	C	186364
Carica papaya	papay (P), pawpaw (E)	pressure, inflammation	fruit	"tea," eat	C	sight record
Cassia occidentales	cafe mocha (E)/cafe zepient (P)	sprains, swelling	seed oil	poultice	C	183945
Cayaponia americana	gwinad (P)	vomiting, loose bowel	fruit	"tea"	N	185568
Cecropia schreberiana	bwa kano (P)	pressure	young leaf	"tea"	C	185566
Cestrum megalophyllum	mi wet (P)	boil	leaf	"tea"	C	185565
Chaptilia nutans	dandilion (E)/do bla and fei do bla (P)	boils	leaf	plaster	C	186363
Chaptilia nutans	dandilion (E)/do bla and fei do bla (P)	buttons, prickle heat, pox, and laxative/ purgative	whole plant	"tea"	C	186363
Chenopodium ambrosoides	worm bush (E)/sime cotwa (P)	worms, stomach gripes, mysterious	all but root	"tea"	N	183860
Chimarrhis cymosa	bwa wivie (P)	headache	leaf	poultice	H	186366
Citrus auruntifolia	lime (E)/citwon (P)	fever	leaf and root	bath/"tea"	N	183840
Cocs nucifera	coconut, jelly (E), koko (P)	inflammation, constipation, pink eye	liquid endosperm	drink, drop in eye	C	sight record
Cordia polycephala	lian la fev (P)	fever	all but root	"tea"	C	185554
Cordyline fruticosa	malvina and san dwagon (P)	cuts, sores	leaf	scrapings on cut	N	185572
Costus sp.	pwev jine (P)	vomiting, gas, "colic"	leaf and stem	"tea"	N	186361
Cymbopogon citratus	lemon grass (E)/citwonel (P)	vomiting	root	"tea"	N	183949
Drymaria cordata	mouwon (P)	throat	whole plant	"tea"	C	185562
Eclipta prostrata	zeb able (P)	pressure, swelling, ulcers, colds, cough, male impotence, inflammation, gonorrhea	whole plant	"tea"	N	185569
Eryngium foetidum	chuk-chuk (E)/chado beni (P)	rheumatism, cough, cold, loose bowel, vomiting, something hurt	all but root	"tea"	H	186380
Eupatorium triplinerve	japana (P)	rheumatism, cough, cold, counters cold-shock	all but root	"tea"	H	186369
Gliricidia sepium	glory cedar and living cedar (E)/glorisida (P)	buttons, rashes	leaf	bath, "tea"	C	186392

TABLE A   PLANTS MENTIONED IN FREELISTS (*continued*)

Species Taxon	Common Name*	Medicinal Use	Plant Part	Preparation	Hum**	ID#***
Gossypium barbadense	black cotton (E)/kouton nue (P)	fright, "pain in heart"	leaf	"tea"	H	186416
Hyptis pectinata	pachuri (P)	rheumatism, cough, cold	all but root	"tea"	H	186348
Jatropha gossypifolia	metsien beni (P)	sore	leaf	poultice	N	186374
Jatropha gossypifolia	metsien beni (P)	fright, mysterious	leaf	"tea"	N	186374
Lantana camara	wild sage (E)/mavizo (P)	loose bowel, ulcers	all but root	"tea"	N	183937
Lepiantes peltata	mal estomak (P)	boils	leaf	poultice	C	183831
Lycopersicum escuelantum	tamatoz (E), tomat (P)	throat	green fruit	gargle	C	sight record
Malvasviscus arboreus	closed-flower hibiscus (E)	colds	flower	"tea"	H	183951
Mangifera indica	mango (E)	loose bowel	leaf	"tea"	H	183833
Mentha pulegium	peppermint (E)/petimant (P)	colds, gas	all but root	"tea"	N	186407
Mentha spicata	black lamant and black mint (E)/lamant nue (P)	gripes, "colic," blood clots, arthritis, fright	all but root	"tea"	N	185580
Mikania micrantha	bitter caapi (E)/kapi vulkan (P)	loose bowel, vomiting, diarrhea, fever	all but root	"tea"	C	185587
Mirabilis jalapa	koko katwe and katwe (P)	sprain	corm	poultice with corm	C	185574
Momordica charantia	ceresse (E)/koukouli (P)	buttons, prickle heat	whole plant	bath	C	183935
Momordica charantia	ceresse (E)/koukouli (P)	cooling, cleans blood, reduces fever	whole plant	"tea"	C	183935
Musa acuminata	fig E/FP, banana (E)	boils	fruit	poultice	C	sight record
Nicotiana tabacum	black tabacco (E)/tabak (P)	boils	leaf	poultice	H	186395
Ocimum basilicum	wild basil (E)/basilik fwanze and basilik (P)	fatigue, flavor for tea, incense	all but root	"tea"	H	186355
Opuntia stricta	wachet (P)	boil	stems	poultice	C	186377
Opuntia stricta	wachet (P)	inflammation	stems	eat, "tea"	C	186377
Paspalum conjugatum	gazon (P)	sprains, strains	whole plant	poultice	N	185570
Passiflora quadrangularis	babadin (P)	buttons, prickle heat	leaf	poultice	C	186418
Peperomia rotundifolia	giwon fle (P)	child colds	whole plant	"tea"	H	183850
Persea americana	avocado (E)/zaboka (P)	indigestion, loose bowels	leaf	"tea"	N	183855
Petiveria alliaceae	kojuruk and kudjuruk (P)	sore throat	all but root	gargle with "tea"	N	186412
Petiveria alliaceae	kojuruk and kudjuruk (P)	headache	leaf	sniff crushed leaves	N	186413
Pilea microphylla	moss and small thyme (E) /limu (P)	fright	whole plant	"tea"	H	185575
Pimenta racemosa	bay, bayleaf (E)/bwa den (P)	rheumatism, flavor	leaf	"tea"	H	183834
Plantago major	plantain (E)/plante and planten (P)	sore throat	whole plant	"tea," gargle	C	183948
Plantago major	plantain (E)/plante and planten (P)	sores, ulcers, skin disease [mix w/sorrel]	whole plant	poultice	C	183948
Plectranthus amboinicus	go djai and go di te (P)	fright, "pain in heart"	leaf	"tea"	H	186388
Pluchea symphytifolia	tobak zombi (P)	for coughs, flu, something hurt	all but root	"tea"	H	183841
Polygala paniculata	estwa fwagil (P)	colds, prevents curse, brings good fortune	whole plant	"tea"	N	183932
Portulaca oleracea	koupiye (P)	worms, inflammation	whole plant	"tea"	C	183851
Psidium guajava	guava (E), goiyav (P)	nausea, loose bowel	young leaves	"tea," eat leaves	C	183852
Rincus communis	castor bean tree (E)/kawapat (P)	soreness, strain, swollen glands	seed oil	massage	N	183950
Rincus communis	castor bean tree (E)/kawapat (P)	constipation, punishment	seed oil	ingest	N	183950
Saccharum officinarum	cane, sugarcane (E)	something hurt	stalk	chew, suck stalk	N	sight record
Sambucus canadensis	siyo (P)	colds	all but root	"tea"	H	183859
Sechium edule	christophine (E)/kristofin (P)	buttons, prickle heat, pressure	eat	fruit	C	186402
Senna bicapsularis	sou mache (P)	inflammation, prickle heat	all but root	bathe, "tea"	C	185584
Stachytarphete jamaicensis	veng-veng latjewat (P)	pressure, swelling, ulcers, colds, coughs, female menstrual "colic"	all but root	"tea"	N	183857

Species Taxon	Common Name*	Medicinal Use	Plant Part	Preparation	Hum**	ID#***
Suavagesia erecta	timayok (E)/ti-maniok and zeb mayok (P)	colds, flu	all but root	"tea" or bath	H	186358
Symphytum officinale	comfrey (E)/konsut and konfou (P)	cold, cough, hernia	leaf	"tea"	H	186353
Symphytum officinale	comfrey (E)/konsut and konfou (P)	cramps, muscle aches	leaf	rub leaf directly	H	186353
Syzygium aromaticum	klou giwav (P), clove (E)	vomiting, toothache	flower (dried)	"tea," place on gum	N	sight record
Thymus vulgaris	thyme (E)/ti di te (P)	fright, loose bowel	all but root	"tea"	H	186354
Triphasia trifolia	small lime (E)/ti sitwon (P)	fever	whole plant	bath, "tea"	C	185581
Unidentified	zanana falez (P)	cuts, sores	leaf	scrapings on cut	N	186397
Unidentified	moube (P)	buttons	bark	soak	C	186428
Unidentified	moube (P)	inflammation	bark	"tea"	C	186429
Zingiber	ginger (E)	stomach gripes, cold	root	"tea"	N	183844

*E = English common name, P = Patwa common name
**Plant's humoral quality. C = cold, H = hot, N = neutral
***Accession number at the Dunn-Palmer Herbarium, University of Missouri

Appendix B

TABLE B   NONHERBAL BUSH MEDICINE TREATMENTS AND INGREDIENTS FOR COMMON ILLNESSES IN BWA MAWEGO*

Nonherbal Cures	Preparation	Use
Ashes	Mix with poultice	Boils
Black [shoe] polish	Topical rub	Sprains
Blue soap (lye soap with bluing)	Make soapy water	Gargle for sore throat
Brandy	Topical rub	Rheumatism
Charcoal	Boil for "tea"	Gargle for sore throat
Cold water	Bathe	Fever
	Drink plenty	Fever
Earth (dirt)	Boil for "tea"	If something "hurts" you
"Food" (dasheen, plantain, tannia, breadfruit, or yams)	Roast over fire and eat	Diarrhea
Honey	Ingest (alone or in tea)	Colds, sore throat, asthma, sprains
Ice	Suck	Sore throat
Kaka poul, "fowl shit"	Roast, then boil for "tea"	Fright
Kerosene	Topical rub	Cough
Kulbwa, Woodant nest	Boil for "tea"	If something "hurts" you
Lard	Eat	Inflammation, pressure
	Topical rub	Rheumatism, buttons
Leaches	Place topically	Rheumatic joints, sores
Pee-pee (Urine)	Topical rub	Sore throat, asthma, stings and bites
Rum, *won*	Drink	Loose bowel
	Tincture base	Various
	Topical rub	Fever, scrapes
Salt	Apply directly	Cuts and sores
Saltfish (cod) skin	Tie directly over	Boils
Saltwater	Drink	If something "hurts" you
	Soak	Cuts and sores
Shark oil	Topical rub	Rheumatism, sprains, strains
Skin of what "hurt" you (pineapple, fish, etc.)	Boil for "tea"	If something "hurts" you
Snake oil (boa constr.)	Topical rub	Rheumatism, sprains, strains
Soft [tallow] candle	Drip wax on skin	Use to paste leaf over a boil, rub for sprains

Nonherbal Cures	Preparation	Use
Starch (arrowroot, manioc, corn, etc.)	Topical rub	Prickle heat
Sticks (1/2" diameter)	Wear behind ears	Vomiting, nausea
Sulpher from hot spring	Topical rub	Tinea versicolor, cuts and sores
	Ingest with water	Tinea versicolor
Turpentine	Ingest few drops	"Fits" or "fixes" of worms
	Topical rub	Rheumatism
Turtle oil	Topical rub	Rheumatism, sprains, strains
Vinegar	Drink	Fright
	Topical rub	Jellyfish stings and insect bites
Zandoli (small lizard)	Boil tail in milk	Asthma
Ziziye poul (yellow membrane of a chicken gizzard)	Boil for "tea"	Vomiting, nausea

*Includes foraged animal and mineral ingredients and purchased ingredients.

Appendix C

Botanical Species	Family	Common Name	Illnesses
Aloe barbadensis	Liliaceae	aloz, *lalue*	inflammation, buttons
Ambrosia hispida	Asteraceae	*set vil*	upset stomach, worms
Aristolochia trilobata	Aristolochaceae	*twef*	upset stomach, worms
Cannabis sativa	Cannabaceae	*kalí, ganja, zeb*	asthma
Carica papaya	Caricaceae	pawpaw, *papay*	inflammation, buttons, pressure
Chenopodium ambrosioides	Chenopodiaceae	*sime kontwa*	upset stomach, worms
Citrus auruntifolia	Rutaceae	lime, *sitwon*	fever
Cocos nucifera	Aracaceae	*koko,* jelly	rheumatism (oil) inflammation (water)
Cordyline terminalis	Agavaceae	*malvina, san dwagon*	cuts
Eryngium foetidum	Apiaceae	*chado beni*	if something hurt
Gliricidia sepium	Papilioniaceae	glorisida, *lecidra*	inflammation, buttons
Gossypium barbadense	Malvaceae	*kouton nue*	fright
Hyptis pectinata	Lamiaceae	*pachuri*	cough, colds
Lepianthes peltata	Piperaceae	*mal estomak*	boils
Lycopersicon escuelantum	Solanaceae	tomatoz, *tamat*	throat
Momordica charantia	Cucurbitaceae	*koukouli*	inflammation, buttons
Peperomia pellucida	Piperaceae	*zeb kwes,* kouklaya	buttons
Petiveria alliacea	Phytolaccaceae	*kojourouk*	headache
Pimenta racemosa	Myrtaceae	*bwa den,* bay	rheumatism, sprain
Plantago major	Plantaginaceae	*plante*	boils
Plectranthus amboinicus	Lamiaceae	*go djai, go di te.*	fright
Pluchea carolinensis	Solanaceae	*tobak zombi*	asthma, cough
Psidium guajava	Myrtaceae	*gwiyav,* guava	diarrhea, upset stomach
Rincus communis	Euphorbiaceae	*kawapat,* caster	rheumatism, sprain
Sauvagesia erecta	Ochnaceae	*ti manyok, zeb mayok*	cough, colds
Stachytarphete jamaicensis	Verbenaceae	*veng-veng latjewat*	pressure
Syzygium aromaticum	Myrtaceae	*klou giwav,* clove	diarrhea, upset stomach
Thymus vulgaris	Lamiaceae	*ti di te*	fright
Zingiber officinale	Zingiberaceae	*Janjam,* ginger	diarrhea, upset stomach

Glossary

affine   a relative by marriage.

alternate leaves   leaves that occur at different levels on opposite sides of a stem. No two leaves are directly across from each other.

analgesic   a substance causing insensibility to pain without loss of consciousness.

antiemetic   a substance that tends to prevent vomiting.

antimicrobial   the destruction or inhibition of growth of microorganisms such as bacteria.

antispasmodic   the prevention or reduction of convulsions or spasms (involuntary, abnormal contractions of muscle or muscle fibers or of a hollow organ).

authority   appears at the end of a species name, and refers to the botanist who gave the plant its taxonomic (species) name.

body image   all the conceptions a person has about his or her body. It is influenced by growing up in a particular culture and family, and includes beliefs about the body's (1) ideal shape and adornment (beauty), (2) structure and functions (anatomy and physiology), and (3) boundaries (public/private parts and propriety about physical distance/touching in differing social circumstances).

bronchodilator   a drug that relaxes bronchial muscle, causing expansion of the bronchial air passages.

couvade   sympathetic, ritual pregnancy or childbirth on the part of a man.

Creole   a language whose vocabulary comes largely from a colonial or trade language, but whose grammar is unique to the Creole form.

culture-bound syndrome   recurrent, specific pattern of aberrant behavior (usually with accompanying physical symptoms) that occurs within a particular

culture and does not absolutely fit with a Western psychiatric diagnosis.

cytotoxicity   being toxic to cells.

decoction   liquid preparation made by boiling plant parts in water.

dialect   a variety of a language spoken in a particular group or in a particular region.

disease   a physiological abnormality that a professional can observe and measure objectively.

domain   cluster of words with a core meaning that relates to one topic (e.g., names of body parts, colors, tools, etc.).

elliptic   the broadening about the center and narrowing equally toward each end.

emic   the viewpoint of individuals inside a particular cultural system. Compare with etic.

enculturation   the pattern by which one gradually learns and assimilates the expected belief and behaviors of a society.

epidemiologists   practitioners of epidemiology.

epidemiology   the study of factors that determine disease frequency and distribution.

escape   a cultivated plant successfully growing in the wild.

ethnobotany   the study of the interrelation between cultures and the plants in their environments.

ethnology   the study of differences and similarities across cultures.

ethnomedicine   the culturally structured medical theory and practice.

ethnopharmacology   the study of medications used by people of a particular ethnic group.

ethnophysiology   the culturally patterned beliefs about the body's inner workings.

etic   an objective viewpoint from outside a cultural system.

etiology   the assignment of a cause, or reason, for a medical disorder.

explanatory model (of health/illness) the patient/practitioner explanation of health or sickness based on notions about how to maintain health, an illness's cause, its effects on body functions, the course of the illness in terms of symptoms and duration, and appropriate treatments for the condition.

fallow   land left unplanted to regenerate the soil.

freelist   interview in which a person is asked to list as many members of a domain as he can think of.

holistic   an analysis that deals with wholes, or complete systems, rather than treatment of, or dissection into, parts.

humor   a vital force in the body, often associated with blood and other body fluids.

humoral medicine (humoral theory, humoral system)   tradition viewing health and healing as the result of balanced exposure to opposing forces such as heat and cold, fire and water or dryness and wetness.

illness   physical or mental unwell state including measurable and indefinite symptoms.

incidence   frequency at which a condition occurs in a specific population.

infusion   a solution in which soluble elements or active principles have been extracted through steeping.

insult   a bodily injury, irritation, or trauma.

internal logic   the necessary ideas and ways of expressing and establishing such ideas from within a particular culture or system of thought.

lanceolate   shaped like a lance head, tapering to a point at each end.

lexicon   a language's words and their meanings, approximated by a dictionary.

limited good, image of   a view associated with peasants in which all desired things (e.g., health, love, wealth) are finite, and usually in short supply within a community. It follows that one individual's betterment may come at the expense of his neighbor.

locus of control   a scale, ranging from internal to external, that measures an individual's assessment of his or her control over life circumstances. People with an internal locus of control perceive that their own actions fully determine their circumstances, while people with an external locus of control view their circumstances as resulting from actions of powerful others or fate.

manioc   the root crop from which tapioca is obtained. It is a food staple of much of the American tropics (a.k.a. cassava, yuca).

medical pluralism   multiple therapeutic options available to a patient, each with a different way of illness explanation, diagnosis and treatment.

menstrual taboo   common cross-cultural practice in which a woman follows various special rules for conduct and restrictions during her menstrual periods.

methodology   the body of methods used in a particular research endeavor.

naturalistic illness   illnesses blamed on exposure to naturally occurring (as opposed to supernatural) risks in one's environment.

neotropical   the American tropics, i.e., the geographic/biological region that extends south, east, and west from the central plateau of Mexico.

obeah   a form of magico-religious sorcery of African origin, practiced in some parts of the Caribbean and nearby tropical America.

obeahmen   specialists who perform cures, curses, and other spells using obeah.

opposite leaves   leaves arranged in pairs in which two leaves grow directly across from each other on each side of a stem.

organoleptic quality   the impression produced on the organs of touch, taste, smell, or sight. Organoleptic treatments include eating a banana that has been fire-roasted until brown to treat constipation, drinking tomato juice to strengthen blood, or eating piquant scotch bonnet peppers to treat a "cold" condition.

participant-observation   living/working among the people being studied and taking part in activities to gain first-hand knowledge about the culture.

pathogenic   causing disease.

pathology departure from a healthy, normal body function; also, the study of the nature of disease and its causes, processes, development, and consequences.

patrilineal based on or tracing descent through the male line.

peasants communities of people who produce food largely for their own subsistence, but who regularly sell part of their surplus into a larger urban economy.

personalistic illness an illness blamed on purposeful supernatural intervention.

petiole the stalk of a leaf.

phoneme a single, distinguishable unit of sound, such as the one English phoneme represented by the letters "f" in fish, and "ph" in phone.

pile sort an interview method to find a subject's cognitive domains by requesting that he or she group similar items into piles.

prophylactic prevents or wards off a condition or disease.

protein complimentarity eating legumes together with starches to approximate the amount of nine essential amino acids present in animal foods. Amino acids that are abundant in legumes compensate for those same lacking amino acids in starchy vegetables and vice versa.

public health the science of improving the health of a community via preventive medicine, health education, control of communicable diseases, and application of sanitary measures.

purgative medicine that purges or cleanses by causing evacuation of the bowels.

rapport a relation characterized by understanding, unity, and mutual trust.

Rastafarian an adherent to a largely Caribbean, Christian-based religious-cultural movement in which the last emperor of Ethiopia, Haile Selassie, also named Ras Tafari (died 1975), is a prophet. Rastafarians tend to reject European market-based culture in favor of a return to nature and are particularly noted for their use of marijuana. Reggae music is heavily influenced by Rastafarianism.

reciprocity offering goods and services with expectation that the gift be returned.

salience score value achieved by ranking freelisted items according to order of mention (relative list position) summing the ranks, and dividing by the number of informants. The resulting scores reveal the relative salience (cognitive and cultural significance) of each item.

shaman a religious-magical-medical specialist common in tribal and band level societies, who heals, guides and prophesizes, typically on a part time basis.

sorcery deeds practiced by individuals who inflict harm or manipulate reality to their advantage via alleged learned rituals and knowledge.

syncretic combining different forms of belief or practice.

syntax the rules of a language.

taboo a ritual avoidance, proscribed for symbolic rather than pragmatic reasons.

tincture liquid preparation made by soaking plant parts in alcohol to release active properties.

umbel flat-topped cluster of flowers generally formed like an umbrella, i.e., the flowers are on several separate stalks that radiate from a central point.

vector a carrier or bearer of a disease-causing agent (e.g., a mosquito serves as the vector that carries the infectious agents [Plasmodium parasites] that cause malaria).

voucher specimen documented, preserved, mounted plant samples deposited in herbaria (plant museums) for the scientific record.

witchcraft deeds practiced by individuals with accepted intrinsic, inborn abilities to inflict harm or manipulate reality to their own advantage.

Bibliography

Adjanohoun, E., L. A. Assi, P. Chibon, S. Cuffy, J. J. Darnault, M. J. Edwards, C. Etienne, J. Eyme, E. Goudote, J. Jeremie, A. Keita, J. L. Longuefosse, J. Portecop, A. Soopramanien, and J. Troian (1985). *Medecine Traditionnelle et Pharmacopee: Contrabution aux Etudes Ethnobotaniques et Floristiques a la Dominique* (Commonwealth of Dominica). Paris: Agence de Cooperation Culturelle et Technique.

Agar, M. H. (1980). *The Professional Stranger*. New York: Academic Press.

Agar, M. H. (1973). *Ripping and Running*. New York: Academic Press.

Alcorn, J. (1995). The Scope and aims of ethnobotany in a developing world. In R. E. Schultes and S. V. Reis (Eds.): *Ethnobotany: Evolution of a Discipline*. Portland, OR: Dioscoirdes Press.

Allaire, L. (1985). *L'Archiologie des Antilles: Grand Atlas de l'Archeologie Universalis*. Paris: Encyclopoedia Universalis.

Almeida, C. E., M. Karnikowski, R. Foleto, and B. Baldisserotto (1995). Analysis of antidiarrhoeic effect of plants used in popular medicine. *Revista de Saude Publica* 29:428–433.

American Psychiatric Association (1994). *Diagnostic and Statistical Manual of Mental Disorders, Fourth Edition* (DSM-IV). Washington, DC: American Psychiatric Association.

Anyinam, C. (1987). Availability, accessibility, acceptability and adaptability: Four attributes of African ethnomedicine. *Social Science and Medicine* 25:803–811.

Arvigo, R., and Balick, M. (1998). *Rainforest Remedies: One hundred healing herbs of Belize* (2nd ed.). Twin Lakes, WI: Lotus Press.

Ausprey, G. F., and P. Thornton (1955). Medicinal plants of Jamaica: Part III. *West Indian Medical Journal* 4:69–82.

Ausprey, G. F., and P. Thornton (1954). Medicinal plants of Jamaica: Part II. *West Indian Medical Journal* 3:17–41.

Ausprey, G. F., and P. Thornton (1953). Medicinal plants of Jamaica: Part I. *West Indian Medical Journal* 2:233–252.

Ayensu, E. S. (1981). *Medicinal Plants of the West Indies*. Algonac, MI: Reference Publications.

Balick, M. J., and P. A. Cox (1996). *Plants, People, and Culture: The Science of Ethnobotany*. New York: Scientific American Library.

Barnet, H. S. (1990). Divorce stress and adjustment model: Locus of control and demographic predictors. *Journal of Divorce* 13:93–109.

Beard, J. S. (1949). *The Natural Vegetation of the Windward and Leeward Islands*. Oxford: Oxford University Press at Clarendon.

Beckles, H. M. (1990). *A history of Barbados: From Amerindian settlement to nation-state*. Cambridge, England: Cambridge University Press.

Berlin, E. A., and B. Berlin (1996). *Medical Ethnobiology of the Highland Maya of Chiapas, Mexico: The Gastrointestinal Diseases*. Princeton, NJ: Princeton University Press.

Bernard, H. R. (1995). *Research Methods in Anthropology*. Walnut Creek, CA: AltaMira Press.

Bernard, H. R. (1994). *Research Methods in Cultural Anthropology*. Newbury Park: Sage.

Bispo, M. D., R. H. Mourao, E. M. Franzotti, K. B. Bomfim, M. F. Arrigoni-Blank, M. P. Moreno, M. Marchioro, A. R. Antoniolli (2001). Antinociceptive and antiedematogenic effects of the aqueous extract of *Hyptis pectinata* leaves in experimental animals. *Journal of Ethnopharmacology* 76:81–86.

Booth, S., T. Johns, and C. Y. Lopez-Palacois (1993). Factors influencing self-diagnosis and treatment of perceived helminthic infection in a rural Guatemalan community. *Social Science and Medicine 37*:531–539.

Boster, J. S. (1987). Introduction. *American Behavioral Scientist 31*:150–162.

Brodwin, P. (1996). *Medicine and Morality in Haiti*. Cambridge: Cambridge University Press.

Brosschot, J. F., G. L. R. Godaert, R. J. Benschop, M. Olff, R. E. Ballieux, C. J. Heijnen (1998). Experimental stress and immunological reactivity: A closer look at perceived uncontrollability. *Psychosomatic Medicine 60*:359–361.

Brown, M. (1987). Toward a human ecology: Medical etnobotany and the search for dynamic models of plant use. *Reviews in Anthropology 14*:5–11.

Brown, C. (1979). Folk zoological life-forms: Their universality and growth. *American Anthropologist 81*:791–817.

Brown, M. (1976). Patterns of variability in two folk systems of classification. *Michigan Discussions in Anthropology 2*:76–90.

Browner, C., B. Ortiz de Montellano, and A. Rubel (1988). A methodology for cross-cultural ethnomedical research. *Current Anthropology 29*:681–702.

Brussell, D. E. (1997). *Potions, Poisons, and Panaceas: An Ethnobotanical Study of Montserrat*. Carbondale, IL: Southern Illinois University Press.

Bryant, C. A., A. Courtney, B. A. Markesbery, and K. M. DeWalt (1985). *The Cultural Feast*. St. Paul: West Publishing Co.

Campbell, F. A., M. R. Tramèr, D. Carroll, D. J. M. Reynolds, R. A. Moore, and H. J. McQuay (2001). Are cannabinoids an effective and safe treatment option in the management of pain? A qualitative systematic review. *British Medical Journal 323*:13–16.

Centers for Disease Control and Prevention (1998). *CDC Travel information: Health information for travelers to the Caribbean*. Atlanta: Author.

Chagnon, N. A. (1974). *Studying the Yanomamo*. New York: Holt, Rinehart, and Winston.

Chandra, O., K. C. Singhal, and K. P. Gupta (1969). A study on the local anaesthetic activity of the acetone extract of Lycopersicon esculentum leaves. *Japanese Journal of Pharmacology 19*:625–626.

Christie, P. (1990). Language as expression of identity in Dominica. *International Journal of the Sociology of Language 85*:61–69.

Clements, F. E. (1932). Primitive concepts of disease. *University of California Publications in Archaeology and Ethnology 32*:185–252.

Coborn, J. (1991). *Atlas of Snakes*. Neptune, NJ: T. F. H. Publications.

Coe, F. G., and G. J. Anderson (1999). Ethnobotany of the Sumu (Ulwa) of Southeastern Nicaragua and comparisons with Miskitu plant lore. *Economic Botany 53*:363–386.

Cohen, S., D. A. Tyrrell, and A. P. Smith (1991). Psychological stress and susceptibility to the common cold. *New England Journal of Medicine 325*:606–612.

Compas, B. E., and M. C. Boyer (2001). Coping and attention: Implications for child health and pediatric conditions. *Journal of Developmental & Behavioral Pediatrics 22*:323–333.

Coreil, J. (1983). Parallel structures in professional and folk health care: A model applied to rural Hati. *Culture, Medicine and Psychiatry 7*:131–151.

Coreil, J., and P. A. Marshall (1982). Locus of illness control: A cross-cultural study. *Human Organization 41*:131–138.

Crandon-Malamud, L. (1991). *From the Fat of Our Souls: Social Change, Political Process, and Medical Pluralism in Bolivia*. Berkeley: University of California Press.

Dalziel, J. M. (1937). *The Useful Plants of Tropical West Africa*. London: Crown Agents for Oversea Governments and Administrations.

D'Andrade, R. G. (1987). Modal Responses and Cultural Expertise. *American Behavioral Scientist 31*:194–202.

Dantzer, R. (2001). Stress, emotions and health: Where do we stand? *Social Science Information/Information Sur Les Sciences Sociales 40*:61–78.

Davis, E. W. (1995). Ethnobotany: An old practice, a new discipline. In R. Schultes and S. vonReis (Eds.):

Ethnobotany: Evolution of a Discipline. Portland, OR: Dioscorides Press.

de Lima, T. C., Morato, G. S., and Takahashi, R. N. (1991). Evaluation of antinociceptive effect of Petiveria alliacea in animals. *Memorias do Instituto Oswaldo Cruz* 86:153–158.

Desmarchelier, C., S. Barros, M. Repetto, L. R. Latorre, M. Kato, J. Coussio, and G. Ciccia (1997). 4–Nerolidylcatechol from *Pothomorphe* spp. scavenges peroxyl radicals and inhibits Fe(II)-dependent DNA damage. *Planta Medica* 63:561–563.

Desmarchelier, C., E. Mongelli, J. Coussio, and G. Ciccia (1997). Inhibition of lipid peroxidation and iron (II)-dependent DNA damage by extracts of *Pothomorphe peltata* (L.). Miq. *Brazilian Journal of Medical and Biological Research* 30:85–91.

Desmarchelier, C., K. Slowing, and G. Ciccia (2000). Anti-inflammatory activity of Pothomorphe peltata leaf methanol extract. *Fitoterapia* 71:556–558.

DeSmet, P. G. A. M. (1992). The adverse effects of herbal drugs. In P. G. A. M. DeSmet, K. Keller, R. Hansel, and R. F. Chandler (Eds.): *Adverse Effects of Herbal Drugs.* Berlin: Springer-Verlag, p. 1.

Dobkin de Rios, M. (1985). Saladera: A culture-bound misfortune syndrome in the Peruvian Amazon. In R. C. Simons and C. C. Hughes (Eds.): *The Culture-Bound Syndromes: Folk Illnesses of Psychiatric and Anthropological Interest.* Dordrecht, Germany: D. Reidel, pp. 351–369.

Eisenberg, L. (1977). Disease and illness: Distinctions between professional and popular ideas of sickness. *Culture, Medicine and Psychiatry* 1:9–23.

El-Mofty, M. M., V. V. Khodoley, S. A. Sakr, and N. F. Ganem (1992). Induction of neoplasms in Egyptian toads Bufo regularis by oil of Chenopodium. *Oncology* 49:253–255.

Eno, A. E., O. I. Owo, E. H. Itam, R. S. Konya (2000). Blood pressure depression by the fruit juice of Carica papaya (L.) in renal and DOCA-induced hypertension in the rat. *Phytotherapy Research* 14:235–239.

Etkin N. L. (2001). Perspectives in ethnopharmacology: Forging a closer link between bioscience and traditional empirical knowledge. *Journal of Ethnopharmacology* 76 (2):177–182.

Etkin, N. L. (1996). Ethnopharmcology: The Conjunction of Medical Ethnography and the Biology of Therapeutic Action. In *Medical Anthropology: Contemporary Theory and Method.* Revised edition. C. F. Sargent and T. M. Johnson, Eds. New York: Praeger Publishers, pp. 151–164.

Etkin, N. L. (Ed.). (1994). *Eating on the Wild Side: The Pharmacologic, Ecologic, and Social Implications of Using Noncultigens.* Tucson: University of Arizona Press.

Etkin, N. L. (1988). Ethnopharmacology: Biobehavioral approaches in the anthropological. *Annual Reviews in Anthropology* 17:23–42.

Etkin, N. L. (Ed.). (1986). *Plants in Indigenous Medicine and Diet: Biobehavioral Approaches.* New York: Gordon and Breach Science Publishers.

Evans-Pritchard, E. E. (1937). *Witchcraft, Oracles, and Magic Among the Azande.* London: Oxford University Press.

Fabrega, H., Jr. (1975). The need for an ethnomedical science. *Science* 189:969–975.

Fabrega, H., and D. B. Silver (1973). *Illness and Shamanistic Curing in Zinacantan: An Ethnomedical Analysis.* Stanford: Stanford University Press.

Farnsworth, N. R. (1988). Screening plants for new medicines. In E. O. Wilson (Ed.): *Biodiversity.* Washington, DC: National Academy Press, pp. 83–97.

Fernandez, M. A., A. Alvarez, M. D. Garcia, and M. T. Saenz (2001). Anti-inflammatory effect of Pimenta racemosa var. ozua and isolation of the triterpene lupeol. *Farmaco* 56:335–338.

Fernandez, M. A., M. P. Tornos, M. D. Garcia, B. de las Heras, A. M. Villar, and M. T. Saenz (2001). Anti-inflammatory activity of abietic acid, a diterpene isolated from Pimenta racemosa var. grissea. *Journal of Pharmacy and Pharmacology* 53:867–872.

Finerman, R. (1993). Annex 2: Culture-specific disorders. In *The ICD-10 Classification of Mental and Behavioural Disorders: Diagnostic*

Criteria for Research. Geneva: World Health Organization, pp. 176–187.

Finerman, R. (1991). The forgotten healers: Women as family healers in an Andean Indian community. In *Women as Healers: Cross-Cultural Perspectives*, C. S. McClain (Ed.). New Brunswick, NJ: Rutgers University Press, pp. 24–41.

Fleisher, M. S., and J. A. Harrington (1997). Freelisting: Management at a Women's Federal Prison Camp. In V. de Munck and E. Sobo (Eds.), *Using Methods in the Field*, Walnut Creek, CA: Altamira Press.

Flinn, M. V. (1999). Family environment, stress, and health during childhood. In *Hormones, Health, and Behavior*, C. Panter-Brick and C. Worthman (Eds.). Cambridge: Cambridge University Press, pp. 105–138.

Flinn, M. V., and B. G. England (1997). Social economics of childhood glucocorticoid stress response and health. *American Journal of Physical Anthropology 102*:33–53.

Flinn, M. V., and B. G. England (1995). Childhood stress and family environment. *Current Anthropology 36*:854–866.

Flinn, M. V., D. V. Leone, and R. J. Quinlan (1999). Growth and fluctuating asymmetry of stepchildren. *Evolution and Human Behavior* 20:465–480.

Flinn, M. V., R. Quinlan, M. T. Turner, S. D. Decker, and B. G. England (1996). Male-female differences in effects of parental absence on glucocorticoid stress response. *Human Nature 7*:125–162.

Fontaine, M. D. (1992). *Lekol Kweyol*. Roseau, Dominica: Folk Research Institute, Old Mill Cultural Center, Division of Culture, Ministry of Community Development.

Foster, G., and B. Anderson (1978). *Medical Anthropology*. New York: Wiley.

Foster, G. M. (1994). *Hippocrates' Latin American Legacy: Humoral Medicine in the New World*. Langhorne, PA: Gordon & Breach Science Publications.

Foster, G. M. (1976). Disease etiologies in nonwestern medical systems. *American Anthropologist 78*:773–782.

Foster, G. M. (1965). Peasant society and the image of limited good. *American Anthropologists 67*:293–315.

Frankel, S. (1985). Mogo Laya, A New Guinea Fright Illness. In R. C. Simons and C. C. Hughes (Eds.): *The Culture-Bound Syndromes: Folk Illnesses of Psychiatric and Anthropological Interest*. Dordrecht: Reidel, pp. 399–404.

Frazer, J. G. (1911). *The Golden Bough* (3rd ed.). London: Macmillan.

Fulder, S. (1988). *The Handbook of Complementary Medicine* (2nd ed.). Oxford: Oxford University Press.

Funch, D. P., and J. R. Marshall (1984). Self-reliance as a modifier of the effects of life stress and social support. *Journal of Psychosomatic Research 28*:9–15.

Gabe, J. (Ed.) (1998). *Medicine, Health and Risk: Sociological Approaches*. Oxford, England: Blackwell, p. 176.

Gatewood, J. B. (1984). Familiarity, vocabularity size, and recognition ability in four semantic domains. *American Ethnologist 11*:507.

Good, B., and M. J. D. Good (1982). Toward a meaning-centered analysis of popular illness categories: Fright illness and heart distress in Iran. In A. J. Marsella and G. M. White (Eds.): *Cultural Conceptions of Mental Health and Therapy*. Dordrecht, Germany: Reidel, pp. 150–158.

Gonzalez, N. L. S. (1969). *Black Carib Household Structure*. Seattle: University of Washington Press.

Grisebach, A. H. R. (1864). *Flora of the British West Indian Islands*. London: Lovell Reeve & Co.

Gross, D. (1985). Time allocation: A tool for the study of cultural behavior. *Annual Review of Anthropology 14*:214–255.

Hamburg, D. A., G. R. Elliot, and D. L. Parron (Eds.) (1982). *Health and Behavior: Frontiers of Research in the Behavioral Sciences*. National Academy Press: Washington, DC.

Hames, R. (1991). Time allocation. In E. A. Smith and B. Winterhalder (Eds.) *Evolutionary Ecology and Human Behavior*. New York: Aldine de Gryuter.

Hanson, F. A. (1975). *Meaning in Culture*. London: Routledge & Kegan Paul.

Handwerker, W. P. and S. P. Borgatti (1998). Reasoning with numbers. In H. R. Bernard (Ed.) *Handbook of Methods in Cultural Anthropology*. Walnut Creek, CA: Altamira Press.

Hatfield, G. (1994). *Country Remedies: Traditional East Anglian Plant Remedies in the Twentieth Century.* Woodbridge, England: Boydell Press.

Hard, D. V. (1985). Lanti, illness by fright among Bisayan Filipinos. In R. C. Simons and C. C. Hughes (Eds.) *The Culture-Bound Syndromes: Folk Illnesses of Psychiatric and Anthropological Interest.* Dordrecht, Germany: Reidel, pp. 317–397.

Hartl, G. (1996). Tackling sources of stress in high-risk groups. *World of Work 18*:13–16.

Harwood, A. (1971). The hot-cold theory of disease: Implications for treatment of Puerto Rican patients. *Journal of the American Medical Association 216*:1153–1158.

Haviser, J. B. (1997). Settlement strategies in the Early Ceramic Age. In S. M. Wilson (Ed.) *The Indigenous People of the Caribbean.* Gainesville: University Press of Florida.

Helman, C. G. (1994). *Culture, Health, and Illness* (3rd ed.). Oxford, England: Butterworth-Heinemann Ltd.

Hewitt, H., S. Whittle, S. Lopez, E. Bailey, S. Weaver (2000). Topical use of papaya in chronic skin ulcer therapy in Jamaica. *West Indian Medical Journal 49*:32–33.

Hmamouchi, M., M. Lahlou, and A. Agoumi (2000). Molluscicidal activity of some Moroccan medicinal plants. *Fitoterapia 71*:308–314.

Hodge, W. H. (1954). Flora of Dominica, B.W.I., Part I: Monocotyledoneae. *Lloydia 17*:1–238.

Hodge, W. H., and D. Taylor (1957). The ethnobotany of the Island Caribs of Dominica. *Webbia 7*:513–643.

Honychurch, L. (1995). *The Dominica Story: A History of the Island.* London: Macmillan Education.

Honychurch, P. N. (1986). *Caribbean Wild Plants and Their Uses.* London: Macmillan Caribbean.

Horner, K. L. (1996). Locus of control, neuroticism, and stressors: Combined influences on reported physical illness. *Personality & Individual Differences 21*:195–204.

Hoyos, J. F. (1985). *Flora de la Isla Margarita.* Caracas: Sociedad y Fundacion LaSalle de Ciencias Naturales.

Hughes, C. C. (1990). Ethnopsychiatry. In T. Johnson and C. Sargent (Eds.) *Medical Anthropology.* New York: Praeger.

Hutchens, A. R. (1991). *Indian Herbology of North America.* Boston: Shambhala Publications.

Johnson, A., and R. Sackett (1998). Direct systematic observation of behavior. In H. R. Bernard (Ed.) *Handbook of Methods in Cultural Anthropology.* Walnut Creek, CA: AltaMira Press, pp. 301–331.

Joly, L. G., S. Guerra, R. Septimo, P. N. Solis, M. Correa, M. Gupta, S. Levy, and F. Sandberg (1987). Ethnobotanical inventory of medicinal plants used by the Guaymi Indians in Western Panama, Part I. *Journal of Ethnopharmacology 20*:145–171.

Kahn, R., and C. E. Jarvis (1989). The correct name for the plant known as Plucha symphytifolia (Miller) Gillis, Asteraceae. *Taxon 38*:659–663.

Kainer, K. A., and M. L. Duryea (1992). Mapping women's knowledge: Plant resource use in extractive resources, Acre, Brazil. *Economic Botany 46*:408–425.

Kapadia, G. J., E. G. Chung, B. Ghosh, Y. N. Shukla, S. P. Basak, J. F. Morton, and S. N. Pradhan (1978). Carcinoginity of some folk medicinal herbs in rats. *Journal of the National Cancer Institute 60*:683–686.

Karasek, R. (1990). Lower health risk with increased job control among white collar workers. *Journal of Organizational Behavior 11*: 171–185.

Kerns, V. (1997). *Women and the Ancestors: Black Carib Kinship and Ritual.* Urbana: University of Illinois Press.

Khafagi, I. K., and A. Dewedar (2000). The efficiency of random versus ethno-directed research in the evaluation of Sinai medicinal plants for bioactive compounds. *Journal of Ethnopharmacology 71*:365–376.

Kleinman, A. (1980). *Patients and Healers in the Context of Culture.* Berkeley: University of California Press.

Kloss, J. (1972). *Back to Eden.* Riverside, CA: Lifeline Books.

Kroeger, A. (1983). Anthropological and socio-medical health care research in developing countries. *Social Science and Medicine 17*:147–151.

Laguerre, M. S. (1987). *Afro-Caribbean Folk Medicine*. South Hadley, MA: Bergin & Garvey Publishers.

Lajide, L., P. Escoubas, and J. Mizutani (1993). Comparative effects of aristolochic acids, phenanthrene, and 1,3–benzodioxole derivatives on the behavior and survival of Spodoptera litura larvae. *Journal of Agricultural & Food Chemistry 41*:2426–2430.

Landy, D. (1974). Role adaptation: Traditional curers under the impact of Western medicine. *American Ethnologist 1*: 103–127.

Lans, C., T. Harper, K. Georges, and E. Bridgewater (2000). Medicinal plants used for dogs in Trinidad and Tobago. *Preventive Veterinary Medicine 45*:201–220.

Leonti, M., O. Sticher, and M. Heinrich (2002). Medicinal plants of the Popoluca, Mexico: Organoleptic properties as indigenous selection criteria. *Journal of Ethnopharmacology 81*: 307–315.

Lewis, W. H., and M. P. F. Elvin-Lewis (1977). *Medical Botany*. New York: John Wiley.

Li, Y., H. Matsuda, J. Yamahara, and M. Yoshikawa (2000). *European Journal of Pharmacology 392:71–77.*

Logan, M. H. (1973). Humoral medicine in Guatemala and peasant acceptance of modern medicine. *Human Organization 32*:385–395.

Lowenthal, D. (1972). *West Indian Societies*. New York: Oxford University Press.

Lust, J. (1974). *The Herb Book*. New York: Bantam.

MacCormack, C. P. (1982). Biological, cultural, and social adaptation in human fertility and birth: A synthesis. In C. P. MacCormack (Ed.) *Ethnography of Fertility and Birth*. London: Academic Press.

Mace, M. E., R. D. Stipanovic, A. A. Bell (1993). Toxicity of cotton phytoalexins to zoopathogenic fungi. *Natural Toxins 1*:294–295.

Madsen, W. (1955). Hot and cold in the universe of San Francisco Tecospa, Valley of Mexico. *Journal of American Folklore 68*:123–139.

Malcolm, S. A. and E. A. Sofowora (1969). Antimicrobial activity of selected Nigerian folk remedies and their constituent plants. *Lloydia 32*:512–517.

Manuck, S. B., J. J. Hinrichsen, E. O. Ross (1975). Life-stress, locus of control, and treatment-seeking. *Psychological Reports 37*:589–590.

Martin, G. (1995). *Ethnobotany: A Methods Manual*. London: Chapman & Hall.

Maxwell, L. (Ed.) (1997). *The Caribbean Handbook 1997/98*. Road Town, Tortola, BVI: FT Caribbean (BVI) Ltd.

McCubbin, M. (2001). Pathways to health, illness and well-being: From the perspective of power and control. *Journal of Community & Applied Social Psychology 11*:75–81.

Messer, E. (1981). Hot-cold classification: Theoretical and practical implications of a Mexican Study. *Social Science and Medicine 15B*:133–145.

Millspaugh, C. (1892). *Medicinal Plants*. Philadelphia: John C. Yorston & Co.

Munroe, R. L., R. H. Munroe, and J. W. M. Whiting (1973). The couvade: A psychological analysis. *Ethos 1* (1):30–74.

Myers, R. A. (1984). *Island Carib cannibalism*. New West Indian Guide: Utrecht.

Nahas, G., K. Sutin, and W. M. Bennett (2000). Review of Marihuana and Medicine. *New England Journal of Medicine 343*:514–515.

Naroll, R., and R. Cohen (Eds.) (1970). *A Handbook of Methods in Cultural Anthropology*. New York: Natural History Press.

Neuenswander, H. L., and S. D. Souder (1977). El sidrome calient-frio, humedo-seco entre los Quiches de Joyabaj: Dos modelos cognitivos. In H. L. Neuenswander and D. E. Arnold (Eds.) *Estudios Cognitivos del Sur de Mesoamerica*. Dallas: SIL Museum of Anthropology.

Nicholson, D. H. (1991). *Flora of Dominica, Part 2: Dicotyledoneae*. Washington: Smithsonian Institution Press.

Nichter, M. (1992). Ethnomedicine: Diverse trends, common linkages. In M. Nichter (Ed.) *Anthropological Approaches to the Study of Ethnomedicine*. Amsterdam: OPA for Gordon Breach Science Publications.

Nolan, J. M. (2002). Wild plant classification in Little Dixie: Variation in a regional culture. *Journal of Ecological Anthropology* 6:69–81.

Nolan, J. M., and M. C. Robbins (1999). Cultural conservation of medicinal plant use in the Ozarks. *Human Organization* 58:67–72.

Oakes, A. J., and M. P. Morris (1958). The West Indian weedwoman of the U.S. Virgin Islands. *Bulletin of the History of Medicine* 32:163–170.

Osato, J. A., L. A. Santiago, G. M. Remo, M. S. Cuadra, and A. Mori (1993). Antimicrobial and antioxidant activities of unripe papaya. *Life Sciences* 53:1383–1389.

Otwell, W. S. (1989). *Ciguatera*. National Food Safety Database SGEF-11 (http://vm.cfsan.fda.gov/~ear/CIGUAT.html).

Outwater, A., L. Nkya, E. Lyamuya, G. Lwihula, E. C. Green, J. Hogle, S. E. Hassig, G. Dallabetta (2001). Health care seeking behaviour for sexually transmitted diseases among commercial sex workers in Morogoro, Tanzania. *Culture, Health & Sexuality* 3:19–33.

Patrick, G. B. (1980). Marijuana and the lung. *Postgraduate Medicine* 67:116–118.

Pearsall, D. M. (2000). *Paleoethnobotany: A Handbook of Procedures* (2nd ed.). San Diego: Academic Press.

Pelto, P. (1970). *Anthropological Research: The Structure of Inquiry*. New York: Cambridge University Press.

Pereda-Miranda, R., L. Hernandez, M. J. Villavicencio, M. Novelo, P. Ibarra, H. Chai, and J. M. Pezzuto (1993). Structure and stereochemistry of pectolides A-C, novel antimicrobial and cytotoxic 5,6–dihydro-alpha-pyrones from Hyptis. *Journal of Natural Products* 56:583–593.

Pertwee, R. G. (2001). Cannabinoids and the gastrointestinal tract. *Gut* 48:859–867.

Phillips, D. (1996). Medical professional dominance and client dissatisfaction. *Social Science and Medicine* 42:1419–1425.

Pliskin, K. L. (1987). *Silent boundaries: Cultural constraints on sickness and diagnosis of Iranians in Israel*. New Haven, CT: Yale University Press.

Prance, G. T. (1995). Ethnobotany Today and in the future. In R. Schultes and S. vonReis (Eds.) *Ethnobotany: Evolution of a Discipline*. Portland, OR: Dioscorides Press.

Quinlan, M. B. (1995). *Medical pluralism and the problem of discordant classification: A Caribbean case study*. Annual Meeting of the Society for Applied Anthropology, Albuquerque, NM.

Quinlan, M. B., R. J. Quinlan, and J. M. Nolan (in press). Ethnophysiology and herbal treatments of intestinal worms in Dominica, West Indies. *Journal of Ethnopharmacology*.

Quinlan, M. and R. Quinlan (n.d.) An ecological explanation of menstrual taboos. *In preparation*.

Quinlan, R. J. (2001). Effect of household structure on female reproductive strategies in a Caribbean village. *Human Nature* 12:169–189.

Quinlan, R. J. (2000). *Household Composition and Reproductive Strategies in a Caribbean Village*. Doctoral dissertation, University of Missouri-Columbia.

Quinlan, R. J. (1995). *Father Absence, Maternal Care & Children's Behavior in a Rural Caribbean Village*. Masters dissertation, University of Missouri-Columbia.

Rahim, M. A., and C. Psenicka (1996). A structural equations model of stress, locus of control, social support, psychiatric symptoms, and propensity to leave a job. *Journal of Social Psychology* 136:69–84.

Rietveld, S., I. van Beest, and W. Everaerd (1999). Stress-induced breathlessness in asthma. *Psychological Medicine* 29:1359–1366.

Rivers, W. H. R. (1924). *Medicine, Magic and Religion*. New York: Harcourt, Brace & Co.

Robbins, M. C., and J. M. Nolan (1997). A measure of dichotomous category bias in free-listing tasks. *Cultural Anthropology Methods Journal* 9:8–12.

Roberts, P. A. (1988). *West Indians and Their Language*. Cambridge: Cambridge University Press.

Rotter, J. B. (1966). Gerneralized expectancies for internal versus external control of reinforcement. *Psychological Monographs* 80:1–27.

Rubel, A. J., C. W. O'Nell, and R. C. Ardon (1984). *Susto, A Folk Illness*. Berkeley and Los Angeles: University of California Press.

Rubel, A., and M. Hass (1990). Ethnomedicine. In T. Johnson and C. Sargent (Eds.) *Medical Anthropology: Contemporary Theory and Method*. New York: Praeger.

Ryan, G. W., J. M. Nolan, and S. P. Yoder (2000). Successive free-listing: Using multiple free lists to generate explanatory models. *Field Methods* 12:83–107.

Saler, B. (1967). Nagual, witch and sorcerer in a Quiché village. In J. Middleton (Ed.) *Magic, Witchcraft and Curing*. New York: Natural History Press.

Scartezzini, P. and E. Speroni (2000). Review on some plants of Indian traditional medicine with antioxidant activity. *Journal of Ethnopharmacology* 71:23–43.

Schaubroeck, J. J., Jr., and J. J. Xie (2001). Individual differences in utilizing control to cope with job demands: Effects on susceptibility to infectious disease. *Journal of Applied Psychology* 86:265–78.

Schultes, R. E., and A. Hofmann (1992). *Plants of the Gods*. Rochester, VT: Healing Arts Press.

Schultes, R. E., and R. F. Raffauf (1990). *The Healing Forest: Medicinal and Toxic Plants of Northwest Amazonia*. Portland, OR: Dioscorides Press.

Seeman, T. E. (2000). Health promoting effects of friends and family on health outcomes in older adults. *American Journal of Health Promotion* 14:362–370.

Simons, R. C. (1985). The fright illness taxon: Introduction. In R. C. Simons and C. C. Hughes (Eds.) *The Culture-Bound Syndromes* Dordrecht: Reidel, pp. 329–332.

Smith, J. J. (1993). Using ANTHROPAC 3.5 and a spreadsheet to compute a freelist salience index. *Cultural Anthropology Methods Newsletter* 5:1–3.

Snow, L. F. (1978). Sorcerers, saints and charlatans: Black folk healers in urban America. *Culture, Medicine & Psychiatry 21*:69–106.

Sobo, E. J. (2000). The sweetness of fat: Health, procreation, and sociability in rural Jamaica. In J. Eicher, S. Evenson, & H. Lutz (Eds.), *The Visible Self: Global Perspectives on Dress, Culture, and Society* (reprinted from N. Sault, ed., *Many Mirrors*, 1995, and C. Counihan and P. Van Esterik, (Eds.), *Food and Culture: A Reader*, 1997). New York: Fairchild Books.

Sobo, E. J. (1997a). Caribbean health traditions. In S. Heffner (Ed.), *Ancient Health: Unlocking the Mysteries of Health & Healing Through the Ages*, pp. 339–367.

Sobo, E. J. (1997b). Reproductive health traditions in the Caribbean. *Journal of Caribbean Studies. Special issue: Health and Disease in the Caribbean* 12:72–94.

Sobo, E. J. (1996a). Abortion Traditions in Rural Jamaica. *Social Science and Medicine 42*(4):495–508.

Sobo, E. J. (1993). *One Blood: The Jamaican Body*. Albany: State University of New York Press.

Sobo, E. J. (1992). "Unclean deeds": Menstrual taboos and binding "ties" in rural Jamaica. In M. Nichter (Ed.), *Anthropological Approaches to the Study of Ethnomedicine*. Philadelphia: Gordon and Breach Science Publishers.

Spinu, K., V. Vorozhbit, T. Grushko, P. Kintia, P. Skofertsa, V. Vutkaryov, V. Bologa (1996). Antiviral activity of tomatoside from *Lycopersicon esculentum* Mill. *Advances in Experimental Medicine & Biology* 404:505–509.

Stepp, J. R., and D. E. Moerman (2001). The importance of weeds in ethnopharmacology. *Journal of Ethnopharmacology* 75:19–23.

Steptoe, A. (1991). The links between stress and illness. *Journal of Psychosomatic Research 35*:633–644.

Strassmann, B. I. (1992). The function of menstrual taboos among the Dogon: Defense against cuckholdry? *Human Nature 3*:89–131.

Straus, S. E. (2000). Immunoactive cannabinoids: Therapeutic prospects for marijuana constituents. *Proceedings of the National Academy of Science of the United States of America* 97:9363–9364.

Stuart, S. (1993). Dominican Patwa-mother tongue or cultural relic? International *Journal of the Sociology of Language 102*:57–72.

Taylor, D. (1977). *Languages of the West Indies*. Baltimore: Johns Hopkins University Press.

Thoits, P. A. (1995). Stress, coping, and social support processes: Where are we? What next? *Journal of Health & Social Behavior extra issue, v. 36*: 53–79.

Tona, L., K. Kambu, N. Ngimbi, K. Cimanga, and A. J. Vlietinck (1998). Antiamoebic and phytochemical screening of some Congolese medicinal plants. *Journal of Ethnopharmacology 61*:57–65.

Tramèr, M. R., D. Carroll, F. A. Campbell, D. J. M. Reynolds, R. A. Moore, and H. J. McQuay (2001). Cannabinoids for control of chemotherapy induced nausea and vomiting: Quantitative systematic review. *British Medical Journal 323*:16–21.

Trimble, M. R., and J. Wilson-Barnet (1982). Neuropsychiatric aspects of stress. *Practitioner 226*:1580–1586.

Trotter, M., and M. Logan (1986). Informant consensus: A new approach for Identifying potentially effective medicinal plants. In N. Edkin (Ed.), *Plants in Indigenous Medicine and Diet: Biobehavioral Approaches*. Bedford Hills, NY: Redgrave Publishing.

Vallis, C. P., and M. H. Lund (1969). Effect of treatment with Carica papaya on resolution of edema and ecchymosis following rhinoplasty. *Current Therapeutic Research, Clinical and Experimental 11*:356–359.

Vogel, V. J. (1970). *American Indian Medicine*. Norman, OK: University of Oklahoma Press.

Vom Eigan, K. A. (1992). *Science and Spirit: Health Care Utilization in Rural Jamaica*. Doctoral dissertation, Columbia University.

Vorob'ev, A. A., A. S. Seleznev, L. A. Pavlova, A. B. Kapitanov, A. Yang, N. N. Ershova (1998). Otsenka antibakterial'noi aktivnosti maslianogo ekstrakta miaslianogoekstrakta miakoti tomatov v eksperimente [Experimental evaluation of the antibacterial activity of tomato pulp oil extract]. *Zhurnal Mikrobiologii, Epidemiologii i Immunobiologii 6*:8–11.

Wallston, K. A., B. S. Wallston, and R. DeVaellis (1978). Development of the Multidimensional Health Locus of Control (MHLC) scales. *Health Education Monographs 6*:160–170.

Weller, S., and A. K. Romney (1988). *Systematic Data Collection*. Newbury Park, CA: Sage Publications.

Weller, S. C. (1987). Shared knowledge, intracultural variation, and knowledge aggregation. *American Behavioral Scientist 312*:178–193.

Weniger, B., M. Rouzier, R. Daguilh, D. Henrys, J. H. Henrys, and R. Anton (1986). La medecine populaire dans le plateau central d'Haiti. 2. Inventaire ethnopharmacologique. *Journal of Ethnopharmacology 17*:13–30.

White, L. A. (1928). *A comparative Study of Keresan Medicine Societies*. Proceedings of the Twenty-third International Congress of Americanists, New York, NY.

Whiting, B. B. (1950). *Paiute Sorcery, Viking Fund Publications in Anthropology No. 15*. New York: Wenner-Gren Foundation.

Whiting, J. W. M., and I. L. Child (1953). *Child Training and Personality: A Cross-Cultural Study*. New Haven: Yale University Press.

WHO (1999). *Health for All Database*. Geneva: World Health Organization.

Williamson, E. M., F. J. and Evans (2000). Cannabinoids in clinical practice. *Drugs 60*:1303–1314.

Wilson, S. M. (Ed.). (1997). *The Indigenous People of the Caribbean*. Gainesville: University Press of Florida.

Wong, W. (1976). Some folk medicinal plants from Trinidad. *Economic Botany 30*:103–142.

Yap, P. M. (1977). The culture-bound reactive syndromes. In D. Landy (Ed.), *Culture, Disease and Healing*. New York: Macmillan, pp. 340–349.

Zhu, M., and J. D. Phillipson (1996). Hong Kong samples of traditional Chinese medicine "Fang Ji" contain aristolochic acid toxins. *International Journal of Pharmacognosy 34*:283–289.

Index

African-Caribbean peoples, 14
Alcohol, 85, 86
Aloe barbadensis, 93
Aloz, 73
Alternanthera flavescens, 59
Amaranthaceae family, 59
Ambrosia hispida, 88, 94
Amerindians, 13
Apiaceae family, 59
Arawaks, 13
Aristolochia trilobata, 94, 119, 120
Artemissia absinthium, 94
Asthma, 53, 93, 95

Bay leaf, 80
Bay oil, 30, 74, 100, 101
Bay trees, 23
Behavioral scans, 41
Bignoniaceae family, 59
Biomedicine, 64, 122, 123
Blood disorders, 80, 81
Boa constrictor oil, 93
Body fluids, 82
Body image, 71–86
Body's basic requirements, 75
Boils, 93, 110
Bush medicine, 2, 63, 87–120
  for common illnesses, 93, 94
  conclusions about, 124
  future of, 129
  illnesses treatable by, 90
  influence on biomedical care, 124
  internal logic of, 2
  key informant interviews on, 43
  as primary care, 126
Bush tea, 31, 76, 77, 102, 116
Buttons, 93, 105, 109
Bwa Mawego, 21–35
  body image in, 71–86
  bush medicine in, 87–120
  daily round in, 31
  diseases in, 52, 53
  earning a living in, 29
  ecology of, 23
  ethnomedicine of, 2
  health care sectors in, 62–70
  history of, 23
  illness domains of, 91

illnesses in, 54
physical appearance of peoples on, 28
population of, 24, 25
residences of, 26
site of, 22
situation of, 23
village life in, 31

Cajanus cajun, 80
Camellia sinensis, 76
Cannabis sativa, 93, 96
Caribbean region
  common diseases in, 54
  ethnology of medicine in, 44
Caribs, 13
Caricaceae family, 108
Carica papaya, 93, 108
Centella asiatica, 59
Cerebral palsy, 53
Chenopodiaceae family, 59, 115
Chenopodium ambrosioides, 59, 77, 94,
  115, 116
Chicken pox, 53
Cholera, 54
Circulatory system, 79
Citrus aurantifolia, 93, 104
Cocos nucifera, 93
Cold illnesses, 92
Colocasia esculenta, 23
Contraceptives, 25
Coolings, 109
Cordyline, 26
Cordyline fruticosa, 113, 114
Cordyline terminalis, 93
Costus sp., 65
Cough, 92, 93
Couvade, 84
Creole languages, 16–19
Cuts, 93, 112

Dengue fever, 54
Diabetes, 53
Diablés, 56
Diarrhea, 94, 117
Digestive system, 78
Dió, 60
Dioscorea, 23

Dirts, 78, 81, 82
Disease
    defined, 51
    incidence of, 52
Disease-illness dichotomy, 51
Djombi, 56, 99
Dominica, 8–20
    climate of, 10
    colonial control of, 15
    language in, 16
    physical environment of, 9
    socioeconomics of, 19
    vegetation of, 10
Dominicans, 8–20
    ethnohistory of, 13
Dracaena, 113
Dysentery, 54

Edema, 111
Elephantiasis, 53
Epidemiologists, 52
Epilepsy, 53
Eryngium foetidum, 93
Estwa fwajil, 59
Ethnobotany, 4
Ethnographic cone, 40
Ethnographic fieldwork
    data in, 37
    methods of, 36–50
    rapport in, 37
Ethnomedicine, 2
    in study of ethnobotany, 4
Ethnopharmacology, 4
Ethnophysiology, 55
Etiology, 36

Family health surveys, 42
Farín, 30, 31
Ferns, 59
Fever, 93, 103
Folk medicine, 67, 123
Foods, common, 23
Forests, 10–12, 23
Freelist interviews, 47
Freelist remedies, 49
Fright, 55, 85, 93, 98

Gardens, 12, 29
Garlic, 59
Gas, 115
Gliricidia sepium, 93
Glorisida, 88
Goits, 100
Goiyav, 117, 118
Gossypium barbadense, 93

Gossypium hirsutum, 99
Gripes, 115

Headache, 93, 102
Head cold, 92, 93
Health care
    conclusions about, 121–130
    sectors of, 62–70
Health record collection, 43
Hepatitis A, 54
Herbs to ward off witches, 59
High Science, 67
Holistic medicine, 4
Home remedies, 1–7
Hot illnesses, 103
Household, defined, 26
Humoral system, 6, 71, 125
    of common illnesses, 76
    neutrality in, 75
    in plants, 72, 73
    rural Dominican, 72
Humoral theory, 61, 71
Hypertension, 53
Hyptis pectinata, 93–95

Illness, 54
    bush treatments for, 87–120
    defined, 51
    domains of, 89, 91
    etiologic background of, 6
    freelisted, 47, 90
    humoral quality of, 76
    naturalistic, 51, 54, 61
    personalistic, 51, 54, 59, 60
    pile sorts of, 48
Image of limited good, 59
Inflammation, 93, 105
Influenza, 53
Injectionists, 69
Island-Caribs, 13

Jah, 60

Kalí, 74, 96
Key informant interviews, 43
Kojourouk, 102, 103
Koukoulí, 74, 106
Kouton nué, 74, 99
Kul bwa, 74

L'aluwé, 73
Latin species names, 23
Laurel leaf, 101
Laurus noblis, 101

Lepianthes peltata, 93, 110, 111
Lespwi lom, 59
Lime, 35, 74, 104
Loose bowel, 117
Lougawou, 56
Lycopersicon esculentum, 93, 105

Malaria, 54
Malestomak, 74, 110, 111
Malvaceae family, 99
Malvina, 113, 114
Manihot, 23
Manihot esculenta, 30
Manioc, 23, 30
Mansoa alliacea, 59
Marijuana, 86, 96
Maroons, 14
Meals, common, 76, 77
Measles, 53
Medicine
    and culture, 1–3
    path to treatment for, 69, 70
    pluralism of, 62
Menstrual taboos, 84
Mental illness, 98
Midwives, 67
Momordica charantia, 93, 106
Mube, 80
Musa sp., 23
Myrtaceae family, 100, 117

Nervous system, 85
Nettles, 73
Nutrition, 76

Obeah, 45, 59, 123
Obeahmen, 45, 55, 67
Over-the-counter medications, 69, 122

Pachurí, 74, 92, 94, 95
Papaya, 74, 109
Papilion glirisida, 88
Participant-observation (P-O), 38, 40
Pathology, defined, 51
Patwa, 16, 17
Pawpaw, 74, 108, 109
Peperomia pellucida, 93
Petiveria alliacea, 93, 102, 103
Phytolaccaceae family, 102
Pile sorts, 48, 89
Pimenta racemosa, 23, 93, 100, 101
Pityrogramma chrysophylla, 59
Plantago major, 93

Plants
    collection of, 45
    organoleptic qualities of, 73
Plectranthus amboinicus, 93
Pluchea carolinensis, 93
Pogostemon patchouli, 94
Polygalaceae family, 59
Polygala paniculata, 59
Portulaca oleracea, 94
Posttraumatic stress disorder, 99
Pregnancy, 84
Pressure, 93, 105, 107
Prickle heat, 105, 109
Priest healers, 67
Protein compliments, 76
Psidium guajava, 94, 117, 118
Pteridophytes family, 59
Public health programs, 62
Pwa angol, 80
Pwev jine, 65

Rain forest, 11, 12, 23
Rastafarians, 44
Remedies, freelist of, 49
Reproductive system, 83
Research
    fundamental exploration in, 40
    systematic exploration in, 46
Research team, 37
Rheumatism, 93, 100
Rincus communis, 93

Salience score, 48, 89
San Dwagó, 113, 114
Sauvagesia erecta, 93
Schistosomiasis, 54
Seizures, 115
Semantic domain, 47
Set vil, 88
Seventh Day Adventists, 44
Shamans, 2, 69
Shingles, 53
Sime kontwá, 59, 77, 115, 116
Sinusitis, 53
Sleep, 75
Something hurt you, 93, 97
Sorcery, 55
Sores, 93, 112
Sore throat, 93, 104
Soukwayan, 56
Sprains, 93, 112
Stachytarphete jamaicensis, 93
Staphylococcus, 109
Stomach conditions, 113

Symphytum officinale, 93
Syzygium aromaticum, 94

Taboo, 61
Tallow candle, 93
Tea, 31, 76, 77. *See also* Bush tea
Termite nest, 93
Tinea, 53
Ti plant, 26, 59
Tomatoz, 74, 105
Tombe-leve, 59
Tuberculosis, 53
Twef, 119, 120
Typhoid fever, 54

Upset stomach, 94, 118
Urinary system, 78
Uterus, mechanical, 83

Vomiting, 118
Voucher specimen, 45

Washouts, 109
Win, 57
Witchcraft, 55, 58, 59, 123
Won, 77
Woodants' nest, 97
Worm bag, 78, 113
Worm bush, 59
Worms, 94, 113

Xanthosoma sp., 23

Zingiber officinale, 94
Zoutí, 73